Parti ———————————————————— *Brazil*

Participatory Institutions in Democratic Brazil

Leonardo Avritzer

Woodrow Wilson Center Press
Washington, D.C.

The Johns Hopkins University Press
Baltimore

EDITORIAL OFFICES

Woodrow Wilson Center Press
One Woodrow Wilson Plaza
1300 Pennsylvania Avenue, N.W.
Washington, D.C. 20004-3027
Telephone: 202-691-4029
www.wilsoncenter.org

ORDER FROM

The Johns Hopkins University Press
Hampden Station
P.O. Box 50370
Baltimore, Maryland 21211
Telephone: 1-800-537-5487
www.press.jhu.edu/books/

2 4 6 8 9 7 5 3 1

Library of Congress Cataloging-in-Publication Data

Avritzer, Leonardo.
   Participatory institutions in democratic Brazil / Leonardo Avritzer.
      p.   cm.
   Includes bibliographical references and index.
   ISBN 978-0-8018-9174-8 (hardcover : alk. paper) —
   ISBN 978-0-8018-9180-9 (pbk. : alk. paper)
   1. Democratization—Brazil.   2. Local government—Brazil.   3. Local budgets—
Brazil—Citizen participation.   4. Collective behavior—Political aspects—Brazil.
5. Political culture—Brazil.   6. Political participation—Brazil.   7. Brazil—Politics
and government—1985–2002.   8. Brazil—Politics and government—2003.   I. Title.
JL2481.A87 2009
323′.0420981—dc22

                                                                  2008051222

**Woodrow Wilson
International
Center
for Scholars**

The Woodrow Wilson International Center for Scholars, established by Congress in 1968 and headquartered in Washington, D.C., is the living, national memorial to President Wilson.

The Center is a nonpartisan institution of advanced research, supported by public and private funds, engaged in the study of national and world affairs. The Center establishes and maintains a neutral forum for free, open, and informed dialogue.

The Center's mission is to commemorate the ideals and concerns of Woodrow Wilson by providing a link between the world of ideas and the world of policy, by bringing a broad spectrum of individuals together to discuss important public policy issues, by serving to bridge cultures and viewpoints, and by seeking to find common ground.

Conclusions or opinions expressed in Center publications and programs are those of the authors and speakers and do not necessarily reflect the views of the Center staff, fellows, trustees, advisory groups, or any individuals or organizations that provide financial support to the Center.

The Center is the publisher of *The Wilson Quarterly* and home of Woodrow Wilson Center Press, *dialogue* radio and television, and the monthly newsletter "Centerpoint." For more information about the Center's activities and publications, please visit us on the web at www.wilsoncenter.org.

Lee H. Hamilton, President and Director

Contents

Tables and Figure

Tables

Figure

Acknowledgments

This book is the result of almost ten years of empirical research on Brazil's new participatory institutions. My interest in these institutions began in 1999 when I spent a month in Porto Alegre researching participatory budgeting for a Ford Foundation project on civil society and public space in Latin America. A year later I coordinated a Ford Foundation project on participatory budgeting that led to the book, *A Inovação Democrática no Brasil*. Many people in Porto Alegre, Belo Horizonte, and other cities participated in different phases of the research I conducted on participatory budgeting; among them I would like to give special thanks to Zander Navarro, Adalmir Marquetti, Marcelo Silva, Luciana Tatagiba, Ana Claudia Teixeira, Claudia Feres Faria, and Brian Wampler. Along the years I also interacted with many people who were doing research on the same topic and whose work influenced me. I would like to mention Evelina Dagnino, Yves Sintomer, Gianpaolo Baiocchi, and Giovanni Alegretti.

My research on participatory budgeting led me to study other forms of participation in Brazil. I started working on participation in São Paulo in 2002 and researched voluntary associations in the city. In São Paulo I interacted with many people; among them I would like to mention Felix Sanchez, Vera Schattan Coelho, Marisol Recaman, and Gustavo Venturi. Our joint work led to another book, *A Participação em São Paulo*. At the same time, I was doing research on councils in Belo Horizonte, where I got the help of excellent research assistants. I would like to mention only a few: Roberto Pires, Eleonora Schetini, and Aurea Motta. It was during the same period that John Gaventa and Gary Hawes invited me to start working on the Statute of the City as part of a project they were coordinating at the Institute of Development Studies at the University of Sussex. This project gave me the opportunity to establish the comparative framework that led to this book, and I am very thankful to them.

Most of this book was written at the Woodrow Wilson International Center for Scholars in Washington, D.C., during the winter and spring of 2006. Many people at the Wilson Center and in the Washington area gave me invaluable contributions while I was finishing the book. Enrique Peruzzotti, Jonathan Fox, John French, Wendy Hunter, Andrew Seele, and Margaret Keck have been excellent commentators. I also have had the opportunity to present the book's arguments at Brown University, Georgetown University, and the University of Massachusetts at Amherst. Among the excellent comments I received at that point were those of Patrick Heller, Richard Snyder, and Sonia Alvares. I would like to thank the Woodrow Wilson Center Press, in particular Joe Brinley for his enthusiasm for the book since our first talks. I would also like to thank Alberto Olvera for his encouragement in having the book translated into Spanish.

Participatory Institutions in Democratic Brazil

1

Toward a Theory of Participatory Institutions in Brazil

In just a few decades, Brazil has been transformed from an authoritarian regime in which most citizens did not participate in any form of voluntary association to a democracy in which citizens are mobilized in a broad mix of civil and political interactions in new participatory institutions. These participatory institutions have expanded citizenship at the local level by effectively creating opportunities for the deliberation of new claims for rights and urban services and for the redistribution of power between central and local authorities. Participatory institutions in Brazil became well known worldwide because of their capacity to attract the participation of poor citizens and to redistribute public goods. Many international institutions and public administrations in Latin America, Europe, and Africa decided to implement participatory budgeting, the most important of Brazilian participatory institutions. Now that the self-congratulatory moment seems to be over, the academic debate on the success of these institutions is only beginning. Is the Brazilian experience a model for increasing participation elsewhere? Can the successful experiences in Brazilian cities be reproduced in places where the conditions may be very different? And under what conditions can participatory institutions succeed?

To answer these questions, we need a theory of the relationships among civil society, political society, and institutional design. We also need to identify the conditions necessary for the emergence and success of participatory institutions. This chapter aims to develop such a theory and, throughout the book, I strive to figure out the conditions under which participatory institutions can succeed, as a way of broadening participation in Brazil and other recently democratized countries.

1

The Democratization of Brazil

Since the withdrawal of the military from Brazilian politics in 1985, Brazil has gone from being a country with low levels of citizen participation and mobilization to a country known for its participatory institutions (Santos, 1998, 2002; Abers, 2000; Avritzer, 2002a; Baiocchi, 2005; Avritzer and Navarro, 2003; Tendler, 1997; Dagnino, 2002; Fung and Wright, 2003; Wampler and Avritzer, 2004; Cornwall and Coelho, 2007). The Constituent Assembly, which drafted the country's 1988 Constitution, began the process of building an amazing infrastructure for participatory democracy. Although the 1988 Constitution was considered conservative when it was ratified, because it did not embrace some progressive views on issues such as the duration of President José Sarney's mandate and the organization of the political system (Zaverucha, 1998; Whitaker et al., 1989), a more historical perspective suggests a radically different picture.

The 1988 Constitution opened the way for important changes in Brazil regarding access to social services and the creation of participatory institutions. It has 14 devices that allow for participation, starting with its article on sovereignty, which allows a mixture of representation and participation (Vitale, 2004). The key participatory articles concern healthcare, social assistance, the environment, and urban organization (Avritzer and Pereira, 2005). These articles prompted the emergence of a large participatory infrastructure in contemporary Brazil, which now includes 170 experiences of participatory budgeting and many thousands of health councils. The Statute of the City, approved in 2001 to authorize cities to develop their own master plans, has also added to the range of participatory experiences.

The expansion of participation in Brazil has become a benchmark for participatory policies in the rest of Latin America (Romero, 2006; Peruzzotti, 2007), as well as in Europe (Bacqué, Rey, and Sintomer, 2005; Alegretti, 2006) and parts of Southeast Asia (Heller and Isaac, 2006). In Latin America, leftist actors, local political players, and international agencies such as the Inter-American Development Bank and the World Bank have all advocated the expansion of participation (Cornwall and Brock, 2005). For leftist actors, participation is part of the reconstruction of a broader conception of democracy (Gret and Sintomer, 2002). For international agencies, the participation of citizens and communities is a new way to promote more accountability (Fox, 1998). Thus, participation is being sponsored today by many actors with different purposes: for some of them participation means empowering social actors; for others it means sharing control over decision-making processes or implementing a new conception of democracy. A common thread, however, is that none of the actors has yet developed a way to evaluate whether participation leads to its presumed results.

The Importance of Context

This book argues that the expansion of participatory institutions may produce different results depending upon context. In Brazil and the rest of Latin America and Europe, participation has been linked to empowerment (Abers, 2000; Avritzer, 2002a; Baiocchi, 2005), to political cooptation (Silva, 2003; Wampler, 2008) or implemented under political conditions that rendered it ineffective (Silva, 2003). Although many recent books deal with participation in Brazil (Abers, 2000; Avritzer, 2002a; Baiocchi, 2005; Nylen, 2003; Santos, 2006) and all deal with the experience of participatory budgeting in Porto Alegre,[1] few consider the specific characteristics of civil and political society in Porto Alegre (Avritzer, 2006) and even fewer, the difficulties of reproducing these characteristics elsewhere (Wampler, 2008). This book broadens the scope of analysis to include the main forms of participation in Brazil—participatory budgeting, health councils, and city master plans—as well as to analyze them in different contexts.

The Importance of Definitions

The most important works on participation do not even agree on the meaning of the term. Abers refers to participation as "increasing citizens' control over the state and improving the capacity of ordinary people to understand and decide about issues affecting their lives" (2000: 5). Nylen refers to democratic participation as "the exercising of real power over decisions" (2003: 28). Baiocchi links the origins of participation in Brazil to social movements that challenge "representative democracy by calling for participatory reforms" (2005: 11). For Fung and Wright, participation refers to "the commitments and capacities of ordinary people to make sensible decisions" (2003: 5). Even this small sample illustrates a point that remains problematic in the literature: none of the authors provides a comprehensive theory of participation or proposes a theory of participatory institutions.

---

1. There is also an emerging literature that deals with participation in comparative perspective. Goldfrank has studied forms of participation in three Latin American cities, Porto Alegre, Caracas, and Montivideo. Wampler has studied eight cases of participatory budgeting in Brazil. Both forthcoming.

Moreover, most of these authors do not differentiate between participation and participatory institutions. In my view, the definitions are muddled because participation can be regarded theoretically as a sociological concept concerning the intention of the subject to participate (Melucci, 1996) or as a political concept involving the organization of the polity on a purely participatory principle (Bachrach and Baratz, 1962, 1975; Pateman, 1970). Practically, however, none of the participatory experiences studied in this work has those purely abstract characteristics. In most cases, participation takes place within specially designed institutions. Thus, we are no longer talking of participation as an alternative to representation or as an activity of social actors, but rather as an outcome of institutions designed to promote participation. In this sense, a new way of doing politics is being practiced, but remains theoretically unaccounted for. This chapter reviews the debates on democratic theory and participation, showing how they have missed the institutional dimension of participation, and proposes a theory of participatory institutions. At the end of the chapter, an overview summarizes the book's structure and principal arguments.

Democratic Theory and Participation

The recent emergence of participatory institutions in both the developing and developed world (Santos, 2006; Avritzer, 2002a; Heller and Isaac, 2006; Baiocchi, 2005; Abers, 2000) represents a break with most of twentieth-century democratic theory. In the first half of the twentieth century, democratic theory rejected most of the elements of a theory of participation that had been at its root (Rousseau, 1997). That rejection arose out of a perceived link between participation and irrationality.

Theories of the Irrationality of Popular Sovereignty

Both Max Weber and Carl Schmitt pointed out in the first decades of the twentieth century that participation would not necessarily lead to rational results. For Weber, the classic author in this literature, the clash of values in modern political society led to moral relativism (Weber, 1968; Habermas, 1984), which involves the impossibility of linking morality and truth. With such incommensurate moral values, he argued, it is not possible to establish the desirability of democracy, because democracy is only one moral conception among the many available. Weber's model for understanding political domination poses three value-neutral conceptions of legitimacy—

traditional, charismatic, and rational domination—but does not allow us to normatively choose one over the others (Breiner, 1996: 2). Thus, we cannot deduce from Weber's theory any normative foundation for a theory of democracy or participation.

Weber's idea was followed up by many theorists, most importantly the Austrian-American economist and political scientist Joseph Schumpeter. Schumpeter transformed Weber's skepticism and moral pluralism into a challenge to participation and popular sovereignty. For him, what was irrational was not participation in itself, but rather the idea that popular sovereignty could produce rational results. Like Weber, Schumpeter challenged popular sovereignty's founding pillars by raising the same issues raised by mass society theory. Mass society theory holds that the opinions of the majority are not necessarily democratic. Citing examples such as sixteenth-century witch hunts and the persecution of the Jews in the twentieth century, Schumpeter showed that the preferences of the majority, inherent in the concept of popular sovereignty, might legitimize antidemocratic attitudes sanctioned not by rational political actors but by the irrational masses (Schumpeter, 1942: 242). Thus, to uphold the concept of popular sovereignty it is necessary to indicate clearly how and by whom decisions are to be made. Schumpeter's solution was to reduce the scope and meaning of the concept of sovereignty, transforming it from a process of forming the general will into a process for authorizing the exercise of power by members of representative political bodies (Avritzer, 2002a: 17–19). Schumpeter's theory became the classical view of participation that postwar democratic theory would uphold. His proposal for democratic organization was widely accepted in the postwar period, even in Europe.

The Italian thinker Norberto Bobbio reconnected the democratic elitist tradition with debates over the meaning of sovereignty and forms economic management within the European left and liberal camps. Bobbio approached the gap between democracy as popular sovereignty and democracy as a rule for selecting governments in terms of "unfulfilled promises," as ideas proper to the democratic tradition, yet impossible to satisfy in complex societies. Like Schumpeter and Weber, he noted the increasing complexity of both the economy and the state, and he claimed that "the project of political democracy was conceived for a society much less complex than the one that exists today" (Bobbio, 1987: 37). For Bobbio, the growth of administrative complexity and technical education contradicts the pursuit of participatory democracy. These processes expand the domain of technocrats at the expense of the autonomy of the common citizen: "Technocracy and democracy are antithetical: if the expert plays a leading role in the industrial society he cannot be considered as just any citizen. The hypothesis which underlies democracy is that all are in a position to make decisions about everything" (Bobbio, 1987: 37). Hence Bobbio, like Schumpeter, proposes to reduce the scope of decision-making to make democracy compatible with growing complexity. Both authors acknowledge that the transition to a modern and highly differentiated society brings many gains, but also a sharp political loss expressed in the inevitable necessity of narrowing the scope of political participation.

The trend established by Schumpeter in the United States and Bobbio in Europe set a standard for democratic theory. Contemporary authors such as Sartori or Dahl operate within this framework, either by conceiving of democracy as the government of the "active minorities" (Sartori, 1987: I, 147) or by assuming that political incorporation can take place only by including new groups in the representative system (Dahl, 1990).

Theories of Collective Action and Cultural Pluralism

This narrowing of democratic participation has been continuously challenged around the world since the 1970s on two main fronts: the first was the emergence of the so-called new social movements in Europe and the United States (Melucci, 1980, 1996; Cohen, 1985, 1996; Tilly, 1985, 2006). Social movements such as the environmental movement (Kaase and Newton, 1995) and the human rights movements (Jelin and Hershberg, 1996) are forms of collective action characterized by the formation of solidarity among different social actors, the public presentation of an existing conflict through demonstrations and other forms of direct action, and a breach of the limits of the representative system. Each of these characteristics allows a new way of dealing with cultural pluralism. However, European and North American social movements did not generate a new form of institutional participation. On the contrary, they obeyed the cyclical logic of mobilization and demobilization proper to collective action. In this sense, it is very difficult to ground a theory of participatory institutions on social movement theory, despite a few overlapping issues, such as a vindication of the rationality of social actors (Melucci, 1996; Cohen, 1996; Tilly, 2006; Avritzer, 2002a).

The second break with democratic elitism's antiparticipatory tradition came with the emergence of civil society movements during the democratization of Eastern Europe and Latin America (Arato, 1981; Cohen and Arato, 1992; Kaldor, 1995; Stepan, 1988; Alvarez and Escobar, 1992; Alvarez, Dagnino, and Escobar, 1998; Avritzer, 2002a; Dagnino, Olvera, and Panfichi, 2006). Civil society is a concept that bridges many theoretical traditions and can be understood in a nonparticipatory way (Shils, 1991; Roniger and Ayata, 1995), as well as in a participatory way (Cohen and Arato, 1992; Habermas, 1995; Oxhorn, 1995; Dagnino, 2002). Civil society in its participatory version can be understood "as self-limiting democratizing movements seeking to expand and to protect spaces for both negative liberty and positive freedom and to recreate egalitarian forms of solidarity" (Cohen and Arato, 1992: 17). In Latin America and Brazil, in particular, civil society was linked to the reconstitution of social ties among the poor (Oxhorn, 1995; Alvarez, Dagnino, and Escobar, 1998; Avritzer, 1999) and middle-class sectors (Weffort, 1989; Stepan, 1988; Aguayo, 1996; Olvera, 1997; Peruzzotti and Smulovitz, 2006) during the authoritarian regimes of the 1970s. Civil society was employed to establish a watershed between the actions of an authoritarian regime and its political opposition (Weffort, 1989). In this context, civil society is a concept distinguishing the newly emerging social and political actors from the market, understood as the private economic interests associated with the authoritarian regime, on one side, and the authoritarian state, on the other.

However, two major limits of civil society theory emerged once democratization took place in Latin America and civil society actors started to join participatory institutions. First, the demarcation between civil society and the state could not explain the entry of civil society actors into political arrangements (Dagnino, 2002). Civil society and the state started to overlap and to act together, requiring a new theory of the encounters between civil society and the state (Dagnino, Olvera, and Panfichi, 2006; Avritzer, 2003, 2004; Santos and Avritzer, 2006). Second, political parties and political society remained undertheorized in most of the literature of participation, because of the elitist character of the literature or the antisystemic conceptions of social movements theory (Alvarez, Dagnino, and Escobar, 1998). Particularly in Brazil, where the Workers Party (called the PT) has led the way in introducing participatory arrangements, the connection between political parties and civil society in implementing forms of participation became a key variable—but one that is not explained in theory.

The Limitations of Current Democratic Theories

Thus, the current democratic theories, even on their divergent paths, face constraints in two directions. The first is a crisis of the elitist theory of democracy, which assumes that representation is enough to deal with all aspects of political participation and that collective action is irrational. This theory, which originated in the aftermath of World War II, cannot explain the proliferation of newer forms of participation, such as mass political parties, in both the developed and the developing worlds.

Second, the available theories of participation, based on social movement theory (Melucci, 1996; Touraine, 1988; 1992; Tilly, 2000), are incapable of grasping the institutional elements of long-term forms of participation between social movements and the state. The same is true of theories of participation whose origins lie in civil society theory (Cohen and Arato, 1992; Oxhorn, 1995; Habermas, 1995). They cannot account for the reduced autonomy of civil society actors in participatory arrangements or the new forms of relations between civil society and political society. Thus, a new theory of the emerging forms of participation is needed. I call it a theory of participatory institutions.

The Nature of Participatory Institutions

During most of the twentieth century, participation and institutionalization remained building blocks of different theoretical traditions. Only in the early 1990s, with democratization in Eastern Europe and Latin America, did they start to overlap. Civil society actors in Brazil and many other Latin American countries promoted participation in public institutions (Avritzer, 2002a; Dagnino, 2002; Whitaker, 2003; Dagnino, Olvera, and Panfichi, 2006). At the same, during Latin American democratization, institutions adapted themselves to participation.[2] Instead of maintaining monopolistic ways of expressing sovereignty, institutions opened themselves to the participation of civil society actors in healthcare, urban policy, social assistance, and environmental protection. Many new institutions emerged in this process. In this book I will call them participatory institutions.

Participatory institutions have four main characteristics: (a) operation simultaneously through the principles of representation and participation, (b) transformation of voluntary characteristics of civil society into forms of permanent political organization, (c) interaction with political parties and state actors, and (d) relevance of institutional design to their effectiveness.

---

2. There are many examples of adapting institutions to the participation of social actors beyond the Brazilian examples described in this book. In Mexico, the classical example is the Federal Electoral Institute (Olvera, 2003; Avritzer, 2002a). In Argentina and Uruguay there are also forms of institutional participation at the local level. See Peruzzotti and Smulovitz, 2006.

Together, these features make participatory institutions a central element in the operation of participation.

Operation by Both Representation and Participation

Participatory institutions are hybrids between participation and representation, as well as between civil society and state actors. In Brazil, they operate simultaneously on the principle of representation and participation. Although state actors still maintain formal sovereignty over the decision-making process in health or urban planning, they transfer this sovereignty to a larger participatory body. Civil society actors take the actions of state actors inside participatory institutions seriously, and the institutions provide a forum where state and civil society representatives may interact directly. Thus, we are seeing a new type of institution formed by two principles— representation and participation—that have remained apart too long in modern politics.

Transformation by Civil Society into Permanent Political Organization

Within participatory institutions, civil society transforms previous practices of social organization into a permanent form of political organization (Avritzer, 2002b). Civil society organizes its participation within institutions in a variety of ways. In participatory budgeting, the operating principle is open entry, according to which every citizen can participate in a regional assembly (Abers, 2000; Baiocchi, 2005). Health councils rely on the preselected representation of civil society actors with two-year mandates (Coelho, 2004; Tatagiba, 2002). In some cases, there is interaction between broad participation and the state. In other cases, there is interaction between a selected group of civil society actors and the state. In both instances, civil society practices become institutionalized as permanent forms of interaction with the state. Although civil society actors are just one type among many actors within participatory institutions, they play the role of bringing claims from the broader environment into a selective institutional environment. As they interact with state actors, the civil society actors tend to lose their autonomy in relation to the state.[3]

3. A systematic discussion of the autonomy of civil society is beyond the aim of this work. In the literature, this concern has come from two different sources. From a theo-

Interaction with Political Parties and State Actors

Political parties and state actors play key roles within participatory institutions. Yet, the way they interact with these institutions is also very specific and goes beyond what most of the literature assumes to be political society's role, namely, aggregating political opinion (Przeworski, 1991) and competing in elections (Linz and Stepan, 1996; Mainwaring and Scully, 1995). Political society within participatory institutions connects grassroots conceptions of participation to civil society actors. In this sense, political society reinforces general conceptions of participation that are at the root of the formation of leftist mass political parties (Offe, 1974; Keck, 1992). Participatory institutions transform diffuse demands for participation at the civil society level into an organized conception of participation at the state level. The PT in Brazil played exactly this role of connecting ideas of participation present in its grassroots with civil society actors' claims for participation. In most of the cases of participation analyzed in this book, the initiative was taken by political society actors.

Relevance of Institutional Design to Effectiveness

Studies of participation have tended to recommend the replication of successful elements of the main participatory institution, namely, participatory budgeting (Fung and Wright, 2003; Bacqué, Rey, and Sintomer, 2004). In this book, I understand design in a participatory way, as an institutional element that unleashes innovation and horizontal political relations. Design is not neutral. On the contrary, different designs have different consequences in the organization of political institutions (Ostrom, 2005). However, when it comes to participatory institutions, this issue is even more important because it involves strengthening horizontal potentials already present in civil society or blocking hierarchical elements already present in

---

. retical perspective, critical theorists defended civil society's autonomy based a new organizing principle beyond the market and the state (Cohen and Arato, 1992). From a practical perspective, the idea of autonomy emerged in Latin America and Eastern Europe based on the idea of a demarcation between state and civil society (Arato, 1981; Weffort, 1989; Dagnino, 1994). Today, the multiple forms of interaction between state and civil society suggest reason to reduce the scope of what is called civil society's autonomy. For the purposes of this work, autonomy means the non-intervention of the state in the organizational characteristics of civil society associations.

the polity. The fine-tuning of participatory designs is essential to making these institutions achieve their potential, and variation in design is a key consideration. This book makes this point by comparing different kinds of participatory designs in Brazil and evaluating their success.

Institutions as a Central Element of Participation

Participatory institutions change the debate on participation in three ways.

- *They insert civil society into the broader polity.* At the beginning of democratization civil society considered itself an autonomous and antistate institution. In contrast, civil society inside participatory institutions plays the role of connecting grassroots actions and political actors.
- *They help recover the grassroots dimension of political society.* Successful leftist parties tend to become completely absorbed by the competition of electoral politics. Participatory institutions restore the capacity of parties to connect with grassroots actors who demand participation.
- *They change the debate on institutional design.* The focus of design moves from one about rules for political competition to one that emphasizes the connection between the state and society.

In this book, I analyze the operation of participatory institutions in Brazil, the country that has implemented the most such institutions and most likely the broadest variety of them as well.

Overview of This Book

In the following part of this book, I analyze how participatory institutions emerged in democratic Brazil using the three variables of civic culture, political environment, and institutional design. In the second part, I examine the design and context of the three main participatory institutions that have succeeded in democratic Brazil: participatory budgeting, health councils, and city master plans. Connecting the two parts is the idea that a successful mix of civil and political society interactions explains the emergence and success of participatory institutions. In the concluding part, I use the eleven cases of participation considered in the book to establish a typology of the effectiveness of participatory institutions in different contexts.

The Emergence of Participatory Institutions

Until the late 1970s, very few active associations existed in the country, and most citizens did not participate in voluntary associations (Conniff, 1975). In a survey conducted in the 1973, Kowarick found that 93 percent of poor Brazilians did not engage in any kind of civic or political participation (1980: 21). In their classic book on participation in São Paulo, Singer and Brant pointed out that voluntary associations in the city during 1946–64 were predominantly recreational in nature (1980: 87). This situation changed fast when a large part of the Brazilian poor joined participatory institutions in the early 1980s (Santos, 1993: 84–85; Avritzer, 2000, 2004: 25; Gohn, 1991; Scherer-Warren, 2000). I argue that this change in associative patterns gave rise to new claims for rights and urban services and allowed the state to join in participatory arrangements, a mode of social action I have called participatory publics in my previous work (Avritzer, 2002a). This argument advances the existing literature on associations in two important ways. First, it goes beyond Robert Putnam's influential density argument by showing that it is not only the number of association that generates democratic change, but also the types of associations and the social actors they bring into politics. Second and more important, it departs from most public policy literature that claims that the poor do not benefit from participatory arrangements (Verba, 1995; Barnes, 1999). Rather, I show that poor social actors participate when institutions are designed taking their needs into account.

Another aspect of the amazing rise in political participation in Brazil was the emergence of a popular mass party, the Workers Party, or PT. Before the 1980 party reform, Brazil had one of the least institutionalized political systems in Latin America (Mainwaring, 1999: 354). This changed in 1980 with the creation of the PT, a mass party with large grassroots support (Keck, 1992; Hunter, 2006). With its origins outside the political system, the PT is a classic mass party (Duverger, 1951; Menegello, 1989: 32–33; Avritzer, 2005) that challenged century-old political practices of clientelism and top-down politics.[4] The PT was crucial in bringing new practices of participa-

---

4. It is impossible to ignore the fact that, as I am writing this book, the government of Luiz Inacio Lula da Silva, the first PT administration at the national level, is involved in a serious corruption case called *mensalão*. It is also impossible to ignore the fact that of all the PT's experiences in power, Lula's administration has been the least participatory. Although the book does not deal directly with the *mensalão* scandal, it provides a framework of participatory and nonparticipatory identities at the local level that can help in better understanding it. On the *mensalão,* see Flynn, 2005.

tory politics from the periphery of the political system into the center. The PT was a key actor in the late 1980s in debates on participation in the health-care system. It was also central to the process of approving participation in the elaboration of city master plans. The PT in Porto Alegre introduced participatory budgeting during its first city administration. I show how the PT changed the established political pattern in Brazil and thus had a huge impact on the emergence of participatory institutions, especially in Porto Alegre, Belo Horizonte, and São Paulo.

By introducing a political variable in the analysis of the emergence and consolidation of participatory institutions, this book departs from the established literature on political parties, which concentrates overwhelmingly on electoral issues and the organizational aspects of party politics (Diamond and Gunter, 2001; Gunther, Montero, and Linz, 2002). I maintain that the distinction between mass parties and electoral parties still stands. In addition, I argue that the identity side of party formation continues to be relevant in the debate on mass political parties (Offe, 1984). I demonstrate that a mass party with external connections to the political system is the ideal vehicle for bringing participatory claims to the state.

The design of participatory institutions was also critical in the rise of participation in Brazil. Brazilian civil society actors and political parties demanded the involvement of grassroots actors in deliberations about public policies in many arenas. New forms of participation assigned full deliberative capacity to social actors or civil society associations (Abers, 2000; Avritzer, 2002a; Baiocchi, 2005). I also argue that the way participatory designs emerged and their bottom-up character was a key element in the success of institutions such as participatory budgeting and health councils. The new participatory institutions could never have succeeded without the willingness of civil society and political actors to radicalize participatory designs by making them bottom-up. Thus, against well-established theories that reduce the success of participation to design (Fung and Wright, 2003), I argue that it is how civil and political societies interact to make designs bottom-up or horizontal that accounts for their success.

The Operation of the Institutions

In Part II, I analyze three types of participatory institutions that emerged with this new framework: participatory budgeting systems, health councils, and city planning processes under the Statute of the City. All three new institutions greatly enhanced participation, by increasing both the number of·

people involved and the extent of power-sharing between the state and civil society actors. Participatory budgeting led to power-sharing in the formulation of city budgets; health councils opened participation in deliberations on health priorities; and the statute of the city required the incorporation of social actors in determining a city's master plan.

All three cases yielded significant outcomes. The first is a dramatic increase in the number of social actors involved in policy-making. In 2004, more than 300,000 people participated in participatory budgets in Brazil. More than 10,000 health and social assistance councils now exist, in which more than 400,000 people participate (IBGE, 2002). Another important result is a democratization of access to public goods. Brazil has long a tradition of increasing access to social services by law without implementing it administratively (Santos, 1979; Holston, 1993; Mendez, O'Donnell, and Pinheiro, 1999). New participatory institutions created new ways of enforcing social policies at the local level. In this way, they opened the way for more democracy and greater access to public goods at the local level. To show how success in the implementation of participatory institutions has varied, I discuss the introduction of the three participatory institutions in four cities: São Paulo, Porto Alegre, Belo Horizonte, and Salvador.

São Paulo

Brazil's largest city is also one of its most unequal cities. Economic growth between 1900 and 1950 led to rapid population growth as well, as the city expanded from 240,000 to 3.5 million people. But growth also yielded stark inequalities across regions and groups. If we divide the city population in five groups according to where they live, we find a seven-fold variation between the annual income of the poorest region (US$400) and the wealthiest (US$3,000) (Torres, 2003). Lack of sewerage, health services, and access to good education are the main issues that create an enormous social divide in São Paulo and gave rise to important social movements during the Brazilian process of democratization.

São Paulo is the home of the civil society movements that triggered democratization (Singer and Brant, 1980; Caldeira, 2000). Many of the movements that led to the participatory institutions discussed in the book, in particular the health and urban reform movements, first emerged there. São Paulo's industrial belt, called the ABC region, is also the home of the PT (French, 2004), where the party had its first core constituencies and leadership (Keck, 1992). I show how scale and the struggle between the political left and right influenced the implementation of participation in the city.

Porto Alegre

Founded in the eighteenth century, Porto Alegre is the most important city of the Brazilian South. Its population has grown more slowly than in other Brazilian cities. In 1964 it was already trailing most Brazilian cities in population growth, and between 1964 and 1985 its population grew modestly from 770,000 to 1,275,000. Nonetheless, slower population growth did not preclude the city from having the same inequality problems that plagued other Brazilian cities. In 1986, 44.8 percent of the city population lived below the poverty line.

In the postwar period, Porto Alegre's singular configuration on the left of the political spectrum distinguishes it from all other Brazilian cities. Between 1946 and 1964, it elected the PTB, a populist leftist party with limited support in Brazil's Southeast, for most administrative positions. During the period of democratization, Porto Alegre civil society quickly reorganized itself, and many new associations emerged (Baiocchi, 2005). Nonetheless, the city's political orientation remained uniquely concentrated within the left. I discuss the implementation of the three participatory institutions in Porto Alegre from this perspective.

Belo Horizonte

Belo Horizonte, at the center of Brazil's third-largest metropolitan region, is the third-largest economy in Brazil and has long been the country's third-largest city. Today, it trails Salvador and Fortaleza, whose populations grew at a much faster rate during the 1980s and the 1990s. Belo Horizonte is a new city founded in 1897 to provide a central economic hub that could substitute for Ouro Preto, the region's historical colonial city. Although Belo Horizonte was a planned city, its planning was quickly undermined, as the illegal occupation of land began within ten years after the city's founding. Belo Horizonte's population grew enormously during the postwar period from 350,000 to 1,770,000, a six-fold increase. Family income in the city averaged R$1,307 in 1996, below the averages of Porto Alegre and São Paulo. Participation in Belo Horizonte involves claiming better access to public goods in a city that could not keep up with its economic and urban growth.

Belo Horizonte has neither the leftist tradition of Porto Alegre nor the contentious city politics of São Paulo, but it is the Southeastern city with the most rapid change in associative patterns during the democratization period. Neighborhood associations, as well as health and professional associations, thrived (Avritzer, 2000). Belo Horizonte's political society has been known as a pole of conservative sectors (Hagopian, 1996), but it also became a PT stronghold. The three participatory institutions will be analyzed from this perspective.

Salvador

In the past 20 years, Salvador has emerged as the most important city in the Brazilian Northeast, a place long held by Recife. Salvador's rapid population growth—from 747,000 in 1964 to 1,811,000 in 1986—continued throughout the 1990s, reaching 2.8 million in 2005 (IBGE, 2007). This huge population growth has led to greater inequality than in other Brazilian cities, many of which had stabilized their population growth in the 1990s. Salvador is the Brazilian capital with the largest number of poor, and almost a quarter of its inhabitants declare they have no income (Boschi, 1999).

Salvador effectively contrasts with the other cities studied here because of its weak civil society and its political conservatism. The government has made no attempt to involve civil society associations in public policy. On the contrary, the oligarchic Magalhães family controls the Salvador government with a strong antiparticipatory bias. It is from this perspective that I will analyze the implementation of health councils and city master plans in Salvador.

The Importance of Context

Context matters when it comes to participatory institutions. Methodologically, then, I employ a subnational comparative method to analyze data on the emergence, consolidation, and expansion of participatory institutions in these four cities. Subnational comparison is superior to quantitative methods when the number of cases involved is low, since it allows the researcher "to construct controlled comparisons" (Snyder, 2001: 94). I find that in each case the quality of civic life and the specific configuration of political society led to different designs and therefore to different degrees of deliberative and distributive effectiveness.

Summary of the Arguments

Overall, this book has three main arguments, one about civil-political society relations, one about institutional design, and one about the success of participatory institutions in delivering public goods.

Civil and Political Relations

I argue that patterns of association or political will alone cannot trigger successful participatory institutions. On the contrary, they need to be the result of a specific interaction between the political will to initiate a participatory process and civil society actors who can join these institutions. In very few cases do these two conditions appear together.

Institutional Design

I distinguish between more participatory designs, which I call bottom-up designs, and more interactive designs, which I call power-sharing designs. I also introduce what I call ratification designs. My main argument concerning participatory designs is that the willingness to introduce a more participatory design is not enough to ensure its success. I show that each one of the three main designs fits a certain context. I also argue that the failure to carry out participation is directly linked to the introduction of bottom-up designs in situations in which they do not fit.

Effectiveness in Distributing Public Goods

I show that participatory budgeting, the most bottom-up of the designs analyzed in the book, is likely to produce the most participation and the widest access to public goods. However, it cannot be introduced where there is too much political contention, because it depends on the political will of the mayor. I show that less bottom-up designs operate better in contentious situations. In conclusion, I present a typology of designs and contexts and propose different participatory institutions according to the organization of civil and political society.

Part I

The Emergence of
Participatory Institutions in Brazil

2

Changes in Civil Society

Participation in democratic Brazil has as its starting point the emergence of a new associative civic culture. Beginning in the 1970s, voluntary associations began to grow in diversity and density across Brazil, transforming the country's weak public sphere by undermining the traditional patterns of patronage, political favors, and privatism. But, the transformation of associative life varied widely from city to city. This chapter argues that the changes in Brazil's civic culture in since the 1970s increased patterns of association and laid the foundation for democratization. I review the literature that has drawn theoretical connections among a country's associative life and its inclinations toward authoritarianism or democratization. Then I examine the specifics of Brazil's experience, in the context for four different cities, to show how new patterns of association combined to produce a new civic culture that could support democratic reforms.

Assessing the Link between
Association and Authoritarianism

Until the 1970s, Brazil was thought to have a weak public sphere and a strong private sphere (Leal, 1977; DaMatta, 1985; Reis, 1995; Roniger and Waisman, 2002; Avritzer, 2002a). The literature on association typically linked authoritarianism in Brazil to the country's weak associative life, particularly the pervasive clientelism and political favoritism. Low levels of association were often linked to the strength of the Catholic Church (Conniff, 1975; Boschi, 1987; Schmitter, 1971).

This analysis followed Alexis de Tocqueville's remarks in *Democracy in America* that the "country in the face of earth where the citizens enjoy unlimited freedom of association for political purposes [is] the same country . . . in the world where the continual exercise of the right of association has been introduced into civil life" (Tocqueville, 1966: II, 213). Tocqueville's remarks provided a useful framework for analyzing cases in which rich associative life did generate a democratic political system. Yet, he was not very specific about political systems with a low associative propensity, as was the case in Brazil for most of its history.

A Comparative Framework for Associative Culture

In the late 1950s, Edward Banfield transferred Tocqueville's framework to the domain of social science by trying to connect low associative density with the failure of political and economic modernization in non-Western countries: "There is some reason to doubt that the non-Western cultures of the world will prove capable of creating and maintaining the high degree of organization without which a modern economy and a democratic political order are impossible" (Banfield, 1959: 8).[1] Banfield illustrated the obstacles to democratization in a nonassociative culture in an empirical study of socialization in a village in southern Italy, Montegrano. For Banfield, the population of Montegrano pursued "amoral familism" in their social relations, following the maxim: "maximize the material, short-run advantage of the nuclear family. Assume that all others will do likewise" (Banfield, 1959: 85). In contrasting Latin and Anglo-Saxon cultural practices,[2] Banfield concluded that the lack of broader, impersonal structures of trust influenced the capacity of a country to become democratic. In this sense, one could say that Banfield provided a framework to analyze Brazil in the first half of the twentieth century.

1. Fukuyama's book *Trust* is a follow up of Banfield's argument. For Fukuyama both the economy and the political democracy require a broad structure of trust to fully develop. Fukuyama goes beyond Banfield in establishing a larger set of trust institutions and expanding the argument beyond the West versus the East. However, Fukuyama is as unable as Banfield to show how trust is created or how structures of trust change. See Fukuyama, 1995, and for a critique, see Offe, 1996.

2. Banfield's framework has many shortcomings. The first is that democracy is not an exclusive institution of the Anglo-Saxon world, having developed in France as early as in the United States. In addition, it is not clear that a nondemocratic and individualistic culture could not be found in democratic countries, just as it is not clear how Montegrano's culture negatively influenced the Italian democracy.

Banfield's generalization about the differences between democratic and nondemocratic cultures was at the root of the concept of civic culture introduced by Almond and Verba in the 1960s. For Almond and Verba "the working principles of the democratic polity and its civic culture—the ways in which political elites make decisions, their norms and attitudes, as well as the norms and attitudes of the ordinary citizens . . . have the diffuse properties of belief systems" (1963: 5). This concept allowed the establishment of a broad cultural divide between Anglo-Saxon and Iberian political cultures, with a high propensity to associate in the former and a low propensity in the latter. Almond and Verba considered voluntary associations to be key players in democracies because they mediated between the individual and the state (1963: 300; Armony, 2004). In the so-called Latin and Iberian cultures, individuals tended not to act collectively because of their attachment to prepolitical institutions, such as the family, and their rejection of a logic of collective gains (Wiarda, 2001; Reis, 1995).

Associative Culture and Democracy

The attempt to associate culture with readiness for democracy received several criticisms, all of them relevant to the analysis of Brazilian democratization. On a methodological level Barry (1970) argued that although Almond and Verba enumerated democratic and nondemocratic elements of different national cultures, they were unable to relate these elements to the existence or breakdown of democracy. He argued that Almond and Verba failed to relate cultural variables with institutional variables and were thus unable to establish a causal relation between the existence of a noncivic culture and the breakdown of democracy (Barry, 1970: 48). Muller and Seligman also challenged Almond and Verba, as well as the continuation of their work by Ingelhart, on a methodological level (Inglehart, 1997). Muller and Seligman maintained that there is a "possibility that civic culture attitudes are an effect rather than a cause of democracy" (1994: 635). Both criticisms were valid for Brazil. It was not clear whether the breakdown of democracy in 1964 was caused by culture or by the action of specific actors, or why other countries with similar characteristics (Mexico, for instance) did not pass through the same form of authoritarian breakdown. It also was not clear whether associative patterns could change or whether they were a structural characteristic, or even how the new Brazilian democracy affected the values of the population.

The attempt to relate culture to democratization regained momentum with the recent work of Robert Putnam. Putnam has two insights central to the debates on democratization in Latin America. The first is that countries can have more than one political culture and structure of trust. Putnam argues that Italy has had both civic and "uncivic" regions. Second, and perhaps more important, Putnam analytically relates political culture not to the presence or absence of democracy, but rather to its quality: "a dense network of secondary associations embodies and contributes to effective social collaboration. . . . In a civic community associations of like-minded individuals contribute to effective democratic governance" (1993: 90). Thus, for Putnam a nonassociative political culture need not lead to the breakdown of democracy. It leads rather to poor administrative performance and the inability of the political system to utilize new and positive elements of a specific culture to improve its legitimacy. Putnam's approach leads to a completely new understanding of democratization, despite its overemphasis of the density of associative life (Armony, 2004).[3]

In this chapter, I will use Putnam's framework[4] to show how a new civic culture emerged in Brazil and how it influenced democratization. To understand the role of associations in the emergence of participatory institutions, I look not only into their density but also into their role in public policy and their articulation with the political system. Specifically, I examine the capacity of voluntary associations to equalize previous material inequalities (Cohen and Rogers, 1995: 43). Voluntary associations are a form of deliberation on public policy that may equalize unequal access to political institutions. In the case of Brazil, the poor population lacked any strong form of organization during the country's process of modernization and urbanization, both in the countryside and in the cities. Thus, Cohen and Rogers's argument is relevant to Brazil because it throws light on changes

3. Armony in his excellent recent book criticizes Putnam concentrating too much on the density issue. For Armony, Putnam focuses almost exclusively on the idea that associations create virtuous cycles of cooperation among individuals. Armony correctly points out that in many nondemocratic or totalitarian situations, such as pre-Nazi Germany or the southern United States, associations played a key role in politics (Armony, 2004: 60–69). To overcome this shortcoming in associative theory, it is important to supplement the density argument with an argument on how associations establish mediations with the state.

4. Putnam's work has also received several criticisms. Some authors claim that he still sticks to a very structuralist approach to the political system, in which the characteristics that he attributes to southern Italy are as permanent as the contrast proposed by Almond and Verba. The main criticism of Putnam's work in my view is the lack of a perspective on how to create social capital or new associative patterns. See Krishna, 2002; Offe, 1996.

in associative patterns that can affect the distribution of public goods. I will show in Chapters 5, 6, and 7 how poor social actors took advantage of their new organizational skills to claim new rights and public goods.

Democratization and Changing Associative Patterns in Brazil

The classic work on associations in Brazil is Phillip Schmitter's *Interest Conflict and Political Change in Brazil*. Schmitter focused on the rise of state-sponsored corporatism in Brazil after Getulio Vargas seized power. However, Schmitter was also concerned with the anticipation of the organization of professional and business sectors before 1930 (Schmitter, 1971: 137). Schmitter started his analysis by pointing out that during the process of colonial formation in Brazil associations, particularly guilds and corporations, did not play the same kind of role they had played in Portugal (ibid.: 138). Schmitter noted that this situation changed during the nineteenth century with the emergence of new workers' professional associations in Recife and Rio de Janeiro. During the first part of the twentieth century, many new forms of voluntary associations emerged in Brazil, particularly in Rio de Janeiro, among them the commercial association of Rio de Janeiro, the first industrial associations, and trade unions representing the professional middle-class sectors (ibid.: 148). Although Schmitter's approach helps us understand the anticipation of corporatist forms of organization in Brazil before 1930, it misses an important dimension of early twentieth century social life in Brazil: the development of horizontal forms of voluntary associations in Rio de Janeiro and the first leisure associations in São Paulo (Singer and Brant, 1980).

Early Patterns of Association

Voluntary associations developed very slowly in Brazil through most of the twentieth century. During Brazil's first experience with democracy (1946–64), the number of voluntary associations fell in Rio de Janeiro (Conniff, 1975; Boschi, 1987) and in most of the rest of the country (Singer and Brant, 1980). The literature on the dominant practices within these associations suggests most focused on leisure and community activities. For example, neighborhood associations (SABs, for Sociedade de Amigo de Bairro) emerged in São Paulo during the 1950s with the reintroduction of the right to vote in capitals in 1953, and their leaders were often incorporated into the city political system (Singer and Brant, 1980; Moisés, 1975; Gohn, 1991). The political committees of Janio Quadros, the winner of the 1953 election, became leisure associations after his election and had the role of gathering demands to be presented to the city administration. Most of these demands were related to leisure and were met by material benefits provided by the state (Singer and Brant, 1980: 87). The city with the best-organized neighborhood movement in Brazil during the 1950s was Porto Alegre, where FRACABs (Federation of Neighborhood Associations) anticipated characteristics of the democratization period of the 1970s and 1980s (Silva, 2001), in particular the critique of clientelism.

We can note three features of voluntary associations in Brazil during its first democratic period. The first is that very few voluntary associations were formed, and very few that claimed public goods from the state. The second point is related to what has been called "civil society regimes" (Baiocchi, 2005). Most voluntary associations in Brazil during the first democratic experience were recreational and hierarchical, and they adapted themselves to the top-down policies of Brazilian populism (Weffort, 1980; Erickson, 1977). The third point is that the civil society regime was not homogeneous: during the 1950s Porto Alegre neighborhood associations were already diverging from the rest of Brazil in their understanding of relations between the state and civil society.

Evidence of Change

Brazil's democratization between 1974 and 1988 was marked not only by the reestablishment of political competition, but also by a marked increase in the propensity to create voluntary and independent forms of association (Santos, 1993; Gay, 1994; Avritzer, 1995, 2000, 2004; Baiocchi, 2005). Boschi (1987) found that more voluntary associations were created in Rio de Janeiro between 1978 and 1980 than during the entire previous democratic period. Santos (1993) showed a similar phenomena for all categories of voluntary associations in the country's largest cities.

Table 2.1 shows the increase in the number of voluntary associations created in São Paulo, Rio de Janeiro, and Belo Horizonte during Brazil's long transition to democracy. The number of associations doubled in São Paulo in the 1970s and tripled in Belo Horizonte in the 1980s. In both cities, that pace was almost twice the population growth rate in the same period the increase was lower in Rio de Janeiro than in the other two cities because,

Table 2.1. Number of associations founded in large Brazilian cities,
1930–1990

City	1941–50	1951–60	1961–70	1971–80	1981–90
São Paulo	288	464	996	1,871	2,553
Rio de Janeiro	188	743	1,093	1,233	2,498
Belo Horizonte	120	204	459	584	1,597

Note: The growth of associations exceeded the population increase in the three cities in the same period. São Paulo's population increased 43 percent between 1970 and 1980, and 13.5 percent between 1980 and 1990, while the number of new associations increased by 88 percent and 36 percent, respectively. Data for Rio de Janeiro and Belo Horizonte are even more compelling.
Source: Santos, 1993; Avritzer, 2000.

for historical and political reasons, Rio de Janeiro already had the most voluntary associations.

The increase in Brazilian associative life was qualitative as well as quantitative. Some forms of voluntary association that were not very strong before the mid-1970s grew in number and influence. For instance, the number of neighborhood organizations increased from 71 to 534 in Belo Horizonte. In Porto Alegre between 1986 and 1990 the number of neighborhood associations rose more than 50 percent from 240 to 380 (Baiocchi, 2005). The increases in São Paulo and Rio de Janeiro were also very impressive: of the neighborhood associations in the two cities, 97.6 percent and 90.7 percent were created after 1970, respectively. Other types of associations were also relatively new in all three cities: 92.5 percent of the health professionals' associations in São Paulo were created after 1970, as were 76.2 percent of the lawyers' associations in Rio de Janeiro (Santos, 1993). In Belo Horizonte, all 29 associations dealing with environmental protection, human rights, and ethnic issues were created during this period. Thus, all three cities experienced an increasing propensity to associate, a greater number of associations, and an emergence of new associations for claiming material benefits, such as community improvement, and for addressing broad nonmaterial claims, such as environmental protection and human rights.

The changing pattern of association in Brazil supports both Putnam's density argument and Cohen and Rogers's equality argument. The rapid growth in the number of associations shows that voluntary associations are not simply linked to the process of historical formation, as Almond and Verba and even Putnam have claimed, but can change relatively quickly in response to political circumstances. In Brazil, the trigger for this change was an authoritarian experience in which the state intervened deeply into the everyday lives of the poor by removing slums from the central areas of Brazilian cities and encouraging a huge migration from the countryside to the cities, without providing adequate healthcare, education, and infrastructure for the poor. The latter phenomenon shows also the egalitarian side of the process of formation of voluntary associations (Cohen and Rogers, 1995: 43). Although many types of voluntary associations grew in Brazil, the ones that grew the most were those that thrust the poor into politics. The poor organized themselves in Brazil to claim access to public goods, a motive that has proved to be a central characteristic of multicentered citizenship in democratic Brazil.

Associations and Informal Affiliations

The academic debate in the 1990s on associative life in Brazil focused on its density, with some authors challenging the growth in the number of voluntary associations after democratization (Ferreira, 1999). In this section, I will respond to authors who have denied the changing character of associative patterns in democratic Brazil by presenting data on associations in São Paulo in 2003.

    While earlier literature had shown a change in number of associations, these authors raised the issue of the stagnation of the associated population, based on survey data gathered by the IBGE, the Brazilian Census Bureau. The IBGE carried out two surveys on association membership, which showed that only affiliation in leisure associations and different types of churches grew in democratic Brazil, as shown in Table 2.2 (IBGE, 1996; IBGE, 1998).

Table 2.2. Distribution of the population affiliated with voluntary associations in the six largest Brazilian cities, 1988 and 1996 (percent)

Group and Type of Association	1988	1996
Total sample	100.0	100.0
Share who are affiliated with associations	14.3	12.1
Neighborhood associations	2.3	2.5
Religious associations	3.6	5.0
Philanthropic associations	—	0.7
Sports and culture associations	7.0	109
Share who are not affiliated	85.7	87.9
Size of sample	25,502	22,474

Source: Ferreira, 1999.

These data clearly contradict the picture of voluntary associations presented above. They show that voluntary association membership overall in the six largest cities of Brazil decreased from 14.3 percent of to 12.1 percent of the population between 1988 and 1996. In addition, affiliation increased only for religious and leisure associations. The data thus seem to deny the hypothesis that affiliation has grown, although it is hard to explain the growth in the number of associations without any parallel growth in affiliation.

Yet, a major caveat remains in the way the IBGE collected its data. It did not ask about collective action and informal affiliation, but rather asked a closed question about a few types of association. As a result, the IBGE data may undercount participation in voluntary associations because it did not count informal affiliation, particularly at the level of popular movements and neighborhood associations. Most popular movements in Brazil do not stress formal membership. They normally accept all those who come to meetings. Thus, the discrepancy between the IBGE numbers and numbers of voluntary associations could be a methodological discrepancy. To test this hypothesis we carried out a survey in São Paulo that asked 2,403 respondents: "Did you participate in the last 12 months in any form of collective activity?" Table 2.3 shows the response, which fully confirms that more people participate informally in voluntary associations in Brazil than do formally. This is expected since in Brazil economic and political ties tend not to be formal. The data thus suggest strongly that the census data dramatically undercounted the extent of affiliation.

Particularly in regard to neighborhood associations and popular associations, informal participation is very important. We found a much higher

Table 2.3. Distribution of the population in São Paulo participating formally or informally in voluntary associations (percent)

Group and Type of Association	Distribution of Total	Distribution of Participants	Link with Association	
			Formal	Informal
Total sample	100	19	7	12
Share who participate in associations	19	100	100	100
Religious associations	10	51	38	59
Civil associations	9	49	62	41
Share who do not participate	81	—	—	—
Size of sample	2,403	448	166	281

Source: Avritzer, 2004.

associated population in São Paulo (19 percent) than the IBGE survey had found (only 12 percent). In the next sections I discuss the different forms of organization of associative life in four cities in Brazil.

São Paulo

São Paulo is the key city for evaluating the changes in Brazilian associative life. It is a very diverse city scattered across a huge territory of close to 100 square miles. Until the 1950s the population was packed into a much smaller territory in which the wealthy owned houses and the poor lived in *cortiços,* squatter settlements concentrated in the central regions of the city (Caldeira, 2000). Beginning in the 1950s the poor moved or were expelled to the outskirts, where there was no infrastructure. This lack of infrastructure has been one of the major engines of association in the city.

In addition to conflicts around the appropriation of goods and land, São Paulo has seen a pluralization of religious denominations. Catholicism has steadily lost ground in the city since the late 1950s to all kinds of evangelical and neo-Pentecostal churches. The Church tried to regain ground during the 1970s and 1980s by organizing the poor, an action that was initially successful, but was halted by the Vatican and led to the division of the archdiocese into four pieces (Doimo, 2004). The religious division is also a territorial division. Catholicism is stronger in the east of the city, while Pentecostal churches are stronger in the south. Participation in voluntary associations is strong in the eastern and central districts and is linked to the emergence of social movements in the late1970s. The health movement and most of the well-organized neighborhood associations emerged in areas such as São Mateus, São Miguel Paulista, Perus, and Butanta.

Since democratization, São Paulo is a city with strong religious and civil associations, which arose from important social movements and forms of collective action of the democratization period. Health associations still play an important role in the city, as do housing and neighborhood associations. About half (51 percent) of participants in voluntary associations are active in religious associations sponsored either by the Catholic Church or Pentecostal denominations. The other 49 percent are affiliated with civil associations. Half of these civil associations are linked to popular civic issues, such as neighborhood, health, and housing conditions. Toward the periphery of the city, associations generally become more religious in orientation, particularly in the south.

How do social actors conceive of their associations? How they see their political participation? Why do they participate? How do they organize

Table 2.4. Participation in voluntary associations, by gender and type of association (percent)

Type of Association	Total	Men	Women
Share who participate in all associations	19.0	17.2	19.9
Religious associations	9.0	7.6	1.1
Trade unions	1.5	1.8	1.1
Neighborhood associations	2	2.2	1.3
Sport associations	1.5	2	1.1
Housing associations	1	0.6	1.6
Political parties	1	0.7	0.6
Professional associations	0.7	0.6	0.5
Educational associations	0.7	0.6	0.6
Health and handicap associations	0.7	0.1	1.2
Other groups	1.0	1	1
Share who do not participate	81	76	77
Size of sample	2,403	1,130	1,273

Source: Avritzer, 2004.

their associations internally? How do they see their relationship with the political system? To answer these questions, we conducted a survey of 2,403 members of associations in São Paulo distributed in the categories in Table 2.4.

The survey data clearly show the small influence of leisure associations,[5] corroborating the argument of a change in Brazil's civil society regime. In addition, the data reveal the importance of neighborhood associations, along with those for the improvement of housing and healthcare. Such associations represented 3.7 percent of the population and close to 20 percent of the associated population, nearly 300,000 people.

To inquire into the characteristics of associational life, we asked how many times a week members meet and what kind of activities they perform; why they participate in associations and if their work is paid or voluntary; and how decisions are made within the associations. We found a very high level of voluntary work, 94 percent, as well as a very high frequency of participation, with 38 percent of respondents stating that they participate once a week or more in their associations. Thus, the first important result is of high-intensity participation in the city. The most common activities within the associated population are participation in meetings (85 percent), food

5. The criteria used to determine affiliation to a voluntary association was much more careful than the one used by IBGE. IBGE did not differentiate between belonging to a sport club and going there to swim and participating in an assembly. In our survey, we differentiated collective action from paid affiliation to entities (Avritzer, 2004).

distribution (32 percent), and participation in association plenaries (22 percent). Data from Belo Horizonte a few years earlier also found high-intensity participation (Avritzer, 2000). Thus, we can say that São Paulo's associative habits seem to be typical. It is interesting to note that high-intensity participation does not necessary mean democratic participation in decision-making. The survey showed that a large proportion of those who participate do not hold positions in the associations' board, as shown in Table 2.5, particularly within religious associations.

These data caught our attention because they show a discrepancy between intensity of participation, on the one hand, and participation in decision-making, on the other. If we compare intensity of participation in São Paulo with the available data for the United States, where less than 10 percent of those affiliated with associations participate in meetings and only 4 percent dedicate more than five hours a week to their associations, we have to acknowledge the high intensity of participation in São Paulo (Verba, 1995: 54). Nonetheless, 48 percent of respondents said that they did not participate in their associations' main decisions, and, among this group, the main characteristics were affiliation with a religious association and/or education of less than four years of schooling.

Thus, the democratizing effect of affiliation with associations is found mainly among those members of civil or popular associations. Not by chance, these are individuals who join participative arrangements in the area of public policy. Here again it is possible to point to elements of change, as well as elements of continuity. Change is expressed by the people who belong to popular associations and participate in the decision-making process in their associations. As I show in Chapters 5 and 6, these are the people who joined participatory arrangements as they were introduced by the state.

Table 2.5. Survey responses to the question, "Which one of these sentences better expresses your participation?" (percent)

Survey Response	Total	Men	Women	Until Fourth Grade	College Education
You do not participate in the main decisions	48	45	50	55	45
You participate in some decisions	27	28	26	25	25
You participate in the main decisions	25	26	24	20	31
Others	—	1	—	—	—
Size of sample	448	194	253	81	126

Source: Avritzer, 2004.

Not all voluntary associations have aims that are immediately political or linked to political themes. Some authors maintain that voluntary associations produce democratic results in spite of having nonpolitical aims (Putnam, 1993), while others maintain that only certain types of associations have democratizing effects on public life (Locke, 1995; Krishna, 2002). São Paulo associative life seems to point in the latter direction. Social activities related to religious life continue to fulfill an important role in the city's sociability. They still make up the main activity of the associated population, accounting for 36 percent of participation. The main activities and aims of associated actors, however, show the presence of São Paulo's most important popular movements, such as the housing and health movements. Ten percent of people who belong to associations say their main aim is to improve housing, while 7 percent say their aim is improve health conditions. We can thus say that São Paulo's associative life is composed of two main activities. One block, formed by religious associations and spiritual and religious activities, is stronger and represents a larger network of actors and associations, while a second block is made up of popular associations whose actions focus on areas such as health and housing. Most of the respondents in both groups (83 percent) regard their participation in associations as a key component of the defense of their interests (Avritzer, 2004). We can also note that membership in popular associations increases when participatory institutions are put in place in the city, and membership contracts when the city administration pursues antiparticipatory politics.

Porto Alegre and Belo Horizonte

The data on associations in São Paulo are important to understanding associative patterns in large Brazilian cities. Yet, São Paulo should be distinguished from other cities in Brazil, in particular those, like Porto Alegre and Belo Horizonte, that have had institutional participation for a longer period. Two characteristics distinguish São Paulo from the two other cities: the thematic nature and contentious politics of associative life in São Paulo. Since the beginning of the democratization period São Paulo has had more thematic movements, particularly to improve health conditions in the east of the city (see Chapter 6) and to improve housing. Belo Horizonte and Porto Alegre, in contrast, saw more general movements, such as neighborhood movements or the umbrella associations of popular movements. Furthermore, São Paulo's political society has been deeply divided about whether to incorporate popular participation. Politics in the city has been contentious, and the question of participation has divided progressive and conservative politicians. Participation is a less contentious issue in Belo Horizonte and Porto Alegre and is generally accepted by politicians of the center.

The Context in Porto Alegre

In the aftermath of democratization in 1985, neighborhood movements emerged in most capitals of Brazil's South and Southeast, but Porto Alegre went farthest in reorganizing neighborhood associations. In Porto Alegre, much as in São Paulo and Rio de Janeiro, new neighborhood associations were created in the late 1970s to demand public goods and access to city services. However, two major issues distinguished the emerging neighborhood movement in Porto Alegre from others in the Southeast. First, Porto Alegre returned to its earlier tradition of a citywide umbrella organization— the FRACAB—which did not exist in São Paulo and was very differently organized in Rio de Janeiro. Second, although the FRACAB was taken over in the late 1970s by the PMDB, the opposition party under authoritarianism, a drive for a new type of umbrella associations was triggered in 1983 and led to the creation of UAMPA. UAMPA initially represented no more than one-third of the city's neighborhood associations, but it proposed the participation of neighborhood associations in budget issues and had an influence on the city proposals for participation (Avritzer, 2002). The number of neighborhood associations in Porto Alegre during the late 1980s increased dramatically (Table 2.6).

According to the IBGE, close to 22 percent of Porto Alegre's population is affiliated with neighborhood associations, making it the best organized of the six large Brazilian capitals.[6] In addition, Porto Alegre's neighborhood associations have practices that are not found in the other large cities of the Southeast: formal affiliation in associations and the payment of monthly fees. Meetings are generally reported in writing and elections for the leadership take place regularly. Thus, Porto Alegre's civic life differs from that in the rest of Brazil not only in its density, but also in the articulation between this density and a different conception of civic life. The most important characteristic of Porto Alegre's civic life in the democratic period is that these associations increased their brokerage power in city politics during

---

6. IBGE data on associations should be taken cautiously, as I have pointed out earlier. However, one characteristic of neighborhood associations in Porto Alegre makes them more accessible to IBGE surveys, namely, the fact that in Porto Alegre, unlike São Paulo and Belo Horizonte, neighborhood associations affiliate their members and require the payment of a monthly fee.

Table 2.6. Share of the population affiliated with neighborhood associations in Porto Alegre, 1985–1986 and 1990

Year	Population Affiliated with Neighborhood Associations (%)	Number of Neighborhood Associations
1985–1986	22	240
1990	—	380

Source: Baiocchi, 2005; IBGE.

the 1980s. Forms of participation at the neighborhood level have grown steadily in the city since the 1980s, generating a strong constituency for participatory politics. The second important characteristic of Porto Alegre's civic life is the continuity of a conception of involving social actors and voluntary associations in city politics. Since the mid-1980s, all Porto Alegre administrations have pursued the same policy, increasing the leeway of neighborhood associations. These two characteristics will serve as a contrast to the organization of civic life in São Paulo.

The Context in Belo Horizonte

The city had very few neighborhood associations until 1970. Until then, roughly one neighborhood association was created in the city per year (Avritzer, 2000). From the late 1970s and mid-1980s, however, the pattern of association changed, and by the late 1980s Belo Horizonte already had close to 500 neighborhood associations. Although there is an important health movement, most participation takes place in general associations such as neighborhood associations.

Being larger than Porto Alegre, Belo Horizonte faces the territorial segmentation of its associative life. Important neighborhood associations emerged in the city in the second half of the 1970s in the Barreiro region, where the Catholic Church was influential and the left diffuse. The first associations created in this period, such as the Lindeia association, mobilized around better access to public goods. During the 1980s neighborhood associations expanded to Venda Nova, a newer region at that point, with less access to public goods. Most of the neighborhood associations that emerged in Belo Horizonte during the 1970s and 1980s were informal, and they were formalized only in the late 1980s in response to a requirement of a milk program instituted by the government of José Sarney. Thus, Belo Horizonte has a tradition of neighborhood associations, but this tradition is more recent than Porto Alegre's and less segmented than São Paulo's.

Similarities to Porto Alegre

Associative life in Belo Horizonte is closer to the Porto Alegre model than to São Paulo with regard to the values of association actors. Belo Horizonte's associations claim as much autonomy from the state and political parties as Porto Alegre's. In 1998 a survey of the city's voluntary associations, we investigated the forms of organization, types of work, and political conceptions of voluntary association members (Avritzer, 2000). Asked whether they belonged to a political party, 79 percent of the respondents in Belo Horizonte answered that they did not. More significantly, asked if they would stop participating in their association if it became linked to a political party, 67.3 percent said they would. Yet, Belo Horizonte's associated actors are the key members of participatory budgeting and health councils. Thus, while association members may oppose subordination to political parties, they are less concerned about their autonomy in relation to the state.[7] In Belo Horizonte, as in Porto Alegre, relations between the state and civil society are marked by the continuity with which participatory policies have been implemented since the early1990s.

Differences from São Paulo

Two characteristics differentiate the associative life of Porto Alegre and Belo Horizonte from São Paulo. The first is related to the thematic orientation versus generalist concern of voluntary association members. Owing to the history of its democratization, São Paulo's main popular organizations have been concerned with health and urban planning issues. These movements emerged in the city and consolidated a leadership there. Belo Horizonte and Porto Alegre had stronger general movements linked to a more general conception of improving the poor's access to public goods. These internal characteristics made a difference in the implementation of participatory policies

7. The Brazilian debate on the autonomy of civil society from the state began during the early 1980swhen the past of the Brazilian left was thoroughly reexamined by the forces of opposition to the authoritarian regime. The Brazilian opposition considered the capacity of the state to intervene in social movements and trade unions the worst characteristic of the previous democratic period and claimed autonomy (Weffort, 1989; Dagnino, 1994). However, the claim for autonomy can be understood in a strong or a light version. In its strong version it meant complete separation between civil society and political society. The problem with the strong version was that it implied a lack of collaboration between the state and civil society in public policies. In its light version it implied that political parties and the state would not interfere with the organization of civil society. This lighter version allowed more interaction between state and civil society.

during the 1990s: one characteristic of participatory politics in São Paulo has been the dispute between thematic movements and more general policies concerning access to public goods.[8] The second difference involves the relationship between civil society actors and the political system. São Paulo's political system has been divided on the question of participation, a division reaches into the PT. Porto Alegre has been united in favor of participatory policies, even outside the PT. Though not as unified as Porto Alegre, Belo Horizonte stands closer to it than São Paulo. I will draw out the implications of these differences for participatory policies in the next two chapters.

Salvador

The case of Salvador reveals interesting differences in the organization of civic life in Brazil, as well as in the relation between the associated population and the political system. Salvador is located in the Northeast of Brazil, a region considered less inclined toward political participation.[9] Salvador diverges from the South and Southeast model of fast economic growth and social change in two important ways. First, it lagged behind the metropolitan regions of the South and Southeast of Brazil in economic growth until the late 1970s and had much higher population growth than the other cities discussed here. Salvador's population grew at 2.98 percent per year in the 1980s and 1.3 percent per year in the 1990s, when the pace of population growth was declining in most large Brazilian cities (Boschi, 1999: 4). Salvador also has higher levels of poverty than most Brazilian large cities, with 23.8 percent of the population earning less than the minimum wage. Thus, Salvador is poorer than most other metropolitan regions and was slower to change its associative patterns.

Civil society organizations in Salvador have been historically weak. One explanation may be the control of social movement activities by the traditional left. The Brazilian Communist Party (PC do B) is strong in the city and was reluctant to introduce bottom-up policies during the democratiza-

---

8. The most important of these disputes took place during the Marta Suplicy administration between the health movement and participatory budgeting.

9. The stratification of participation in Brazil according to regions has to be further qualified, as well as the remark that the Northeast region is homogeneously nonparticipatory. Brazilian regions are not homogeneous, and traditions of participation vary in the different regions. Recife in the Northeast has had a strong tradition of participation, whereas Bahia is considered a less participatory state. The conception of a homogeneously participatory South also needs to be further qualified. Paraná in the sfouth of Brazil has a very weak participatory tradition. See Avritzer, 2007.

tion period.[10] In addition, Salvador's associative life is centered more around race issues, which are portrayed in broad cultural terms (Ireland, 1999), than around distribution. Salvador had few race associations during the first democratic period (1945–64) because it was difficult to legalize black cultural associations in Brazil during the 1950s and 1960s. During the democratization period large new associations emerged, focusing overwhelmingly on racial issues. Olodum is one of these groups. Called the Olodum Carnival Group until 1984, it then changed its name to the Olodum Cultural Group. Olodum's aims include raising black pride and identity, as well as improving living conditions in the Maciel-Pelourinho area in downtown Salvador (Ireland, 1999: 112). Like other black groups, such as Ilaye, Olondum has been much more successful in promoting local culture than in improving the quality of life of the black population. When the Pelourinho area was completely reconstructed by the city, which systematically relocated the poor and transformed the area in a commercial region, black culture associations could do nothing to prevent it (Fischer and Moura, 1996).

Salvadoran civil society is less developed than other civic traditions in Brazil not only because of the internal configuration of its associations, but also because of the dominant trends within its political society. Salvador's political life has been dominated by the Magalhães family for the past 20 years. Antonio Carlos Magalhães was mayor of Salvador and governor of Bahia during the authoritarian period. He played an important role during the transition, supporting Tancredo Neves, the opposition candidate whose winning triggered democratization, and ensuring the survival of the local oligarchy. Since democratization, the opposition has won two elections in the city, the first time with Lidice da Matta in 1993 and the second in 2004. The Da Matta administration tried to implement participatory policies, but it has been boycotted by the Magalhães and finally gave up. In the past 15 years the Magalhães' control over Salvadoran politics has been overwhelming, and they have rejected all forms of public participation.

Although there are not many data on civic associations in the city, one IBGE study reveals an interesting contrast between Salvador and Porto Alegre with regard to the population's contact with politicians (Table 2.7). Thus, it is possible to observe that a low rate of association with a concentration on race and culture has underpoliticized Salvador's civic life. A smaller share of contacts arise from citizens' claims, suggestions, or com-

10. It is beyond the scope of this work to analyze the Brazilian left tradition, but it is important to point out that most civil society organizations during the democratization period were sponsored either by the Catholic Church or by new left sectors. None of them has had a strong presence in Salvador.

plaints in Salvador than in Porto Alegre, while citizens are more often plead-
ing for favors. Despite the importance of Olodum in cultural activities, it
did not have the same impact claiming public services and public goods. In
addition, Salvadoran political society has been conservative and opposed
to participation, reducing the access of the poor to public goods. Table 2.8
summarizes the four cases discussed in this chapter.

*Table 2.7. Distribution of citizens who made
contact with politicians in Salvador and Porto
Alegre, by motive (percent)*

Motive for the Contact	Salvador	Porto Alegre
Ask favors	51.48	37.81
Make claims	21.16	24.39
Make suggestions	14.02	18.46
Make complaints	13.35	19.35

Source: IBGE, 1996.

Table 2.8. Patterns of civil society formation in four Brazilian cities

City	Civic Organization before 1964	Civic Organization after Democratization	Pattern of Interaction with Political Society
São Paulo	Recreational and linked to populist politics.	Huge expansion in the east and west zones of the city.	Contested outside the PT and in same sectors of the PT.
Porto Alegre	More horizontal and with relative independence from politicians.	Huge expansion in some sectors of the city after democ-ratization. After the introduction of participatory budg-eting homogeneous presence in all neighborhoods.	General consensus on par-ticipation within and outside the PT.
Belo Horizonte	Very weakly organized particularly in poor regions of the city.	Huge expansion in some sectors of the city after democ-ratization. After the introduction of participatory budg-eting homogeneous presence in all neighborhoods.	Strong consensus on the PT and within left sectors. Some PT sectors reject broad participation.
Salvador	Very weakly organized particularly in poor regions of the city.	Small expansion linked to black culture.	Strong consensus among the liberal against participation.

We can thus see that the organization of civic life in the four cities followed different patterns, with Porto Alegre assuming the lead in terms of the independence of civic associations and their impact on the political system. Belo Horizonte seems to be the second most successful case, owing to its continuity and the role of participatory budgeting in expanding existing civic networks. São Paulo is the most complicated case, but still a partial success: voluntary associations have not been able to expand to all parts of the city or to create a broad consensus on the desirability of participation. Salvador is clearly the least successful case: the density of associations increased relatively little after democratization and the relation between civil society and the political system is almost nonexistent. In the concluding remarks of this chapter I will relate the changing associative patterns to the question of the emergence of participatory institutions in Brazil.

Associative Life and Participatory Institutions in Brazil

Only with the introduction of participatory institutions did voluntary associations acquire general influence in a few Brazilian cities, such as Porto Alegre and Belo Horizonte. In other cities this drive was not as strong, and opposition by political society sectors prevented its generalization, as in Salvador. Participatory institutions had to deal with this uneven growth, which has influenced their uneven dynamics. Even within cities, affiliation with voluntary associations varied widely across regions, In São Paulo, for example, three districts have affiliation levels of around 25 percent of the population (Lapa, Butanta e Pinheiros, and Freguesia e Casa Verde e Socorro) whereas others, like the very poor regions of Campo Limpo and Boi Mirim, have almost none. Thus, inequality in the associative life in São Paulo is linked to the lack of popular associations in the southern part of the city, where religious associations thrive. This reduces the efficiency and viability of participatory politics in the city, as I will show in Chapter 5.

Belo Horizonte and Porto Alegre are in a different associative universe. Popular associations are better distributed in both cities, owing to long-standing state incentives to create associations in the city's outskirts through participatory budgeting or health councils. Thus, popular associations are not equally distributed in Brazilian cities; rather, they are concentrated in areas with a tradition of popular movements. Associations that demand participation in public policy expand when these policies are implemented. The problem, however, is that the expansion of the influence of democratic civic life remains dependent on political coalitions and practices within political society, which may become a liability.

It is at this level that Putnam's analysis of the density of patterns of association reveals its limits. I have showed in this chapter that change in the density of associative life was an important part of Brazilian democratization. This argument needs to be further qualified because not all areas have seen an increase in density and also because the interaction between civil society associations and the political system becomes a key variable in determining whether the new civic culture manifests itself in participatory institutions.

Two issues become relevant in this context. The first is that not all voluntary associations play the same role. The importance of the Brazilian case is the emergence of associations that forward the interests of the poor population (Cohen and Rogers, 1995: 43; Cohen, 1997). The second issue is that only the interaction between civil associations and a group within political society willing to bring participatory and deliberative practices to the administrative level gives the new associated actors a democratizing role. However, the presence or the lack of a strong associative tradition influences the effectiveness of participatory institutions, as I will show in Chapter 4.

I will also show in Chapters 5, 6, and 7 that changes at the civil society level in large Brazilian cities produced a new dynamic between social actors and local government. In this process different types of voluntary associations were important in different parts of the country: city master planning, health councils, and participatory budgeting are good examples of this relation. In each case, voluntary associations that emerged during democratization played key roles that included organizing the poor, introducing alternative practices, and organizing to propose new legislation on health and urban reform. The spread of these practices, however, remained dependent on a political actor willing to bring them to the center of political power. In the next chapter I will analyze the trajectory of the PT and its role in the emergence of new participatory practices in Brazil.

3

Changes in Political Society

Political parties are often defined by their strategy or their sense of identity (Offe, 1974; Menegello, 1989; Keck, 1992; Przeworski, 1988; Kitschelt, 2000). Parties usually emerge either to compete in elections, in which case building a winning constituency is their main concern, or they are the result of a new identity that has emerged in society, be it that of workers, peasants, environmentalism, religion, or any other broad coalescing vision. Usually those who introduce new party identities tend to downplay the strategic side of political competition (Menegello, 1989; Keck, 1992; Ladrech, 1999). However, every successful mass party has to find the right balance between identity and strategy.

Brazil's Postwar Experience with Political Parties

Latin American party systems have been based more on the competition among elites than on the formation of an identity. Until 1980, Brazil was a classical case of party formation among elites within a very unstable political system.

Parties in the First Democratic Period

Parties did not endure the first democratic experience (1946–64), as emerging mass leaders, such as Getúlio Vargas, Jânio Quadros, and João Goulart, overshadowed formal political institutions (Mainwaring and Scully, 1995). Parties fragmented, and clientelism dominated the politics of the period.

Appropriation of public resources became a common practice of those seeking to build majorities in Congress, while the state tried to insulate bank and state-run enterprises from Congress (Nunes, 1984). No other large country in Latin America showed as little political party stability as Brazil between 1946 and 1980. Thus, identity parties system did not emerge in Brazil during the country's first experience of democracy. Most of the parties emerged from intraelite competition—some sponsored by Vargas, others by his opponents or the opponents of populism.

Parties during the Authoritarian Regime

The authoritarian regime that seized power in 1964 thought exclusively in terms of political strategy. Because it considered its rupture with political normality a provisional break that should not become permanent,[1] the authoritarian regime allowed Congress to continue to operate, but purged it of undesirable Congressmen. The decision to allow the operation of the political and juridical institutions was intended to establish a semidemocratic or semiauthoritarian political order with a combination of electoral and non-electoral mechanisms. Yet the problem of how to build electoral majorities soon emerged: the authoritarian regime needed to compete in and win local elections.

The regime's strategy was to secure "authorization" for the partial functioning of political society. The condition for the operation of the political system was the political society's submission to the authoritarian state. The regime imposed a dualist party structure, with a regime and an opposition party (Alves, 1988), and adopted several tactics to subdue political society to its imperatives. The first was establishing a veto over political will formation by purging deputies; the second, finding a political base outside the large cities, and thus more conservative and more traditional than itself. The presence of clientelism in Brazilian politics was broadened—an act that would have dire consequences for democratic Brazil. The opposition MDB party incorporated the same logic as the party that supported the regime, ARENA,

1. The Brazilian authoritarian regime understood its break with democracy as a provisional break. The reading of the Institutional Act Number 1 and even the introduction to the Institutional Act Number 5, claim the adhesion to democracy in the long run. See Brazil (12/13/1968). Yet, the practice of the authoritarian regime has always been antidemocratic in the sense that it granted itself the prerogative to change political results after the fact.

because this logic was generated by the political system itself (Kinzo, 1988).[2] Only with the party reform of 1979–80 could a new political logic emerge.

Parties during Political Reform and Democratization

Brazil's economic and political crisis in the 1980s triggered a negotiated transition to democracy that was concluded in 1985 (Alves, 1988; Martins and Velasco e Cruz, 1983; Kinzo, 1988; Avritzer, 1999; Ames, 2002). The authoritarian regime began political reform in 1979–80 with strategic intentions. After 1978, elections became plebiscites, and the electorate tended to vote for the opposition. The 1979–80 electoral reform allowed the pluralization of the party structure and led to the emergence of the first mass party in Brazil's history, the PT, or Workers' Party (Duverger, 1964). Since its foundation, the PT has been a mass party in at least four respects: first, it drew on social and political movements—the new unionism and Catholic movements —that emerged outside the political realm (see Chapter 2); second, it created early on a very centralized national political leadership; third, it established a link between its grassroots and the party political life through national and local meetings; and fourth, it adopted a political platform and has sought to act according to this doctrine (Menegello, 1989: 33; Keck, 1992). Every major change of course in the PT's history has reflected a change of political doctrine. For example, party doctrine was revised at the IX National Summit in 1994, when the moratorium on foreign debt was taken out of the party program, and at the Recife Summit that preceded the election of Luiz Inácio Lula da Silva, when some neoliberal elements were introduced into the party's economic policy (Azevedo, 1995: 157; Pallocci Filho, 2003).

The PT changed the political patterns of democratic Brazil, At the level of political practices, the PT challenged several elements of the Brazilian political culture: the lack of party discipline in Congress and the tendency of all political forces to support the federal government; private relations and influence between political parties and the country's main economic groups; and, most important, the century-old practice of exchanging votes for political goods at the local level (Leal, 1977). Thus, the PT represented

---

2. The MDB incorporated into its ranks several politicians who were clientelist and did not share the kind of opposition stand its leadership has had vis-à-vis the authoritarian regime. These politicians were incorporated into the MDB to increase its electoral chances. Orestes Quercia in São Paulo, Newton Cardoso in Minas Gerais, Iris Resende in Goias, and Chagas Freitas in Rio de Janeiro are examples of this move (Hagopian, 1996).

a sharp political renewal in Brazil at least until the emergence of the Mensalão scandal in 2005 (Flynn, 2005).

Over the past 20 years the PT has become the most successful leftist party in the recent history of Latin America. It steadily increased its influence in Brazilian politics over the 1980s and 1990s. In 1988, it won elections in four Brazilian capitals, among them São Paulo and Porto Alegre. Its widely known participatory budgeting was introduced in Porto Alegre in 1990. In 1989, Lula almost won the elections for president after surprising everyone and making his way to the runoff with Fernando Collor de Mello, the candidate of the Brazilian elites. In 1992, the PT played a central role in the impeachment of Collor de Mello and after that became a champion of anticorruption politics in Brazil. The number of cities governed by the PT grew steadily in the 1990s, including Belo Horizonte, Brazil third largest city in 1993, Recife, the most important capital of the Northeast in 2000, and São Paulo in 2000. The party governed 187 cities by 2004, when it was victorious in 400 cities. The PT representation in Congress also grew steadily, from 3 members in 1982 to 92 in 2002, when Lula was elected president of Brazil.

Throughout its short and successful history, the PT has faced the classic dilemma of every leftist mass party between identity and competitive capacity (Offe, 1974). In the early 1980s, the PT understood itself as having a commitment to social movements: it pledged to "not only participate in elections but also in labor's everyday struggles," leading "to the direct exercise of economic and political power" (PT, 1980). In this sense, the PT's early identity was formed by a conception of integrated labor struggles outside and inside parliament. This conception was electorally defeated in 1982 and was changed to a conception of popular government that became successful in the late 1980s. Around that time, the PT built a centralized political machine under the control of José Dirceu.[3] The PT organized its

---

3. José Dirceu is a political actor whose role in the PT rise and eventual demise will still have to be told. He was an important student leader during the 1960s, who went to armed struggle at the end of the decade. He stayed hidden in Brazil during most of the authoritarian period and went back to politics after the amnesty of 1979. Dirceu reconstituted a group of leftist militants in the PT. Most of this group has had a castrist orientation and were not very fond of participatory politics. Dirceu made his way up in the PT by thwarting the candidacy of Francisco Weffort as a Constituent Assembly member in 1986. Defeated in the elections Weffort resigned as general secretary, and Dirceu emerged as the all-powerful leader. Dirceu centralized the party in ways that could not have been envisioned earlier. Dirceu established a proportion mechanism that allowed the majority group within the PT to run the party without consulting other groups. Dirceu

members to run electorally around three major rules: obligatory party contributions; open votes on the party list at party conventions; and joint action in parliament. These three features would distinguish the PT organizationally from other Brazilian political parties. Thus, during the late 1980s the PT constructed itself on two pillars: a pillar of identity based on the idea of popular government, and a pillar of strategy based on the idea of party discipline and self-finance. Both pillars became very well integrated in the 1990s as the PT grew at the local level.

In this chapter, I explain the overlapping factors that allowed the creation of a popular mass party in Brazil in the 1980s after the failure of the Brazilian Communist Party in the previous democratic period. I also explain the Workers' Party's evolution in the 1990s and how it escaped the fate of most leftist parties after the demise of the Soviet Union. I then differentiate PT leaderships according to their participatory identity, showing that a common national orientation for participation led to different local policies. In closing, I propose a model to distinguish among local PT parties in São Paulo, Porto Alegre, Belo Horizonte, and Salvadoran. These differences will account partially for the success or failure of participatory policies in these cities.

The Origin of the PT as a Mass Party

The PT has its political origins outside the Brazilian political system. The Brazilian political system in the late 1970s was absorbed by the moves and countermoves of the authoritarian regime and the opposition PMDB Party. The PMDB pursued the undifferentiated majority strategy of an omnibus party,[4] aiming exclusively to defeat the authoritarian regime in Congress. The new PT, in contrast, tried to challenge the developmental state, the proj-

---

also sponsored the intervention in local electoral directories in Rio de Janeiro and Minas Gerais in preparation for Lula's elections in 2002. Dirceu was considered by the Brazilian Congress the main person behind the Mensalão scandal that has shaken Lula's government.

4. Fernando Henrique Cardoso coined the opposition strategy in Brazil the creation of an omnibus party. According to Cardoso, in an omnibus each passenger could get on where he wishes and get off where he wishes. Cardoso never took a bus in São Paulo. If he had, he would have noticed a common phenomenon in Brazil, which is overcrowded buses that do not allow passenger to get off where they wish, but only where the bus driver stops and most passengers get off. This actual experience seems to represent better the PMDB strategy. Because so many conservative politicians joined the party, they took over the leadership and the Cardoso group eventually had to leave the omnibus party. See Cardoso, 1989.

ect that dominated Brazilian politics from the 1930s to the 1980s. The PT's critique of the developmental state focused on its subordination of labor and social movements to the state (Weffort, 1989; Alves, 1988; Sader, 1988; Keck, 1989, 1992).

A Coalition of Three Diverse Forces

The PT's political project arose from the claims for autonomy from the state made both by the new unionism (Humphrey, 1982; Keck, 1989; Barros, 1999) and the Catholic Church (Casanova, 1994; Doimo, 2004). Autonomy meant something different in each case. For the new unionism, autonomy meant breaking the Ministry of Labor's control over trade union organization.[5] This goal was the origin both of the São Bernardo Movement and of Lula as a political leader. For the Catholic Church, autonomy meant the ability of social actors to claim public goods—land, social services, healthcare, or urban improvements, such as pavement and sewerage—independently from the state. These were the internal origins of a project that also claimed an external heritage, namely, a critique of the uncritical support of the Brazilian left, especially the Communists, for economic development strategies (Chilcote, 1982).

The PT thus represented a particular connection between party and identity. The PT presented itself from the very beginning as a mass working-class party. PT members identified themselves with labor militants demanding autonomous negotiations with the state, poor city dwellers demanding urban infrastructure, and landless peasants demanding land. These identities implied two different kinds of actions that marked the PT from its beginnings: the critique of clientelism and the adoption of participatory democracy. The PT critique of clientelism allowed it to position itself as a modern party, to assume a critical stand against traditional Brazilian politics, and later to present itself critically in several corruption scandals during the 1990s. The PT was the champion of anticorruption politics in Brazil until 2005 (Flynn, 2005). This identity would also allow it to innovate institutionally by introducing forms of participation in budgeting, health, and urban policy.

5. This was a discussion that emerged in Brazil in the mid 1930s. Trade unions were free until Vargas's rise to power in 1930. In 1932 the Ministry of Labor established state control over trade union organization, as it introduced the formal labor registration card. Trade unions fought hard for their autonomy and defeated the Vargas government during the Constituent Assembly of 1933–34. Yet, a few days after the enforcement of the 1934 Constitution the Ministry of Labor reissued a law linking trade unions to the state (Barbosa, 1980).

A Party Forging Its Identity

In its constitution the PT connected the struggle for the autonomy of social actors to grassroots forms of organization.[6] With this move, the party broke with a tradition of elitist democracy that had prevailed in Brazilian politics since at least the 1930s. This break led the PT to react against the elitist transition pact, which did not take into account the demands of social movements and societal interests. It was also the kernel of the PT's proposal for participation in the Constituent Assembly and later, in the 1990s, for participatory budgeting, as well as many other forms of participation at the local level such as city master plans. In this way, grassroots democracy became a means of breaking with an exclusionary political culture and assuming a modern political identity. It allowed the PT to become a legal, open, mass party that defined its political proposals according to its institutional and extrainstitutional experience.

The PT ran in the 1982 elections, the first free elections since 1964,[7] as the direct expression of grassroots social movements. It identified the political limits of Brazilian modernization with class interests. By linking the critique of an elitist political society with both the authenticity of class interests and the direct expression of the socially oppressed, the PT misunderstood the nature of the field of political competition and went down to electoral defeat. At the national level, it did not win even 5 percent of the national vote (Keck, 1992: 149). Indeed, it won more than 3 percent in just two states. It probably got fewer votes than would be expected, given the influence of the social movements to which it was linked. Thus, in its first

6. Fernando Henrique Cardoso was the first to explore the PT's naiveté about democracy. He attributed it to an old conception that related party-building with authentic representation. Cardoso attributed the poor electoral performance of the PT in 1982 to this aspect, to which he contrasted the PMDB as the model of the mass party not built around class interests but rather around "social variation." Cardoso was right on one count and wrong on another. He was correct to suppose that a very strict representation of a grassroots social movement does not lead to broad electoral representation. He was wrong to suppose that the opposition between the PMDB and the PT could be reduced to strict representation of class interests versus social variation. There were other issues involved, such as the possibility of forming a party around the notion of identity and the recovery of a critique of elitist democracy. If the PT critique of representative democracy was naive, its critiques of the specific way political society was organized in Brazil were not. See Cardoso, 1989.

7. The elections of 1982 were not completely free. They involved a dispute over the state administrations as the center of political decision-making. They were also the first elections that were not plebiscites and in which several parties run. However, there were still limits to political propaganda, and the government predetermined that votes could be given to only one party. On the elections of 1982, see Skidmore, 1999.

political stage, the PT sought to make its identity its main competitive asset and was soundly defeated.

After 1985 the PT reworked not only its identity, but also its organizational structure. The new conception of the PT after 1985 had two main dynamics: a societal dynamic linked to social movements and an institutional dynamic of democracy, which referred not only to members of social movements but to the population as a whole. These changes transformed the PT from a class-based party into an electoral party with a strong social movement constituency, allowing it to sharply criticize both the elitist nature of the political system in Brazil and the dominant patrimonial political culture. At the same time, the anticorruption stand of parliament members linked to the PT and the PT's success in local government changed the Brazilian public's view of the party.

The impeachment of Collor de Mello was the first moment in which the PT acted as an anticorruption party in the Brazilian Congress. Collor belonged to a very traditional political oligarchy in Alagoas. The family was used to impunity in the broadest sense of the word.[8] His brother's revelation of a corruption ring in his government destroyed his government. The PT had an active role in the CPI, the parliamentary hearings on this influence ring (Avritzer, 1999). The CPI and the impeachment took place at a moment in which forces of the center were crafting an alliance with Collor. Thus, the impeachment helped to redefine the PT's identity in the 1990s. After the impeachment, the PT's anticorruption stand was reinforced with the so-called budget CPI, which revealed a corruption ring linked to the federal budget. With this second round of corruption hearings, the PT traded its identity as a socialist labor party for that of an anticorruption popular party. This identity involved investigating corruption cases, avoiding mismanagement in its own administration, and having federal deputies who were drawn from outside the political system and who kept close links with public opinion. In the early 1990s the PT redefined itself ideologically and organizationally with its anticorruption stand. It associated its origins outside parliament with a critique of politics as usual. Yet, it was at the local level that the PT most distinguished itself from other parties by becoming the champion of participatory politics. The success of its administrations proved the PT's capacity to govern. However, to understand the successes,

8. In a not very well known case, Collor de Mello's father was involved in a murder case inside the Brazilian Congress in the early sixties. He tried to shoot a deputy who was his enemy but missed the target and killed another deputy. He was later absolved in the criminal case.

as well as the failures of these policies, it is necessary to disaggregate the identity and strategy debate at the local level. The PT has not been as participatory in all states and cities as its national identity might lead us to believe, and the different results in participatory policies can be explained by differences in local identities.

Identity and Strategy at the Local Level

The PT identity was the product of three movements: the new unionism, the grassroots Catholic movement, and the new left. The PT emerged almost simultaneously in three Brazilian states, São Paulo, Minas Gerais, and Rio Grande do Sul, where these movements were strong and the party had the bulk of its support up to the 1989 elections.[9] In the latter two states PT support was concentrated in the capitals, Belo Horizonte and Porto Alegre. Yet each of these movements took a different form in each state and capital, as summarized in Table 3.1 and discussed in detail in the following sections.

São Paulo

São Paulo is a singular case for at least three reasons. The first is an over-concentration of new unionism. Of the 11 members who created the new unionism, 6 were from São Paulo. In addition, São Paulo was the only state in Brazil where PT support extended beyond the capital and reached the metropolitan region in the first six years of the party's existence (1980–86). This support came mainly from the industrial belt of the city, the ABC region. Second, Catholic activism in the city was very uneven, with important grassroots leadership in the east, while the PT was relatively disorganized in other regions, in particular in the south or where it had clientelist constituencies, such as the Tato family.[10] Third, the influence of the organ-

9. In the elections of 1989 Lula went to the runoff in second place, defeating the traditional leftist politician Leonel Brizola. The key states for Lula's electoral success were São Paulo, where he got 17 percent of the total state votes, and Minas Gerais, where he got 23 percent. Rio Grande do Sul strongly supported Brizola in that election, and Lula got 6 percent of the votes there.

10. The Tato family is a classical example of the mix between clientelism and grassroots politics that developed in some parts of Brazil. The Tatos are from a region in the southern district of the city of São Paulo called Capela do Socorro, where they initially organized grassroots constituencies as every other PT group did during the 1980s. In the 1990s they started to move from grassroots to clientelistic policies. For example, they sponsored the occupation of public land reserved for environmental protection in the

Table 3.1. Patterns of grassroots participation in four Brazilian cities

City	Left Sectors	Catholic Sectors	New Unionism
São Paulo	Divided on participation. Jose Dirceu group was more top down and interested in electoral politics.	In favor of participation, but isolated in a few districts of the city.	More interested in corporatist representation after an initial mobilization period.
Belo Horizonte	United on participation, but less radically in favor than in Porto Alegre. The PT was more cautious of the opposition than in Porto Alegre.	In favor of participation in spite of the conservative trajectory of the Catholic Church in the city.	Weak. It has one marginal leadership in the movement.
Porto Alegre	All PT groups were united behind participatory policies that had the support of opposition sectors until 1992.	Weak.	Very progressive and in favor of participatory policies.
Salvador	Left sectors were weak in the PT until the 1990s. Traditional left controlled city left.	Weak within the PT.	Strong and very interested in corporatist representation.

ized left in the city of São Paulo was strong, mainly through José Dirceu, José Genoino, and Rui Falcão, leaders of different leftist factions during the late 1960s and early 1970s, who were in exile or in jail at the beginning of the democratization process. The leftist sectors of São Paulo's PT were not particularly in favor of participation, while its Catholic sector, though in favor of participation, has never able to assume party hegemony.

Thus, the party's national identity as a grassroots socialist party merged with local politics. In the case of the city of São Paulo, the identity of the PT as a grassroots party applied only to the Catholic Church militants and selected sectors of the left. The main group within the left, the Dirceu group, always collided with this grassroots view of politics. Not by chance, Dirceu, Genoino, and Falcão became the main strategists of the PT and also vote

---

southern district of São Paulo, which cast doubts upon their political practices. From then on, the Tatos have operated as an expanded family and have been present in all the political activities of their district. They are considered the large holders of vote blocks within the left in the city of São Paulo today. During the direct elections for president of the PT in 2005, the Tatos were accused of sponsoring generalized fraud (*Folha de São Paulo,* September 2, 2005).

champions within the party. The new unionism was more about interest-based representation than about grassroots participation (Oliveira, 2003). All attempts to introduce participation in São Paulo would be marked by this duality between its grassroots identity and electoral strategy, as I show later.

Belo Horizonte

In the two other states, Minas Gerais and Rio Grande do Sul, PT support was concentrated in the capitals and came mainly from two sectors. In the case of Belo Horizonte, the Catholic Church and the organized left were the main forces, while the new unionism had only a symbolic role in the party's first two years (1980–82) (Lima, 1988; Abers, 1996). Although the Catholic Church in Belo Horizonte had long sided with conservative groups within the National Bishop Conference, the Church allowed grassroots activities in the city's industrial belt (Wanderley, 1998). That stance contrasted with the situation in Rio de Janeiro, where grassroots activism was halted by the Church hierarchy. In Belo Horizonte, Catholic militants linked to the Church emerged in this process, including important PT leaders such as Patrus Ananias, Nilmario Miranda, Tilden Santiago, Raul Messias, and Durval Angelo. The other important source of PT activism in Belo Horizonte was the left. The organized left had an important presence in the city in the late 1960s and had established roots in sectors such as professional trade unions, teachers associations, bank unions, journalists associations, and human rights and environmental groups. Important PT leaders who emerged from these movements include Helena Greco, Luis Dulci, and Virgilio Guimaraes. The initial presence of the PT in Belo Horizonte was small, but it grew quickly after the second round of the 1989 presidential elections, in which Lula won almost 80 percent of the vote. In Belo Horizonte's both leftist and Catholic PT militants favored participation, so that once the PT was in power there was not much conflict over it.

Porto Alegre

Porto Alegre's PT also diverged from São Paulo's. First of all, the new unionism in Porto Alegre was more grassroots-oriented than in São Paulo and also more tolerant of other leftist groups. A very particular sector of the new unionism, represented by Olivio Dutra, also made itself felt in the city. Dutra entered politics after serving as president of the banking clerks' union. In the mid-1980s Dutra crafted strong support that lasted for more than ten years, until his dispute with the Tarso Genro's group about the gubernatorial primaries in 1998.

Two important sectors of the organized left, the Tarso Genro group and the so-called Socialist Democracy group, were part of the PT in Porto Alegre and shared its grassroots identity as a leftist socialist party. Raul Pont, president of teachers' union, and his group Socialist Democracy had a strong presence in many neighborhoods, while Tarso Genro had been in exile during the authoritarian period. What has characterized the Porto Alegre PT is a broad coalition inside and outside the party, with groups of the Labor Democratic Party (*Partido Democrático Trabalhista,* or PDT) also favoring participation.

Salvador

In Salvador, the PT was initially very weak and has had a very uneven presence among Catholic, leftist, and union groups. The Catholic Church is very conservative in the city, and Pope John Paul II nominated as the city bishop one of his closest friends Dom Lucas Moreira Neves. Neves implemented a conservative policy that offered no space for progressive views. At the same time, the new left was very weak in Salvador, and the old left that had not joined the PT continued to be strong in the city. The only group relatively strong in Salvador among the three initial PT groups was the new unionism, with its presence in Petrobras and in telecommunications. Jacques Wagner and Walter Pinheiro were the strong names of the new unionism in the city. Neither has had a strong concern with participatory policies.

Participation at the Local Level

The rise of the PT in municipal elections started in 1988. In that year, the PT elected mayors in four capitals, including São Paulo and Porto Alegre (Table 3.2). The presence of the PT in the city of São Paulo was significant from the very beginning, but its growth was less constant than in Belo Horizonte and Porto Alegre, as we can see from selected results in local elections. In the first elections in 1982 for governor (the first mayor elections took place after democratization in 1986), Lula already received 14.9 percent of the votes in the city of São Paulo—more than PT candidates in other states. In 1988, the PT elected Luiza Erundina and Olivio Dutra in São Paulo and Porto Alegre with a little more than one-third of votes cast (1988 were the last elections without a run-off in cities with more than 200,000 electors). However, in 1992 the PT's share in São Paulo decreased, whereas the party won reelection in Porto Alegre with more votes than in 1988. In the

Table 3.2. Votes cast for the PT in mayoral elections in four Brazilian cities, 1998–2004 (percent)

City	1988	1992	1996	2000	2004
São Paulo	33.0	30.68	24.51	38	35.8
Belo Horizonte	24.0	36.91	22	46[a]	68.4
Porto Alegre	34.34	40.76	55.0	48.7	37
Salvador			29.8	35	21.7

a. In coalition.
Source: Local electoral courts (*Tribunal Regional Eleitoral do Distrito Federal,* or TRE).

case in Belo Horizonte, the first PT candidate elected mayor was Patrus Ananias in 1992, with 36.9 percent of the votes. In the 1996 election, two candidates disputed the continuation of Ananias administration in Belo Horizonte: Guimares of the PT, who won 22 percent of the votes, and the PSB vice mayor Celio de Castro, who received 35 percent in the first round and more than 70 percent in the runoff (TRE, 1996). Castro won the elections and continued participatory policies in the city. Since then the PT has run in a coalition with the PSB and increased its share in the city to 68 percent in 2004. Castro joined the PT in 2001. In Porto Alegre the PT increased its share of the vote until 1996, when it won 55 percent.

Thus, we can establish the following typology of local politics in the three cities. In São Paulo, Belo Horizonte, and Porto Alegre, the PT was initially strong, and strongest in São Paulo. The three groups that gave birth to the PT were not equally represented in the three cities, and they diverged as the party grew, as I will show below. The PT initially grew faster in São Paulo, electing Luiza Erundina as mayor with 33 percent of the votes. That share, however, proved to be the ceiling: Eduardo Suplicy, running for the PT in 1992, received only 30 percent of the votes. The PT's share decreased until 2000, when Marta Suplicy was elected. In contrast, the party's share of votes in Porto Alegre and Belo Horizonte increased almost continually, making PT hegemony in the two cities less contentious. Salvador is again a fourth case. The PT was initially very weak in the city and did not elect a federal deputy for the Constituent Assembly. When the PT grew, its main leaders were trade unionists without a participatory identity.

We can also make a typology of the willingness of the PT to carry out participatory politics based on three elements: party unity on participation; PT electoral hegemony; and the opposition's willingness to accept participatory policies. The three elements express a combination of identity and strategy. The initial basis for participatory politics at the local level is party identification with grassroots politics. It is this element that provided the initial boost for participation, as I will show in the next section of this chapter. However, where this identity is lacking and the PT vote does not grow, there is a strong chance that the PT will trade participation for electoral viability, as happened in São Paulo between 2000 and 2004.

São Paulo

Luiza Erundina was elected mayor of São Paulo in 1988, the most important administrative position the PT had won at that time. Erundina's nomination as the PT's candidate was not smooth: she ran in the primaries against the candidate supported by the national leadership, Plinio de Arruda Sampaio, at that point considered a moderate.[11] Erundina defeated him with the support of the party's left and conducted an independent campaign that to everyone's surprise defeated the favorite, Paulo Maluf.[12] Erundina broke ranks with the national leadership by naming a secretariat that was basically composed of independent intellectuals, such as Paulo Freire, Marilena Chaui, and Paulo Singer, and leftist militants. These nominations were considered a declaration of war by the national PT leadership (Couto and Abrúcio, 2003).

Erundina had problems not only with the PT leadership but also with the São Paulo city council from the very beginning of her administration. In 1988 the PT elected 19 of 53 city councilors and immediately faced fierce opposition from former Malufista members, as well as other conservative and centrist parties such as the PSDB. Unlike Dutra in Porto Alegre and Ananias in Belo Horizonte, Erundina chose not to seek a coalition in parliament. According to her leader in the city council, "Erundina claimed that the PT would not let her move forward in this direction" (Whitaker, 2003; Couto and Abrúcio, 2003). In spite of stiff opposition within the PT and city council, Erundina moved to implement participatory policies: she proposed a very participatory city charter (*Lei Organica Municipal*) reorganizing the use of the urban space (Singer, 1994). Opposition to the master plan proved insur-

11. Plinio de Arruda Sampaio trajectory in the PT gives a good example of the party changes during the 1990s. Sampaio was considered a moderate member of the PT in the late 1980s and ended up being the most radical candidate in the primaries for PT president in 2005. He left the PT for the PSOL, a leftist opposition party to Lula's government a few weeks after the primaries (*Folha de São Paulo,* September 27, 2005).

12. An external fact helped Erundina to defeat Maluf in the last moment. A few days before the elections of 1988 the army killed three workers during a strike in Volta Redonda. To many Brazilians the army actions seemed to suggest a return to authoritarianism, and they changed their votes in the last minute. Erundina was trailing Maluf until election day (*Almanaque Folha,* 2006).

mountable, and the plan was never approved, although Erundina managed to create councils in the areas of healthcare, the elderly, urban policies, and the handicapped (Tatagiba, 2004). She also tried hard to decentralize the city by introducing a council of representatives in each sub-*prefeituras* (Macaulay, 1996). This proposal was not fully approved, and São Paulo had *administrações regionais* until 2002. The councils of representatives were introduced in 2004, but have still not been implemented (Polis, 2005). Thus, all three proposals faced implementation problems both at the city council and at the level of the PT leadership. In the end, São Paulo's administration between 1989 and 1992 was considered unsuccessful, because of fractures within the administration and the lack of a clear agenda and support from the PT leadership (Macaulay, 1996; Couto and Abrúcio, 2003).

São Paulo's second PT administration was different in almost every respect. Marta received 38 percent of the votes in the first round, a higher share than the PT got with Erundina but still very short of its share at that point in Belo Horizonte and Porto Alegre (46 percent and 47 percent, respectively). The Suplicy administration departed from the Erundina administration in two main ways. First, it represented the PT leadership and was able to integrate leftist sectors. The national leadership, José Dirceu in particular, was very close to the secretary of government, Rui Falcao, and at this level there were no conflicts. However, the Suplicy administration was much more skeptical about participation. The administration proposed giving the most important positions in the administration to her political supporters (the Rui Falcão group) and transferring participatory policies to leftist members of her coalition. However, the left's prerogatives on participation were not clearly established at the beginning of her term, and the results of deliberations were not fully implemented.

The second important change was that the administration decided to run a coalition government in order to have a majority at the city council. The PT elected 15 councilors, but had a broader base of support than Erundina's. In addition, Suplicy was willing to trade positions at the sub-*prefeituras* for political support, guaranteeing relatively stable support in the city council.

Suplicy proposed three major actions on participation: introducing participatory budgeting, which had been part of her campaign program (Sanchez, 2004); empowering existing councils, such as the health council (Coelho and Veríssimo, 2004) and creating new ones demanded by social movements, including a housing council, a council on food security, and a council to monitor the street population (Tatagiba, 2004); and, last but not least, decentralizing the city administration by transferring health and education policy to the sub-*prefeituras* (Polis, 2005). These policies worked better than during Erundina's administration, but still cannot be considered successful cases of participation.

As I show in Chapter 5, participatory budgeting did not distribute as many public goods in São Paulo as it did in other Brazilian cities. A few social policies worked well, among them the health and the housing councils, as discussed in Chapter 6 (Coelho, 2004; Tatagiba, 2004). But the main problem with the administration's participatory policies was at the level of the sub-*prefeituras*. Suplicy cut many deals with the conservative PMDB and even Malufistas politicians, and this reduced her ability to carry out participatory policies at the grassroots level (Polis, 2005).

Thus, in the case of São Paulo, the PT ran into two main obstacles to participation. The first was the composition of a hegemonic group within the party and its reluctance to strengthen participation. In the Erundina administration this produced a conflict between the administration and the PT, while in Marta Suplicy's administration it produced a conflict between the administration and more participatory groups within the PT. The result of the two administrations is that participatory groups in São Paulo's civil society are not as widespread as in other cities, and this creates problems for both the implementation and the success of these policies, as I show in Chapter 7. The second problem in São Paulo was the relationship between the administration and the city council. In the best moments, the PT has controlled between one-quarter and one-third of the seats on the São Paulo city council. Erundina tried to defeat the city council by organizing external pressure (Macaulay, 1996: 226), a policy that did not work well. The Marta Suplicy administration tried to co-opt part of the opposition, which thwarted participatory policies where conservative councilors named the sub-*prefeitos*. In the end, both episodes show how difficult it is to combine identity and strategy in São Paulo. Erundina went too far in the direction of grassroots identity and had policies thwarted by city council; Suplicy was concerned with the PT's vote ceiling and sought to limit participatory policies in order to broaden support. This strategy guaranteed neither her reelection nor the success of participatory policies. Civil society, though well organized in many districts, did not broaden across the city as a whole. Only a stronger PT and civil society presence in the southern region of the city may be able to strengthen participation in São Paulo in the future.

Porto Alegre

The PT municipal government in Porto Alegre can be contrasted with the Erundina and Marta Suplicy administrations in almost every respect. In

Porto Alegre, Olivio Dutra took office with the full support of all groups within the PT, leading to a pact according to which each local PT faction would nominate the mayor in each subsequent election. Tarso Genro followed Dutra, and Pont followed Genro, showing how this pact at the leadership level has produced a durable PT hegemony in the city.[13] Furthermore, unlike in São Paulo, the PT's main opposition in Porto Alegre, the PDT, was programmatically and at its grassroots in favor of participation, particularly in the Partenon region of the city (Baierle, 1998; Baiocchi, 2005; Avritzer, 2006). The Porto Alegre PT began its participatory policies by solving two problems that long plagued the party in São Paulo: PT unity around participatory policies and the capacity to approve them in the city council.

Although it had only 9 of the 33 city councilors in 1988, the PT in Porto Alegre did not have as much difficulty implementing participatory policies as did the PT in São Paulo. One reason was the PDT, which also had grassroots support in the city[14] and elected 11 councilors in the same election (Dias, 2002). The strategy the PT used to convince PDT councilors and others to approve participation, particularly participatory budgeting, was to send participatory budgeting councilors and delegates to the city council. Some councilors, like Nereu D'avila of the PDT, complained that "they [the delegates and participatory budgeting councilors] feel themselves as being the legitimate city councilors . . . and in a way they are" (quoted in Dias, 2002). Others argued that the city council never lost any prerogatives because the budget law was never changed (Dias, 2002). In fact, the PT and participatory forces in the Porto Alegre city council increased continually from 9 councilors in 1988 to 12 in 1996, when its coalition won the majority of the votes in the city council.

Other participatory policies in Porto Alegre were also approved without much contention, among them the city master plan of 1997 (see Chapter 7). The city also used participation to define broad guidelines of its planning in the first *Congresso da Cidade*, from which the city master plan and the participatory budgeting thematic meeting emerged. Thus, the organization of political society in Porto Alegre differed from that in São Paulo in three important ways: the Porto Alegre PT was united around participatory policies

13. This pact was broken in the 1998 primaries for PT candidate for governor. In a bitter dispute Dutra defeated Genro, who became convinced of fraud in MST [Movement of Landless Peasants] settlements. Navarro, 2005.

14. The clash between the PT and PDT in Rio Grande do Sul took place in 1992, when Genro defeated Alceu Collares in the mayor elections. At the same time, popular grassroots of the PDT were integrated in participatory budgeting and started to vote for the PT. At this point, the PDT changed its vision on participation.

across different administrations; the largest group within the opposition was not against participation, at least until 1992; and the administration was able to get policies approved at the city council. These three elements again reflect a mix of identity and strategy. The participatory identity in Porto Alegre was broader than in São Paulo in two ways: not only was the PT united around a participatory identity, but the opposition also shared elements of this identity. Strategy in Porto Alegre followed the success of participatory policies, which led to the reelection of PT candidates on three occasions. These elements together facilitated not only the implementation of participatory budgeting, but also the extension of a participatory civil society across the city.

Belo Horizonte

Belo Horizonte also has a more unified PT than São Paulo, despite the fact that the two main groups within the local party never made a pact on turning over power. Guimarães was the main PT leader in Belo Horizonte and ran for mayor twice in the 1980s, receiving a large share of the votes in the 1988 elections. However, the first PT mayor of Belo Horizonte was Patrus Ananias, who was linked to Catholic grassroots groups. In the same election Guimaraes received the most city council votes and assumed the leadership of the administration in the city council. Ananias had problems overcoming opposition to his administration at the city council. He did so by luring the support of Pentecostal members.[15] The elected speaker was a Pentecostal councilor of the PT, giving Ananias control over the city council. Thus, Ananias, like Dutra, solved the two main political obstacles to implementing participatory policies at the beginning of his government. The PT was united behind him, despite previous disagreements between party factions, and he won city council support through its speaker.

The main participatory policies implemented in Belo Horizonte during the first PT administration were participatory budgeting, the strengthening of the city health council, and the approval of a city master plan. Participatory budgeting was more cautiously implemented in Belo Horizonte than in Porto Alegre, because the local PT in Belo Horizonte had a less radical con-

15. In the first meeting to discuss who will be the speaker of the *Camara dos Vereadores,* the PFL, the party willing to make a strong opposition to Ananias, claimed the place arguing that it was the largest party in the House. The PT won only five city councilors in that election. Pentecostals claimed that, although they were not formally a party, they had the largest numbers of city councilors. Alberto Duarte, an evangelical city councilor and member of the PT, was elected city council speaker. Ananias acquired a majority through this coalition between the PT and Pentecostal city councilors.

ception of participation. Belo Horizonte's participatory budgeting lacked a city council, but it acquired a strong record of public works, as I show in Chapter 5. Health council politics were complicated in Belo Horizonte because of conflicts during the second PT-PSB administration. Still, civil society actors managed to elect the president of the city council, showing the level of support for participation in the city (see Chapter 6 for further discussion). In addition, Belo Horizonte has had the least contentious approval process of city master plans.

Patterns of Participation

Thus, we can see three different patterns emerging at the local level in the PT, contributing to or creating problems for the success of participatory processes. Table 3.3 summarizes the different cases according to the configuration of political society.

Despite a national political identity and a strategy based on party centralization, local PT politics followed slightly different logic because these elements of identity and strategy varied at the local level. An identity with participatory politics that was extremely powerful at the national level did

Table 3.3. Configuration of political society in cases of participation in three Brazilian cities

City	Tradition of the Party Leftists	Unity of the Party	Relation with the Opposition	Relation with the City Council
São Paulo	Nonparticipatory.	Party divided on issues. Minority group representative elected mayor in 1988.	Contentious, with most of the opposition including the center.	Contentious. Mayor decided not to negotiate with city council and was defeated several times.
Porto Alegre	Participatory.	A pact on turnover in power.	Contentious, but within the participatory field.	City council accepts pressure to approve participatory policies.
Belo Horizonte	Participatory, with reservations.	Party is united, but does not have an internal pact.	A coalition between the PT and evangelical city council members.	City council approves participatory policies and gets other benefits in exchange.

not prove as powerful in São Paulo as in Minas Gerais and Rio Grande do Sul. Furthermore, although the national PT strategy was very powerful within the São Paulo PT, this position did not necessarily translate into votes. The ceiling of the PT vote remained around 30 percent from 1988 to 2004, when Suplicy lost her reelection campaign. The ceiling shows that civil society actors never really managed to generalize their presence in the city. This inability to extend participatory practices may limit the party's capacity to carry out successful participatory policies in the long run.

This latter point brings us back to the issue of participatory institutions. I argued in Chapters 1 and 2 that success in the implementation of participation cannot be based only on the willingness of state actors to carry out distributive policies and that a new analytical model was required. I showed that the involvement of multiple actors in carrying out participatory and distributive designs was a key element in the success of participatory institutions. Chapter 2 pursued this argument by showing that civil society actors were available at the grassroots level, though in an uneven way. I also argued in Chapter 2 that these actors may advance participatory policies, but to strengthen their political role it was necessary to broaden associative practices that may exist only in a few regions or subdistricts.

This chapter helped us to see the role of political actors in generalizing participation in civil society. These participatory traditions became the defining identity of PT militants in some cities, while in others they were traded for other identities or just cast aside. The political actors who did the most to generalize participation were the ones who identified most with the participatory traditions that emerged at the civil society level. In this sense, there is continuity between a participatory tradition in civil society and a participatory identity in political society at the local level, despite the different roles they play in politics. In addition, once political actors introduced participatory policies in cities such as Belo Horizonte and Porto Alegre, they helped generalize civil society practices that had existed in only a few regions (I develop this argument in Chapter 5). Thus, the most successful cases of participation are the ones that manage to weave together the actions of civil and political society. One additional issue is relevant before discussing participatory policies in depth: how institutional designs operate within this dual setting.

4

Changes in Institutional Design

The new participatory institutions that emerged in Brazil during the past 20 years have introduced huge innovations in design. Such changes would have been inconceivable to many democratic theorists of the postwar period. Their theories initially regarded participation as anti-institutional (Schumpeter, 1942; Sartori, 1973; Bobbio, 1987; Huntington, 1993) or extrainstitutional (Pateman, 1970; Evers, 1985; Alvarez and Escobar, 1992). The central assumption of this debate was that institutions are top-down bureaucratic forms of control (Weber, 1968; Parsons, 1971; Douglas, 1986; Olson, 1971) and that participation is incompatible with hierarchical forms of organization (Melucci, 1996).

The theory of institutional organization has moved recently toward analyzing institutional renewal (Powell and Dimaggio, 1991) and broadening the conception of institutions. According to Hall and Taylor, "institutions are . . . formal and informal procedures, routines, norms and conventions embedded in the organizational structure of the polity" (1996: 949). This definition expands the traditional approach to institutions as being top-down, bureaucratic organizations and admits informal rules or norms (O'Donnell, 1996). Yet, it still falls short of recognizing the different forms that rules and norms of reciprocity can take in different contexts. Networks of trust, for instance, operate with rules and norms that are not always embedded in the organizational structure of the polity (Fox, 1996: 1089). In addition, the specific way that new rules are fixed or negotiated at the micro level was not a major concern for these new institutional theorists (Sommers, 1993). In this chapter, I show that rules and norms of reciprocity that emerge in civil society can be both contested and adopted by political institutions in different

62

contexts. Thus, I seek to broaden the concept of institutional design to include these negotiations and contests.

Another issue in the debates over institutional design concerns forms of participation, what I call the static versus interactive conception of design. Fung and Wright (2003) have proposed a model for the design of participatory institutions based on three elements. First are fixed elements for the organization of participatory institutions. The authors proposed a model based on four successful experiences—neighborhood governance councils in Chicago, habitat conservation planning in the United States, participatory budgeting in Porto Alegre, and panchayats in Kerala. Because the authors narrowed down the analytical frameworks to one successful case for each one of their examples of empowered participation, they could not find any variation in the context for the implementation of participatory institutions (Cohen and Rogers, 2003). Thus, for either analytical or empirical flaws, they generated a model that had as its main assumption that repetition, not variation, of design elements explains success.

Second, Fung and Wright's approach to the enabling conditions for the emergence of participatory institutions falls in the so-called cultural trap. Because their model is based on a heuristic assumption that successful designs may be carried out in different contexts, they suppose that the enabling conditions for participation are the same across different cultures. For them, issues such as literacy or solving specific problems explain the emergence of these institutions. What Fung and Wright miss in their approach is that, moving away from very basic variables, we may see the presence of other variables, such as clientelism or party interest. Those more specific variables may hinder local participation, even when broad enabling conditions are present.

The third element of Fung and Wright's model is the assumption that success in deliberative participation comes from "self-conscious institutional design efforts," that is to say, the social engineering of institutions with a deliberative aim (Fung and Wright, 2003: 23). Again, what this model misses is that in most cases of participatory design the important design elements come from previous cultural and political practices and only later are appropriated in the process of designing institutions.

I call the three assumptions by Fung and Wright the static participatory design model. That model assumes that there is a recipe for success that can be employed across different contexts (Fung, 2003). In opposition to this model, I propose an interactive dynamic model of participatory design. This model is based on the assumption that, although there are enabling conditions for participation, they change according to the role civil society and political society actors aim to play in participation. The dynamic interactive model also assumes that the success of participatory design is not caused by self-conscious design; rather, such success is the unanticipated result of interactions between civil and political society actors that lead to the dismantling of old rules and the fixing of new ones.

Institutional Design as the Interaction
of Civil and Political Society

The new institutions that have recently emerged in Brazil have incorporated cultural and participatory practices that originally developed within voluntary associations during the democratization process and were only subsequently embedded in political institutions. These practices include formulation of bottom-up rules for participation; sharing of power through deliberation; ratification of policies in public audiences; and the adaptation of practices according to context. The new institutions that emerged during democratization incorporated new rules for engagement from Brazilian civil society associations. However, these associations had both good practices and deficits: although they could experiment with and introduce new institutional forms, such as budget control, local assemblies, and monitoring councils, they could not move from local to general rule making (Giddens, 1991). In addition, associations were unevenly distributed in territorial terms and relied on corporatist forms of representation that did not promote the generalization and fairness of the new rules (Schmitter, 1971). Brazilian political society and state institutions interacted with civil society organizations in the creation of new designs. Political society brought its own concerns to these designs, such as making rules for participation universal, creating incentives for broader participation, and expanding good practices geographically. It is this interaction between civil and political society that I call interactive institutional design. New designs were not successful simply because they came from civil society or because they were successfully proposed by a political party. Rather, they were successful because this civil and political interaction made them more appealing to society as a whole.

In this chapter, I argue that participatory institutional designs emerged through the interaction between the innovation and experimentation of civil society, on one hand, and political society's concerns with mandatory deliberation and universal access to public policy-making, on the other. In this sense, design is the place where interaction between civil and political society produces outcomes and creates new patterns of political action. In what follows, I single out the elements of associative pattern that were incorporated into new institutions, as well as the changes in political patterns that helped these institutions become more effective. I also show how variation in the disassembling of old practices and in the creation of new rules that required participation was essential to the emergence of the new participatory designs (Ostrom, 2005: 18). I draw upon both the new institutional and civil society theories to show that the latter can lead to what I call interactive participatory designs. My main argument is that by inserting civil society input into institutional designs, it is possible to adapt designs to variations in context. The theory of participatory designs that I propose allows me at the end of the chapter to differentiate three contexts for the operation of participatory institutions.

The Design Characteristics of Participatory Institutions

Three elements in the design of participatory institutions allow them to innovate more easily than other kinds of institutions: (a) experimentation in the access to power and public goods, so that the design of a new practice can later be modified or expanded; (b) a flexible approach to rules, which allows an incremental approach to participation; and (c) a way of dealing with mandatory rules for participation that strengthens civil society by providing sanctions if rules are not implemented.[1]

Experimentation in Access to Power and Public Goods

Institutions experiment with new practices to disassemble old ones, particularly to ease distortions in public policy formulation or alter unintended results. New institutions experiment at two levels: at the level of power and at the level of access to public goods. In regard to access to power, Brazilian civil society actors introduced more egalitarian forms of interaction be-

---

1. In spite of the new form of sanction introduced by the law, there is still noncompliance with the new design. Noncompliance takes place through the setting up of fake forms of participation.

tween social actors than those available at the beginning of the democratization process. The horizontal neighborhood assemblies that are at the root of participatory budgeting and the councils that are at the root of health policies are goods examples of these practices.

In regard to access to public goods, a similar logic emerged: Brazilian civil society actors introduced new forms of access to goods and public services. These new forms of access broke with the top-down technocratic rationality that governed most decisions during the authoritarian period. Instead of top-down technocratic rationality, Brazilian civil society actors proposed that social actors participate in decision-making. However, the experimental capacity of civil society varies and has limits. Most likely, this experimental capacity is linked to the loose forms of association that civil society organizations enable (Cohen and Arato, 1992). Multiple forms of organization enable multiple forms of experimentation that are at the root of most new experiences.

Flexible Rule-Making

New political institutions also need to propose new rules for hierarchy, as well as for access to public goods. The fact that civil society actors criticize old rules for access to public goods and power does not mean that they have the ability to propose new rules. Rules can be defined as methodical ways of dealing with the interaction among social actors (Giddens, 1984: 18; Domingues, 2006). Rules always involve power and access to resources. Civil society actors change the way rules work by introducing a more horizontal principle into rule-making.

For Brazilian civil society actors, two rules have had key importance in the organization of participatory institutions. The first one is that a civil society actor who participated at the grassroots level could end up being a civil society representative within a participatory institution. This rule applies both to participatory budgeting and to health councils. The second rule is that the operation of these participatory institutions is to be guided by constitutions that are jointly made by state and civil society actors (as has been the case for participatory budgeting and health councils, among other participatory institutions). Thus, power as a top-down resource was refurbished as a societal resource that would allow social actors to move up in the process of claiming public goods. The reinterpretation of the way power operates within participatory institutions led to new institutional formats that did not exist in authoritarian Brazil: regional assemblies, councils, and public audiences.

Participatory institutions in Brazil also introduced a second new way of dealing with rules: the operation of rules in a flexible way. Rules operate in a flexible way when they can be progressively adapted to context. This is an element that differentiates rule-making within participatory institutions from rule-making within representative institutions. In the latter case, rules must be designed with clear boundaries, because of the free rider problem, which is to say that rule-making needs to deal with the risk that someone will use rules in his or her interest (Ostrom, 2005: 260). Participatory institutions operate with a different logic, according to which the problem with rules is that they may not completely fit the civil society context in which they seek to operate. The result is flexibility in rule-making, that is to say, an incremental approach in which state and civil society actors collaborate to craft rules progressively.

Participatory budgeting is a good example of flexible rule-making. When participatory budgeting was introduced in Porto Alegre, the city established the rules for power (how and where to elect delegates), as well as for access to public goods (which goods would be available in which regions). These rules could not be changed during the participatory process. However, after a council was elected, by the end of the first year it was entitled to change the existing rules before the beginning of the deliberative process (Santos, 1998; Avritzer, 2003). Thus, rules receive a different treatment within participatory institutions: they change according to context, making these institutions more flexible in their operation. Changes in the configuration of social actors and in the way they act lead to subsequent changes in rules. This flexibility is important so that participatory institutions can adapt to their context. However, if civil society is weak, such flexibility also carries the risk that the rule will be made by the state and that it may not be adapted to the logic of civil society participation.

A second important example of how rules are flexible within participatory institutions involves the design of the regions in Porto Alegre's participatory budgeting process. During the introduction of participatory budgeting in Porto Alegre, there was a debate on the design of the city's regions (Baierle, 1998). This debate involved a concern with changing the population targeted by social policies to include those who had received less public goods in the past (Baierle, 1998; Abers, 2000). Porto Alegre's administration advanced the debate by introducing the idea of a quantification of previous access to public goods. However, the city did not redesign districts according to the logic of social mobilization of neighborhood associations. UAMPA, the Umbrella Association of Neighborhood Organizations, and important neighborhood associations defended the redesign of Porto Alegre's regions in order to adapt them to social movement dynamics. In the end, most of the 16 districts were redesigned. Flexible rule-making was important in providing participatory budgeting with a capacity for participation, without which it may not have survived during its first years of operation. Thus, flexible rule-making allows civil society and the state to incorporate each other's concerns during the participatory process.

Mandatory Participation

A third dimension of the design of participatory institutions is how they make participation mandatory. Institutions deal with mandatory obligations as constraints that are imposed upon state actors in cases of noncompliance (Hall and Taylor, 1996). However, within participatory institutions mandatory obligations also play the role of creating a more predictable form of action by civil society actors. The reason is linked to the way participatory institutions bridge political society and civil society. By constraining state actors to implement participation, this design creates an enabling side of constraint. This design feature has been common in both health policies and city master plans in Brazil, where there are sanctions for the failure to implement participatory designs. The federal law that instituted health councils at the three levels of government in Brazil stipulated that federal transfers would be suspended if these institutions were not instituted at the local level. Although these sanctions have seldom been used, one exemplary case was the suspension of transfers to São Paulo during the conservative administrations of Paulo Maluf and Celso Pita.[2]

The same feature operated very well in the implementation of city master plans. The first main institutional element in most master plans is mandatory public audiences, which allows for a broadening of interest representation in urban politics. In case of changes in urban regulation, city governments are required to hold public meetings before they submit changes to the city council. Every city in Brazil that has approved a city master plan is required

2. Paulo Maluf, a well-known Brazilian politician, was both mayor and governor of São Paulo during the authoritarian period. Maluf was elected mayor of São Paulo in 1992. There, he implemented a health model, called PAS, which was different from the one required by the constitution. PAS were private cooperatives of doctors and health personnel that would be paid according to the number of appointments held. The system was a private-public partnership that broke with the idea that the state should be a provider of health services. Marta Suplicy discontinued PAS, and it was abandoned as an idea for privatizing health services (Bouquat, Cohn, and Elias, 2006).

to carry out these meetings. Public meetings were demanded in the MNRU's popular amendment to the constitution in the form of a popular veto on the executive branch changes. In its final form, these meetings became a place in which legislation could be reviewed before the city council approved it. This creates difficulties for the type of fast approval of deals between city hall and the city council that is common in Brazil.

All of these new design elements—opportunities for experimentation, flexibility in rule-making, and requirements for mandatory participation—gave participatory institutions a more contextual nature, grounded in the characteristics of their particular locales and constituencies. Each of these elements was related to the experiences and perceptions of civil society actors regarding what had been the hindrances to the implementation of these institutions. As a result, participatory institutional designs vary, and each may be better able than the others to respond to specific challenges or more vulnerable than the others in specific conditions. In this way, an experimental approach to participation produced institutions that are differentially effective according to context. I analyze this variation by classifying participatory institutions into three different types of design.

The Types of Institutional Designs

Most of the participatory institutions that would play a significant role in Brazil either emerged or were proposed during the 1990s. Each of these institutions had a different form, emerged from a different civil society practice, and required different types of action from political parties, in particular the PT. The new participatory institutions that emerged in Brazil in the 1990s involved three different institutional designs: bottom-up designs, power-sharing designs, and ratification designs. This section discusses how they emerged and how they operate in three different contexts.

Bottom-up Designs

Bottom-up designs are the most radically democratic participatory institutions that emerged in democratic Brazil. They are called bottom-up because they are absolutely open ended at the grassroots level: all citizens can participate. Participatory budgeting is the best example of a bottom-up design. Every citizen that lives in a neighborhood may join its regional assemblies. The second characteristic of bottom-up design is the low involvement of the government in the decision-making process. In bottom-up designs, most of the time the government limits itself to facilitating the deliberative process. Here again, participatory budgeting is the best example of a bottom-up design because the city administration does not have a vote (it only has voice) in the participatory process. The third characteristic of bottom-up design is the formation of an all–civil society body at the upper level. This body tends to dispute power with the local administration and represent the overall interests of the whole participatory process. Participatory budgeting is the best example of this design since it has a council that is formed by an all–civil society constituency. Overall, bottom-up designs embody a radical democratic format. They are more democratic than other designs because they are more experimental and more flexible. However, these characteristics make bottom-up designs effective only in situations of deep agreement between civil and political society actors.

Participatory budgeting as a bottom-up design emerged in Porto Alegre as a local compromise between the proposals of UAMPA, a very radical umbrella organization of neighborhood associations, and a very homogeneous political party in the city, the PT. Participatory budgeting emerged as a proposal for deliberation on the distribution of public goods at the beginning of the democratization process in Porto Alegre (Baierle, 1998; Abers, 2000; Avritzer, 2002b; Silva, 2002). In the beginning of this process, UAMPA proposed the participation of the population in regional assemblies in which members of neighborhood associations would decide on budget issues (Avritzer, 2002b). It was UAMPA that rejected the PDT administration's first participatory proposal. In addition, it was members of UAMPA and local neighborhood associations who demanded the redesign of the administrative districts of Porto Alegre in order to adapt them to the participatory dynamics of social movements (Avritzer, 2002b).

The other innovations in institutional design should be attributed to the PT. The PT proposed a council that would work with the local administration on the final budget, as well as technical criteria for deliberating on the distribution of resources for each region. But above all, as I show in Chapter 5, the PT's role in Porto Alegre was to insist that only through the participatory process could social actors and their respective communities get access to public goods. Participatory institutions are not the result of one proposal made by one actor; rather, they are the result of multiple actors' initiatives. In the context of a very active civil and political society, creating a structure that integrated open-access assemblies with a representative council was a good solution for actors from both civil society associations and the PT. However, what most authors who deal with the expansion of participatory budgeting miss is that the institution remains dependent upon the conditions present in its initial context. I get back to this point at the end of this chapter and in Chapter 5.

Power-sharing Designs

The second design evaluated in this book is called a power-sharing design. Power-sharing designs are less participatory than bottom-up designs. Although they do allow for very limited forms of participation at the grassroots level, from the very beginning they also include forms of representation by civil society actors. Civil society associations elect or indicate members of their constituencies to participate in these participatory institutions. Health councils are the best-known case of a power-sharing design. There is, in Brazil, a limited form of participation in healthcare, what are called health conferences. However, most of the daily decisions in the area of health are taken within health councils. The main characteristic of civil society participation in health councils is that it takes place through the election of civil society representatives.[3]

The second characteristic of power-sharing designs is that civil society actors share decision-making with state actors within a common decision-making framework. Again, the health councils are the best example of this kind of design. Within these councils, civil society and state representatives share decision-making power, with each side having half of the members of the council. The third element of power-sharing designs is that they are legally institutionalized, that is, their implementation is required by law. There are policies that can only be carried out through joint decisions between state and power-sharing institutions. A power-sharing design may not be as participatory as a bottom-up design because it is institutionalized and because the state has more prerogatives in the format for participation. However, power-sharing institutions are less dependent upon the will of political society for their implementation. As I show in Chapter 6, this is

3. There is a debate going on in Brazil regarding how civil society can claim representation of constituencies in the areas of health and water, among others. It is clear that representation in this case does not involve an authorization in the same way that electoral representation does. Some authors argue about presumed representation (Houtzager, Gurza, and Charya, 2003), a concept that seems to be misleading because it accepts uncritically the idea of authorization. Other actors are trying to introduce in the Brazilian context the concept of discursive representation (Keck and Abers, 2006).

due to the way their design incorporated mandatory sanctions against governments that fail to implement them.

As with bottom-up participatory institutions, the emergence of power-sharing participatory institutions is a case of interactive design. The origin of the power-sharing format can be traced to the popular movement for the improvement of health conditions that emerged in São Paulo during the late 1970s (Sader, 1988; Doimo and Rodrigues, 2003.The format of health councils emerged in the eastern district of São Paulo at the beginning of the democratization process (Sader, 1988: 276).[4] However, the council format, at that point, did not acknowledge the joint deliberative format between civil society and the state. The councils initially had an all–civil society format during the early 1980s in São Paulo.

It would take two additional moments, the VIII National Health Conference and the Constituent Assembly, for the health movement to reach the power-sharing format. The popular health movement and the sanitary movement combined during the VIII National Health Conference, where the agenda for the Constitutional Assembly was established. The popular health movement demanded a state-run health system, but was defeated by *sanitaristas* and politicians linked to the health movement who advocated a mixed system that became the most popular proposal for the Constituent Assembly. In this mixed system, the idea of local councils with community participation was preserved. Thus, in a way similar to the case of bottom-up participatory budgeting, the case of power-sharing in health councils emerged progressively through the actions of different social actors with different concerns. The popular health movement linked councils to participation, and the *sanitaristas* introduced the state into the participatory equation. Thus, among the main institutional devices introduced in the area of healthcare, civil society played a key role in two: (a) the idea of deliberation by civil society actors and (b) the idea of incorporating regional representatives into health councils. Political society's role in the implementation of participatory institutions in the area of health was to propose a mixed format between civil society and state actors.

One major difference between the cases of participatory budgeting and the health councils emerged from their different paths of construction: par-

4. The tradition of calling councils every institutional format in which civil society actors are represented goes back to the Vargas regime (1930–45). Vargas created the Council of Historic Landmarks in his first tenure, and the CNPq, the Council for Science and Research, during his electoral comeback during the 1950s. Councils during the democratization period brought in the incorporation of civil society actors in the institutional format. On participation during the Vargas period, see Schmitter, 1971.

ticipatory budgeting remains completely dependent upon the will of political society to release its budgeting prerogatives. As I show in Chapter 6,
health councils are less dependent upon the will of political society. Instead,
they are more dependent upon the organizational skill of civil society, which
is a major difference between bottom-up and power sharing designs.

Ratification Designs

The third type of participatory design introduced in democratic Brazil is
what I call the ratification design. A ratification design's first characteristic
is that participation does not substitute for the state's prerogative in a specific policy-making process. Ratification is a participatory act that follows
a proposal for public policy made by the state.

The best example of a ratification design in Brazil is the approval process
for city master plans. These plans are proposed by the administration and
approved or rejected in open-ended public assemblies at the regional level.
Although these assemblies resemble the regional assemblies that are part of
participatory budgeting, they function somewhat differently. In a ratification assembly, participants can either approve or reject state proposals, but
they are not able to deliberate on the content of those proposals, as in participatory budgeting and the health councils.

A ratification design is mandatory in nature. The state or local administration has to prove that it has carried out the public assemblies. Otherwise,
the proposal of a city master plan becomes null. A ratification design is ob-
viously the least empowering among the three designs analyzed in this
book. However, because it is the only one in which noncompliance with participation can block state action, it is also the participatory institution that
is least dependent upon the will of political society.

The emergence of the ratification design is similar to the other two cases.
The MNRU, an umbrella association for urban reform, proposed a popular
amendment during the Constituent Assembly. However, at the last minute,
conservative sectors bound its implementation to infraconstitutional legislation on the so-called Master Plans (I describe this process in Chapter 7).
Thus, the constitutional text provided legal instruments for democratizing
the city, but did not create legal sanctions for noncompliance. The Constitution required what in the Brazilian legal tradition is called "regulamenta-
tion," an infraconstitutional law that aims to establish enforcement mechanisms. Here again, an unanticipated relationship between city master plans
and participation at the urban level emerged in Brazil. A 14-year battle followed the approval of the Constitution, through which the MNRU became

the FNRU (National Forum for Urban Reform). It first tried to find a sponsor for its legislation and later took up the Pompeu de Sousa Law Project, trying to amend it in Congress. Among the main institutional devices of the Statute of the City, the FNRU proposed the following: (a) mandatory popular consultation on urban reform and (b) legal blocking of executive action in urban reform.

The most important element of ratification designs is the possibility of blocking the actions of the executive branch of government. Among the three participatory design types discussed in this book, ratification designs are the least participatory. They keep the prerogatives of the state in making public policy proposals independent of the will of civil society. However, ratification designs are the most effective in situations in which both civil society organizations and progressive political society are not strong.

Consequences and Context

Thus, the consequences produced by different designs are related to the origin of the institutional innovation. I show in the next section of this chapter that these consequences are linked to three characteristics of participatory institutions: the way they propitiate experimentation; the way they allow the crafting of flexible rules; and the way they create binding constraints on state action. Table 4.1 illustrates the variation in the design of participatory institutions.

Table 4.1. Design features of three types of participatory institutions

Type of Participatory Institution	Type of Design	Origin	Main Positive Characteristic	Main Limitation
Participatory budgeting	Bottom-up.	Civil society and political society interaction in Porto Alegre.	Deep distributive effect.	Remains dependent on the characteristics of the initial context.
Health councils	Power-sharing.	Civil society demands on the state in São Paulo.	Relevant distributive effect.	May be implemented in cases of divided political society.
City master plans	Ratification.	Civil society and political society negotiations in Congress.	Can block power-holders in unfavorable situations for civil society.	Least participatory.

Interactive designs respond to context through the variations in their effectiveness, that is, their capacity to introduce democratic practices and to distribute public goods to the poor. The initiative to expand participatory institutions beyond their original places of emergence poses the issue of what makes the implementation of participatory institutions effective. The main thesis of this book, already stated in Chapter 1, is that the willingness to introduce a more participatory design is not enough to ensure its success. Each of the three main designs discussed above fits a certain context, and as I show in the next three chapters, cannot be easily moved to a different one. The failure to carry out participation is directly linked to the introduction of bottom-up designs in situations in which they do not fit.

Participatory Institutions in Four Cities

The core argument of this book is that context matters when it comes to participatory institutions. In the four cases that follow on the rise of participatory institutions in Porto Alegre, Belo Horizonte, São Paulo, and Salvador, I show the way in which context accounts for variations in the emergence, consolidation, and expansion of these institutions. I argue that in each case the quality of civic life and the specific configuration of political society led to different designs and therefore to different degrees of deliberative and distributive effectiveness in each one of the participatory institutions at stake. The role of context for various participatory institutions is summarized in Table 4.2.

Porto Alegre

Porto Alegre has a singular political configuration that distinguishes it from other Brazilian cities. Located in the extreme south of the country and with 1.3 million inhabitants, it was always home to differentiated political movements such as *Castilhismo* in the late nineteenth century (Love, 1971; Baquero, 1995) and *Brizolismo* in the early 1960s. Porto Alegre is the point of departure for the other cases because of it is home to the most radical and bottom-up participatory design, namely, participatory budgeting. By the 1950s, Porto Alegre already had more horizontal forms of association than other Brazilian cities (Silva, 2001), as shown in Chapter 2. Between 1946 and 1964, Porto Alegre elected the PTB, a populist leftist party with limited support in Brazil's Southeast, for most administrative positions. Porto Alegre departed from the Brazilian mainstream in electoral politics during most

Table 4.2. Role of context in the emergence of participatory institutions in four Brazilian cities

Type of Participatory Institution	Porto Alegre	São Paulo	Belo Horizonte	Salvador
Voluntary associations	Politicized during the 1950s, with fast growth during the democratization period.	Recreational during the 1950s, with fast growth during the democratization period.	Little organized before democratization, with the fastest growth during the democratization period.	Very little organized before and after democratization.
Political parties	PT very strong, administered the city for 16 years alone. Later defeated by a center-left coalition.	PT strong, but not dominant. Least administrative continuity.	PT strong, but governs in coalition with other left parties, particularly the PSB.	PT weak. During democratization other left parties were stronger. City controlled by conservatives.
Institutional design	Emergence of new designs.	Partially adopted new designs.	Adopted new designs in a less radical format. Participatory institutions successful.	Rejected participatory designs, even when mandated by law.
New institutions	Effective in deliberative and distributive terms.	Partly effective.	Effective.	Not effective.

of the postwar period, as I showed in Chapter 3. During the period of democratization, Porto Alegre's civil society quickly reorganized itself, and many new associations emerged (Baiocchi, 2005).

After democratization, only Porto Alegre, unlike the other large capitals of the Southeast, concentrated its local politics on the left. The PT and PDT[5] fought for control of the city and did so around issues of participation. The PT won city elections in 1988 and governed Porto Alegre for 16 years, transforming it into a star of the international left (Santos, 1998; 2006; Waller-

5. The PDT is a leftist, populist party that was created by Leonel Brizola when he returned to Brazil from exile in Uruguay in 1979. In the beginning of democratization, the PDT was stronger than the PT and held state governments in Rio Grande do Sul and Rio de Janeiro. The PT struggled with the PDT for hegemony on the left and only consolidated itself as the main left party in Brazil in the mid-1990s (Hunter, 2006).

stein, 2002). Participatory budgeting was introduced in 1990 and attracted international attention. The PT was finally defeated in the 2004 elections. However, in Porto Alegre the most important public policies, such as participatory budgeting, have remained in place. I show in Chapters 5, 6, and 7 that Porto Alegre is the model for successful bottom-up participatory institutions. I also show that power-sharing and ratification designs are successful in the city as well.

Belo Horizonte

Belo Horizonte, Brazil's third-largest city in economic terms, is an interesting second case. It had neither the popular mobilization of Porto Alegre nor the contentious city politics of São Paulo, but was the Southeastern city with the most rapid change in associative patterns during the democratization period. Neighborhood associations, as well as health and professional associations, thrived in the city during the mid-1980s (Avritzer, 2000), as shown in Chapter 2. Belo Horizonte's political society is known as a pole of conservative sectors (Hagopian, 1996), but it also became a PT stronghold during the 1990s. The PT has governed the city for four consecutive terms and introduced most of the characteristic participatory institutions, such as participatory budgeting and health councils, as shown in Chapter 3.

Belo Horizonte's unique experience with participatory institutions demonstrates that bottom-up institutions, such as participatory budgeting, are not singular to the political and social context of Porto Alegre. Belo Horizonte's civil society does not hold the bargaining power it does in Porto Alegre. The weaker bargaining power of voluntary associations in Belo Horizonte is reflected in the design of its participatory institutions. Participatory budgeting in Belo Horizonte does not have a council and distributes fewer public goods than in Porto Alegre. However, it has been able to distribute a great deal of public goods to the poor (see Chapter 5). Nonetheless, power-sharing institutions, particularly health councils, have flourished in Belo Horizonte. Health policies in Belo Horizonte are better organized than in Porto Alegre, and Belo Horizonte has the only health council with a civil society president among all Brazilian large cities. It is important to compare Porto Alegre and Belo Horizonte's participatory institutions to avoid the mistake of defending the uniqueness of Porto Alegre's bottom-up institutions (Cabanes, 2004).

São Paulo

São Paulo, Brazil's largest city, poses the greatest challenges to the implementation of participatory institutions. São Paulo is home to the civil society movements that triggered democratization (Singer and Brant, 1980; Caldeira, 2000). Many of the movements that led to the participatory institutions discussed in this book, in particular the health and urban reform movements, first emerged there, as shown in Chapter 2. São Paulo's industrial belt, called the ABC region, is also the home of the PT (French, 1992; 2004), where the party had its first core constituencies and leadership (Keck, 1992).

Nonetheless, São Paulo is very far from being a city of the left. Since the early 1950s, the ex-mayor and ex-president Janio Quadros has consolidated a lower-middle-class constituency for conservative politics . Quadros was able to defeat Fernando Henrique Cardoso in the first mayoral elections of the new democratic period in 1986, and city politics has alternated between right and left ever since (Avritzer, 2004). The PT won elections in the city twice and governed between 1989–92 and 2001–04. Paulo Maluf, mayor and governor during the authoritarian regime, won one election and was followed in office by his chosen successor. Each time the PT won elections in the city, it introduced participatory institutions. São Paulo has today 22 participatory councils, 9 introduced during the first PT administration and 7 during the second one. Celso Pitta and Maluf together created six new councils (Tatagiba, 2004). In addition to that, Maluf and Pitta reduced the prerogatives of the city's most active council, the city health council.

The presence of social movements in the city is also highly uneven. During the democratization period, social movements were strong in a few regions in the east of the city because of the strong presence of the Catholic Church (Doimo, 2004).[6] This distinction between the eastern and southern districts remains important, with stronger associative patterns in the east (Avritzer, 2004), and the strong presence of evangelicals in the south. The success of participatory policies in São Paulo has thus been checked by strong opposition within political society and by organized conservative sectors. Every time that a conservative or centrist mayor is elected in Sao Paulo, he or she dismantles participatory institutions. Jose Serra (PSDB),

6. It is beyond the aims of this book to analyze the conflicts within the Catholic Church in Brazil. However, it is important to keep in mind that the organization of popular movements in the eastern district of the city is linked to the arrival of a progressive bishop, Dom Angelico Sandalo, in the region. After the partition of the archdiocese, patterns of mobilization in the eastern district were not followed in other districts (Doimo, 2004). However, Church support is not the only criterion for this distinction. Even within the PT, different politicians with different political practices have electoral bases in different regions of the city, with the clientelist Tatos entrenched in the south and supporters of grassroots movements entrenched in the eastern district.

for example, shut down participatory budgeting after his election in 2004. São Paulo is an excellent case to help us discuss the kind of participatory design that can be implemented in unfavorable conditions, one of the aims of this book. I argue in Chapters 5 and 6 that, relative to other design types, power-sharing designs have greater democratizing and distributive effects in the case of São Paulo, because of their mandatory implementation.

Salvador

Salvador contrasts effectively with the other city cases because of its long-term administration by conservatives. Salvador is one of the fastest growing cities in Brazil, with a population growth of 2.98 percent in the 1980s and 1.3 percent in the 1990s (Boschi, 1999). Salvadoran civil society is not strong, because the associative drive that changed patterns in the South and Southeast of Brazil took place only selectively in the Northeast.[7]

Salvador has higher levels of poverty than the other cities studied here, though it is similar to other Northeastern cities in this respect. Civil society associations in the city are weak, and there has been no attempt to involve them in public policy. On the contrary, Salvador has been controlled politically by an oligarchic family, the Magalhães, with a strong antiparticipatory bias. Antonio Carlos Magalhães was mayor and state governor under the military regime. He broke ranks with the regime, played an important role in the transition to democracy, and has participated in every ruling coalition in democratic Brazil, with the exception of the PT government. Salvador was also governed briefly by Lidice da Mata (1993–96), but her administration was considered a disaster. Da Matta came from the left and was a member of parliament for the PC do B (a traditional leftist party with strong roots in Salvador), but her administration faced strong opposition by the Magalhães and was not able to implement participatory policies. Recently, Salvador's city master plan was cancelled in the courts because the minimum mandated participation was lacking.

Salvador's experience shows that a legal mandate is not sufficient to implement participation or make it effective. Salvador is an excellent case to

---

7. Recife and Salvador can be contrasted in this respect. Recife was part of the associative drive of Brazil's democratization and has had very active urban movements since that period. Its participatory characteristics are very similar to those of the Brazilian South. Salvador had fewer social movements and participatory institutions during the same period (Milani, 2006). In this sense, the broad cultural and geographical contrast established by Putnam would not work for Brazil.

discuss the role as well as the limits of participation in hostile environments. In Chapter 7 and in the conclusion of this book, I defend the claim that ratification designs, in spite of their limited democratizing effects, are the ideal participatory institutions to be implemented in environments hostile to participation. In such cases, participation plays one role: that of blocking close deals between power holders and private interests on public policies. In Chapter 8, I propose a typology that relates the context in which participatory institutions emerge to both the design of those institutions and the possibilities for successful participatory policies. I also argue that in many situations the best policy would be to implement participatory institutions in phases.

Part II

The Operation of
Participatory Institutions in Brazil

5

Participatory Budgeting

Participatory budgeting emerged in Porto Alegre in 1990 and became an international reference point for participation during the late 1990s, with more than 20 works published about it (Santos, 1998; Navarro, 1998; Abers, 2000; Avritzer, 2002a; Fung and Wright, 2003; Baiocchi, 2003; Wampler and Avritzer, 2004; Baiocchi, 2005).[1] It exerted considerable influence not only on the political participation literature, but also on participatory practice. Many of Brazil's large cities have practiced it, including Porto Alegre (for 17 years), Belo Horizonte (for 14), Recife (for 6), and São Paulo (for 3). Participatory budgeting has expanded in at least three different senses: it expanded beyond Porto Alegre and large capitals to small and mid-size cities; it expanded beyond the PT to other parties on the left, with the PSB and PSDB accounting for 15 percent of the cases of participatory budgeting in 2004 (Wampler and Avritzer, 2005); and, it has expanded to the country's North and Northeast regions, not known for being highly participatory. Between 1997 and 2000, there were 103 experiences of participatory budgeting in Brazil (Grazia and Ribeiro, 2003); between 2000 and 2004, this number rose to 170 (Wampler and Avritzer, 2005).

The Characteristics of Participatory Budgeting

Participatory budgeting has three prominent features. First, it began as a classic case of bottom-up design, in spite of the local variations in format.

1. Other important works on participatory budgeting are Avritzer and Navarro, 2003; Faria, 2005; Wampler, 2000; Sintomer and Marion, 2002; Bairle, 1998; Sanchez, 2004; and Dias, 2002.

Second, with impetus from the PT, it succeeded in expanding rapidly to many Brazilian cities. Third, it provided a new means of deliberation and distribution of public goods.

Bottom-up Design

Bottom-up design involves open-entry participation at the grassroots level, low involvement of the government in the decision-making process, and formation of a coordinating mechanism at the top. In 1990, Porto Alegre provided the conditions needed for a bottom-up institution to emerge; indeed, it could scarcely have emerged elsewhere for at least three reasons. First, the debate that led to this institutional innovation was specific to Porto Alegre. Alceu Collares, the PDT mayor elected in the first democratic elections after authoritarianism, proposed a form of participation in the *vilas* (slums) of Porto Alegre called *fiscal do orçamento,* while the umbrella association for neighborhood associations (UAMPA) proposed participatory budgeting (Baierle, 1998) with the support of the PT. This was part of a political dispute in Porto Alegre in the mid-1980s concerning which leftist actor was more closely connected to social actors. Second, the contentious nature of Luiza Erundina's administration in São Paulo would not have allowed the implementation of any participatory public policy in that city (Couto, 1995). Erundina, the first PT mayor of São Paulo, faced strong opposition in the city council and inside the PT (1988–92). Third, participation enjoyed more consensus within the Porto Alegre PT than in other strong branches of the party at the time, notably those of São Paulo and Minas Gerais,[2] although the implementation of participatory budgeting was not consensual under Olivio Dutra's administration and likely led to the resignation of the planning secretary, Clovis Ingelfriz. This chapter tries to show why and how participatory budgeting emerged in Porto Alegre and how it has spread to other cities with mixed success. By analyzing the problems faced by participatory budgeting in São Paulo and Belo Horizonte, I show that par-

---

2. A few talks over the years with key people in Minas Gerais and São Paulo led me to this argument. A high official of the Luiza Erundina administration in São Paulo mentioned to me that organizing participation in the city was a demand from above, made by the mayor office, but he personally was skeptical. In the case of Belo Horizonte the core members of the city administration were initially skeptical at least of how participatory budgeting was implemented in Porto Alegre. Their solution was to implement it without a council, but with two rounds of mandatory deliberation attended by the population.

ticipatory budgeting as a bottom-up design has limits linked to the civil and political society configuration in the cities in which it is implemented.

Rapid Expansion

The second issue related to the success of participatory budgeting is its rapid pace of expansion. Participatory budgeting expanded dramatically in Brazil in between 1992 and 2006, especially if we keep in mind that there was no law requiring it at the federal level. The number of cases grew from 36 in 1996 to 103 in 2000 to 170 in 2004 (Avritzer, 2006). This expansion was based mainly on the political will of PT and non-PT mayors to expand the practice where it had not been available or to continue it when the PT was defeated (in Belo Horizonte in 1997–2000 and Porto Alegre and Ipatinga after 2004). In this sense, the influence of political society has been decisive in the expansion of participatory budgeting, especially insofar as it has become a standard PT policy at the local level.[3] In the states of Rio Grande do Sul and São Paulo many of the PT's competitors decided to implement participatory budgeting for electoral purposes. There is, however, some question about the quality of participatory budgeting in cities where it has expanded at the PT's initiative but civil society associations are lacking.[4] Thus, two other issues I address in this chapter are the conditions for the expansion of participatory budgeting to other large cities in Brazil and the conditions for its successful implementation in these cases. Here I deal mostly with Belo Horizonte and São Paulo as in-depth cases of expansion. My argument is that the expansion of participatory budgeting is mostly related to political society, but that its success depends on the interaction between political society and civil society actors. Thus, under unfavorable political conditions, participatory budgeting is much less likely to be effective in increasing deliberation or the distribution of public goods.

Deliberation and Distribution of Public Goods

The third issue I address in this chapter is what leads to the deliberative and distributive characteristics of the participatory budgeting. Unlike city mas-

3. However, not all PT administrations implemented participatory budgeting. In 2000–4, the PT governed 187 cities, but only 122 cities administered by the PT had participatory budgeting experiences.

4. I have been pursuing a polemic on this issue with my friend Gianpaolo Baioc-

ter plans and health councils discussed in Chapter 6 and 7, participatory budgeting is not legally institutionalized.[5] Nevertheless, in some cities participatory budgeting has taken root in the public imagination. The population at large knows the cycle of meetings, that participatory budgeting is the place to claim material goods, and that it reverses decades-old practices for claiming material improvements through politicians.[6] In this sense, participatory budgeting generates deliberative and distributive outcomes. There have now been a handful of cases of this type, the most important being Porto Alegre.[7] I differentiate the deliberative elements and distributive ca-

chi. Baiocchi argued in his article for the Fung and Wright collection that there was a decisive increase in civil society organization after the introduction of participatory budgeting. I argued in a comparative article on Porto Alegre and Belo Horizonte that the increase was much lower than Baiocchi assumed. Baiocchi counterargued, presenting more moderate data on neighborhood association growth, but still sticking to the same analytical model and presenting the example of the Nordeste Region in Porto Alegre, where there were very few associations before the introduction of participatory budgeting and the number increased rapidly afterward. My reply to Baiocchi is that he still has a case, Porto Alegre, in which civil society exists and is strong in some regions, such as Partenon, and the experience of independence and organization there is to be emulated. Other experiences with participatory budgeting where civil society organization is weak, as it is in Viamao, Gravatai, or Icapui, show that participation has not had too much effect on civil society organization. See Baiocchi, 2003; 2005; Avritzer, 2002a; 2006; Avritzer and Navarro, 2003; and Silva, 2001.

5. There has been a huge discussion on whether participatory budgeting should become a law. The discussion that emerged in Porto Alegre has to do with whether a law should be promulgated to make participatory budgeting the official budget-making institution. The city of Porto Alegre never proposed such a law, based on the argument of social movement activists that it would make the rules for engagement and participation more bureaucratic. In this sense, the lack of institutionalization means the lack of a formal law, even though participatory budgeting as an institution creates a pattern of social actors behavior that is predictable. See Santos, 2006; Avritzer, 2003.

6. One of the most standard forms of clientelism in Brazil is distribution of public goods by politicians. During electoral processes city council candidates go to neighborhoods and promise material improvements to be delivered if they are elected. This creates a grassroots basis of support for the politician. See Mainwaring, 1999.

7. Ipatinga is not studied much, despite its relevance for participatory budgeting. Ipatinga is the headquarters of an important steel mill on the outskirts of Belo Horizonte. The city had an important labor movement in the pre-1964 period, and a massacre of labor activists took place there at that time. The labor movement in Ipatinga continued to be strong during the democratization period, and its main leader Chico Ferramenta became city mayor in 1988. His administration was successful, participatory budgeting was implemented in the city, and the PT was reelected three times. Although the PT was defeated in the 2004 election, as the PSDB candidate withdrew in favor of the current mayor, participatory budgeting is still implemented in the city. See Wampler, 2008.

pacities of participatory budgeting, comparing the cases of Porto Alegre, Belo Horizonte, and São Paulo (there was no participatory budgeting in Salvador until 2005) and showing that in its most successful cases it has become the main instrument for broadening citizenship at the local level. Before describing participatory budgeting, I briefly describe the lack of access to public goods that led to participatory budgeting.

Origins in Urbanization and Inequality

To understand the importance of participatory budgeting for the Brazilian poor, we must look briefly at the history of their access to public goods at the urban level. Throughout the twentieth century, Brazilian cities grew in an unfair, disorganized, and illegal way, as rural people flooded in from the countryside. At the beginning of the century, more than 70 percent of Brazil's population was rural, but by the end of the century more than 70 percent was urban. Unfairness was the result of a process of modernization that proceeded without any kind of planning or with inadequate plans that did not reserve spaces for the poor population, as has been the case in Belo Horizonte and Brasília (Brasil, 2004; Caldeira, 2000). In these planned cities, the poor population was ignored and had to occupy urban plots of land illegally. In Belo Horizonte, fewer than ten years after the formation of the city, slums were already developing because poor migrants lacked areas to settle with access to public goods. Areas occupied by the poor did not initially have access to treated water, sewerage, or even electricity.

Disorganization and illegality were the result of an absurd process of land concession during the colonial and imperial periods, which created a legal chaos in large cities such as São Paulo and Rio de Janeiro (Holston, 1993). A civil code, written in 1916 for a rural society, did not provide adequate legal instruments for urban policies as the country modernized (Fernandes, 2002). The result was a process of urbanization completely out of control at the peak of Brazil's economic growth during the 1970s. Large urban areas in the eastern zone of São Paulo opened to the poor population faced problems of indeterminate property rights, with two or more people claiming the same property. These areas suffered with lack of infrastructure and poor public health. In addition, the state lacked the means to legalize urban tenure for the poor or to generalize access to public goods. For example, in the city of Porto Alegre in 1990, 99 percent of the streets in the center region of the city were paved, whereas only 12 percent of the

streets in the extreme south and 65 percent of the streets in northeast regions of the city were paved. These sharp inequalities, which also extended
to health and education, illustrate the lack of access of the poor to public
goods in Brazil. During democratization, the issue of a better access of the
poor population to urban services was on the top of the agenda of many
civil society and political society actors. Participatory budgeting would
emerge to address this issue.

The Emergence of Participatory
Budgeting in Porto Alegre

The social and political origins of participatory budgeting must be traced
back to the tradition of mobilization in the city of Porto Alegre in the postwar period. The origin of popular movements in Porto Alegre was marked
by the formation of Fracab, the Federation of Community Associations in
Rio Grande do Sul, in the second half of the 1950s (Silva, 2001: 79).[8] Porto
Alegre neighborhood associations in the 1950s aimed to foster a "human-
ist, antipaternalist" form of participation. (Silva, 2001: 81). Porto Alegre
had a strong tradition of leftist politics, which can be traced back to the same
period. Between 1947 and 1963, the PTB (Brazilian Labor Party) received
the largest share of the votes in all the elections for the city council.

At the time of democratization (1985–88), when most Brazilian capitals
were occupied with contests between candidates of the left and the right,
Porto Alegre was clearly on the left. There, the dispute was between the
PDT, a center-leftist party which sought to retrieve the populist past, and
the PT, which sought to renew the Brazilian left and proposed popular councils to govern cities (Keck, 1992; Abers, 1996). In the first round of this
contest, the PDT won the first elections for mayor and tried to introduce
participatory policies. Neighborhood associations and the PT, however,
claimed that the forms of participation were too limited. It was in this
context that UAMPA, the União de Associações de Moradores de Porto
Alegre, launched the idea of participation in the budget-making process

8. Gianpaolo Baiocchi in his excellent book on the participatory budgeting in Porto
Alegre makes an important argument on civil society regimes. According to Baiocchi
Porto Alegre civil society was paternalistic during the 1950s and 1960s. Although I agree
with the idea of civil society regimes and I think it helps to explain changes in state-civil
society patterns of interaction, I think that it is important to make the point that in Porto
Alegre there were anticipations of the new pattern that emerged in Brazil still in the
1950s. See Baiocchi, 2005.

(UAMPA, 1986). Porto Alegre was thus the only city in Brazil in which political competition in the aftermath of democratization occurred among sectors of the left and centered on the issue of local participation. It was in this context that Olívio Dutra was elected mayor of Porto Alegre in 1988 and introduced participatory budgeting as a means of deliberating on the distribution of public goods by his administration.

New Participatory Institutions

Participatory budgeting in its Porto Alegre version (1990–2005), introduced four new institutions, three of them with strong deliberative elements: the regional and thematic assemblies, the Council of Participatory Budgeting (COP), and the determination of the rules for decision-making.[9]

Regional and Thematic Assemblies

The regional and thematic assemblies are places where participants make claims, criticize the administrative actions of local authorities, and negotiate among themselves about their priorities. In Porto Alegre there are 16 regional and 5 thematic assemblies. The format of the regions was a point of conflict between social movements and the administration. Social movements pressed hard to maintain the pattern of collective action in the city's regions, arguing that the administrative design of districts would collide with the mobilization of many community movements (Baierle, 1998). The city agreed to redesign the regions in a way that overlapped with existing forms of mobilization. Thus, the first element of the deliberative process was an attempt to combine the logic of collective action and administration, starting the participatory process from the bottom.

An analysis of the socioeconomic characteristics of the participants in regional and thematic assemblies shows the strong presence of poor city-dwellers in the regional assemblies: 30 percent of the participants make no more than twice the minimum wage, and 25 percent make two to four times the minimum wage, indicating that participants in participatory budgeting closely approximate the socioeconomic condition of the population at large. In each assembly, 45 minutes are open for the contributions of the participants. Presence in the assemblies does not necessarily translate into equal-

9. There are many useful descriptions of the functioning of participatory budgeting, which I will not repeat here. For a full description of the process, see Baierle, 1998; Santos, 1998; Abers, 2000; Avritzer, 2002c; Baiocchi, 2002.

Table 5.1. Socioeconomic condition of all participants and those who never spoke in the assemblies in Porto Alegre

Income (multiples of minimum wage)	Participants in the Assemblies	Share of Participants Who Never Spoke in the Assemblies
Up to 2	30.22	47.30
2 to 4	25.51	37.90
4 to 8	20.60	37.20
8 to 12	9.43	27.10
Others	14.24	—
Total	100	—

Source: Cidade, 1999.

ity in other levels, as indicated in Table 5.1, which correlates income with active participation in Porto Alegre's participatory budgeting.

We can thus note several deliberative characteristics of the regional assemblies in Porto Alegre. First, they express the social diversity of the city, a characteristic that, as I show below, establishes a new social balance in deliberation about the distribution of public goods. Second, although there are still some inequalities in gender or class participation, there is rough gender equity in the number of interventions. Women participate in participatory budgeting meetings slightly more than men (51.4 percent of participants are women) and are also more willing to speak. We should also note, however, that socioeconomic condition sharply predetermines inclination to speak. Among the participants who make up to twice the minimum wage, which is the largest single group, almost half (47.30 percent) never spoke in an assembly. The lower a participant's income, the less likely he or she was to speak up.

The Participatory Budget Council

A second deliberative body of participatory budgeting is the COP, the participatory budget council. The COP is formed during the second round of regional assemblies, when the region elects councilors. This process leads to the formation of a council composed as follows: two councilors from each of the 16 regions (32), two from each of the five thematic assemblies (10), and one each from the UAMPA and the public service trade union (2). The COP has 44 members. Administration members do not vote, although they participate regularly and wield considerable influence.[10]

10. To my knowledge there was only one city in which the administration members could vote in the participatory budget council, the city of Santo Andre. Santo Andre changed the composition of its participatory budget council in 2004 and cancelled voting prerogatives of the administration personnel.

The COP is a deliberative body in which two types of negotiations take place: between community members on their priorities and between community members and the administration on the final format of the budget. Several decisions are made at this level, among them the substitution of previous assembly deliberations by other deliberations as a result of what is called a technical veto, when the administration disallows the decisions of regional assemblies on technical grounds. The most common vetoes involve environmental, property, and financial issues. Common environmental vetoes in Porto Alegre include the channeling of local creeks, which the population demands but the administration regards as a cause of summer floods.[11] Property issues involve the misidentification of land as belonging to the city; when it turns out to be owned by state companies, the state, or the union, the cost of public works increases. Financial issues, finally, involve the cost of extending sewerage or water pipelines. In all these cases, there is vigorous debate between the members of the COP and the administration, with mixed results.

One of the important results of these debates is the requirement imposed by the administration that the technicians attend the regional and thematic assemblies and discuss their positions on these issues with the population. Again, it is important to note that the presence of the technicians in popular assemblies enhances their deliberative nature. The council is also a key element of bottom-up design. It is an institution constituted at the end of open-entry assemblies. Although councilors are chosen representatives, they are strongly linked to the regional leaderships from the places in which they have been elected. The presence of participatory budget councils is a key element of bottom-up design because it expresses the concentration of most of the decision-making process in the hands of civil society actors.

Rule-making

The third deliberative element of participatory budgeting is the process of decision-making on rules for deliberation. Porto Alegre inaugurated a rule-making process that has been followed by other cities in Brazil. In this process, the city determines the initial rules for deliberation (*regimento*), then the COP is able to change them starting the next year. These rules in-

11. Pavement has been the public good most demanded in Porto Alegre since the emergence of participatory budgeting. Paving amounting to 6 million square meters has been done. As a consequence of the increase in pavement in the city, much of the city surface has become impermeable, and summer flooding has increased. This has led to a technical veto on new channeling of creeks.

volve the composition of the COP; the attributions of the COP; rules for the election of local delegates; conditions for losing a mandate; rules for argumentation in the COP; rules for the election of a coordination body within the COP; and, last but not least, rules by which the COP can change the rules for deliberation. Thus, the COP may be understood as a body that sets up its own forms of regulation, from its composition to its rules for deliberation. It shares some of its prerogatives with other bodies, such as the CRC (Coordination of Relations with the Community) and the GAPLAN (Planning Cabinet). However, the final budgetary deliberation takes place in the COP and includes making rules for the COP's future operation.

Expansion of Participation

The most familiar theories about Porto Alegre's participatory budgeting argue that participation increased quickly because of the process's deliberative elements (Avritzer, 2002a; Baiocchi, 2003; Wampler and Avritzer, 2004; Santos, 2006). Despite low initial rates, participation in the new institution grew rapidly, and it is worth exploring the details of the process. Regions with previous traditions of participation, such as Partenon or the east zone of the city, had relatively high initial levels of participation, whereas regions without such traditions, such as Restinga and Navegantes, had low initial levels (Table 5.2). Here we see again the importance of civil society organization for the emergence of the institutional innovation. Without the participation of neighborhood association members in the initial deliberations, the process could have collapsed. Learning and demonstration effects occurred as the neighborhoods singled out above received more benefits than the least

Table 5.2. Participation in participatory budgeting in selected regions of Porto Alegre, 1990–1998

Region	1990	1992	1994	1996	1998
Regions with strong associative traditions					
Leste	152	510	339	623	710
Lomba	64	569	575	973	638
Partenon	75	1,096	661	809	805
Cruzeiro	181	297	494	649	604
Regions with weak associative traditions					
Navegantes	15	165	135	495	624
Nordeste	33	276	350	682	906
Restinga	36	369	1,096	763	1,348
Centro-Sul	101	591	352	1,513	1,461

Source: Municipal Administration of Porto Alegre, Center for Community Relations.

organized regions, leading to the reorganization of the more clientelistic neighborhoods (Abers, 2000; Wampler and Avritzer, 2004; Baiocchi, 2005).

Participatory budgeting in Porto Alegre has enjoyed steady growth, rising from 976 people in 1990 to 26,807 in 2000. This evolution tells us something important about the relationship between civil and political society in the consolidation of participatory arrangements. Civil society was responsible for the initial success of the arrangement by providing the participatory institution with actors capable of fulfilling the roles required of them: attending meetings, identifying neighborhood problems, and participating and deliberating in councils (Wampler and Avritzer, 2004). Political society and the state then generalized previously existing practices to the rest of the city: they extended forms of participation to other neighborhoods and ensured that these forms would be the only way of claiming public goods in the city. Together, the two actions led to the consolidation of participatory budgeting in the early 1990s as a strongly deliberative institution.

The Role of the PT

Although the bottom-up design of Porto Alegre's participatory budgeting process arose from a local consensus and caught the attention of many Brazilian political actors, the spread of participatory budgeting from Porto Alegre to other cities in Brazil was due mainly to the initiative of the PT. From 1993 to 1997 the number of participatory budgeting cases expanded to 103, among them 37 (49 percent) belonged to PT administrations. Although most of the expansion of participatory budgeting from 1993 on was based on the bottom-up design of Porto Alegre, most of the new cases adapted the design to make it more palatable to both the local PT and city hall. In Belo Horizonte and São Paulo, participatory budgeting underwent important changes related to the characteristics of its civil and political society, as described in the following section.

The Expansion of Participatory Budgeting
to Belo Horizonte and São Paulo

Participatory budgeting in Belo Horizonte and São Paulo differed from the process hat originated in Porto Alegre.[12] In this section, I describe only the

12. Participatory budgeting forms of organization are different in almost every city. There is what we in Brazil call the Porto Alegre model, which usually involves regional

changes in bottom-up format of the participatory budgeting in Belo Horizonte and São Paulo. I then move to the general characteristics of participation in both cities.

Belo Horizonte

Participatory budgeting was introduced in Belo Horizonte in 1993 immediately after the inauguration of Patrus Ananias as mayor. Ananias, a leftist lawyer linked to the Catholic Church, decided to implement participatory budgeting even before it was the national and international star of participatory politics. Nonetheless, the success in Porto Alegre and the centrality of participatory policies, compared with other policies such as the *etatization* of the transportation system in popular administrations, were already becoming clear.[13] It is also important to note that the political society in Belo Horizonte was fairly willing to support the mayor's introduction of participatory budgeting. The PT defeated the PSDB, which in the state of Minas Gerais is more participatory and further to the left than it is in São Paulo. Mayor Ananias did not face initially strong opposition; to the contrary, his long-standing links to the Catholic Church, as well as his council speaker's relation to evangelical politicians, gave him a comfortable majority in city hall (see Chapter 3).

Borrowing the Bottom-up Features of Porto Alegre

Participatory budgeting in Belo Horizonte maintained some of Porto Alegre's features, but changed others. It maintained the two rounds of regional assemblies, one of the key characteristics of bottom-up formats. Assemblies take place in the neighborhoods and are open-entry assemblies. Delegates are elected in these assemblies in a way similar to Porto Alegre's. However,

---

assemblies, a participatory budget council, and the elaboration of the budget by the mayor's office or by an institution linked to it (GAPLAN in the case of Porto Alegre). Variations involve mainly the existence or not of a participatory budget council and the place were the budget is elaborated. Many cities have given to participatory budgeting elaboration the status of a secretary, who has to dispute power with other sectors of the administration. (Grazia and Ribeiro, 2003).

13. There was a dispute within the Brazilian left in the early 1990s on what should be the priority of a leftist agenda. In the case of Luiza Erundina's administration, the control by the city of the transportation system acquired priority. Brizola assumed control of city transportation in Rio de Janeiro at the same time, and this discussion was strong in Porto Alegre, too. See Baiocchi, 2005.

these assemblies do not lead to a council, a second important element of bottom-up format. The lack of a council made Belo Horizonte's participatory budgeting a bottom-up institution with fewer power-sharing elements. The administration has most of the prerogatives on the final format of the city budget. What makes Belo Horizonte's design a bottom-up format is the fact that decisions on public works in the regional assemblies are final.

New Devices and Institutions

Belo Horizonte's participatory budgeting also created a few new devices for the participatory process. The first of them is an administrative device, an index to orient distribution of resources to the regions. The IQVU, for the Index for Urban Quality of Living, functions like Porto Alegre's evaluation of previous access to public goods as a means of allocating resources to underserved areas, but in Belo Horizonte the index is applied to only half of the available resources. Half of the resources available for participatory budgeting are evenly divided among the regions, and half are allocated according to this index. Thus, Belo Horizonte, unlike Porto Alegre, gives more weight to technical criteria for the distribution of public goods and reserves more resources for deliberation by the public administration. Thus, Belo Horizonte's process for participatory budgeting moderates the bottom-up features of the original participatory institution.

Two features of Belo Horizonte's participatory budgeting are completely new. One is an internal process of negotiation among the claimers of public goods, called the "priorities caravans." At the stage in which each community has proposed a public project, the city starts a process of mutual visitation by each one of the communities to the other communities. This is an important moment in the deliberative process, in which each one of the claimers evaluates how needy its community is compared with other poor communities. On this basis, different communities start to support one another's claims, forming coalitions that will be decisive in the deliberative process.

The second feature introduced by Belo Horizonte's participatory budgeting is the forum of regional priorities. In this forum, tickets are formed with coalitions of proposals from different subregions. The representatives then vote on these tickets. Unlike in Porto Alegre, the decisions of the regional forums are final. The public works approved by the delegates are then integrated into the budget proposal. One-fifth of the delegates present at the regional forums become members of the *Comforças,* a monitoring body that follows the bidding on public works and negotiates substitutions in case of

technical problems. Thus, it is clear that the participatory design in Belo
Horizonte is still bottom-up, but has more moderate elements than the Porto
Alegre model. I show below how this affects participation and distribution.

Attracting Different Participants

Participation in Belo Horizonte's participatory budgeting institutions varies
more than in Porto Alegre's. The average participant in Belo Horizonte
makes in between two and five times the minimum wage, close to the city
average (Avritzer, 2006). As far as regional variations are concerned, the
Barreiro and Venda Nova regions of Belo Horizonte play similar roles to
Partenon and the east zones in Porto Alegre (Wampler and Avritzer, 2004).

In the first year of participatory budgeting in Belo Horizonte, participation was high because of the demonstration effect of Porto Alegre: the population had good reason to assume that it was participating in an effective
process. Participation increased once its effectiveness at the city level became clear. In its second year, participation grew more than 50 percent over
the previous year, but then decreased in 1996 when doubts emerged about
the future of participatory budgeting. In that year's elections, there were serious doubts about whether the PT candidate would win and thus about
whether the participatory budget decisions would be implemented. Participation decreased again in 1997 because, despite the fact that the new, non-
PT administration promised to continue participatory budgeting, people
doubted that it would. However, once it become clear that it would respect
the deliberations, participation grew again (Table 5.3). Thus, participation
follows both the initial logic of civil society organization and the logic of
uncertainties produced by the electoral competition of political society.

*Table 5.3. Participation in participatory budgeting in Belo Horizonte,
1993–2000*

Year	First Round	Second Round	Third Round	Regional Forum	Total
1993–94	3,671	4,215	6,202	1,128	15,216
1994–95	5,796	5,323	14,461	1,243	26,823
1995–96	5,801	11,796	17,597	1,314	36,508
1996–97	2,938	9,586	17,937	1,334	31,795
1997–98	3,416	3,081	11,871	1,050	19,418
1999–2000	stage suppressed	2,905	16,323	1,947	21,175

Source: Planning secretary of Belo Horizonte.

Differences between Porto Alegre and Belo Horizonte

At least four other differences between Porto Alegre's and Belo Horizonte's participatory budgeting bear emphasis. The first is that each city stresses deliberation in a different way. In Porto Alegre, deliberative capacity is expressed in the way the assemblies are connected with the COP. Porto Alegre's COP can check the power of the mayor, whereas Belo Horizonte's Comforca members can at most supervise the implementation of participatory budgeting projects. However, Belo Horizonte's participants are less dependent on leaders at the city level: once they make a decision, it has to be implemented. To this extent, Belo Horizonte's participatory budgeting places a higher emphasis on local decision-making. In the first regional assemblies, neighborhoods pick public goods they want to see delivered and, through a process of discussion and voting, make a final decision. The city must then implement the assembly's decision. In Porto Alegre, in contrast, the COP and GAPLAN have more leeway to rank and implement the decisions of regional assemblies.

The second difference between the two cities concerns the role of the council. Belo Horizonte did not have a council between 1993 and 1996. At that stage participatory budgeting was a method for distributing public goods at the local level. In 1999 the city administration decided to create a city council, the *Conselho da Cidade,* but it has never acquired the kind of prerogatives the Porto Alegre COP has, like vetoing the city budget. According to a provision in Porto Alegre, the COP is entitled to examine the proposed city budget and to veto it with a two-thirds majority. Although this has not yet occurred, it gives a good idea of the Porto Alegre council's powers. Belo Horizonte and São Paulo never gave their councils similar prerogatives. Thus, in Porto Alegre participatory budgeting is both a local deliberative institution and a social movement body to pressure the city administration, whereas in Belo Horizonte it is just a local deliberative body.

The third difference is the leverage of technical personnel in the deliberative process. Every participatory budgeting system can be constrained by technical personnel. In Porto Alegre, the most important constraints have been limitations on paving because of concerns about the permeability of the soil and limitations on extending city pipelines, so that they followed a linear pattern (Avritzer, 2002b). In Belo Horizonte, these technical constraints are stronger. The IQVU, the urban quality of living index, strictly limits the resources that social actors can shift from one region to another, as well as the kinds of goods they can ask for. Moreover, Belo Horizonte has seen more technical control over its participatory budgeting in the past few years.

The fourth and final issue is the size of investment in participatory budgeting programs. This is one of the most contentious issues in many cities (Wampler and Avritzer, 2004). Every Brazilian city has its finances split between maintenance and investments. A typical Brazilian city reserves close to 50 percent of its budget to maintenance, which includes all the expanses related to maintaining paved streets, sewerage, and water networks. The rest of the resources are divided between personal and investment resources. Porto Alegre has established the tradition of separating for participatory budgeting a certain percentage of investment resources (Table 5.4). That percentage has been relatively high, because Porto Alegre has the advantage over almost all other Brazilian cities of having a municipal water company.[14] Since most participatory budgeting investments have been made in the areas of pavement and sewerage, owning the water company has allowed Porto Alegre to increase its investment in sewerage and pavement by about 5 percent of its yearly budget.[15] Beyond this administrative advantage, the city has also been able to increase these investments either through fiscal reform or by changing the ratio between administrative and social policy employees (Marquetti, 2003).

Thus, we see many differences in the organization of participatory budgeting in the two cities. Porto Alegre implemented a stronger process of deliberation from the very beginning. Its COP is a central element of this process because it is where the city administration and the local associations interact the most. The Porto Alegre participatory budgeting process also decides on more investments, although Belo Horizonte has already implemented nearly 1,000 public works decided by its process. Can we attribute these differences to the cities' respective configurations of civil and politi-

---

14. It is beyond the aims of this book to discuss the specific configuration of each of the city administrations studied. Yet, the configuration of water and sanitation services is an important topic. Until 1988, all large Brazilian states with the exception of Rio Grande do Sul had state-controlled water companies. This was true of Minas Gerais, Rio de Janeiro, and Sao Paulo. The decision to transfer the control of water companies to the state was taken by the authoritarian regime and was meant to transfer city resources to poor areas of these states. Porto Alegre kept its water company, as the state of Rio Grande do Sul managed to keep a different telecommunication and electricity structures. The fact that the city has a local water company allowed it to make more investments in sewerage and sanitation.

15. This is difficult to estimate. This estimate has been made for me by former Belo Horizonte planning secretary, Mauricio Borges Lemos.

Table 5.4. Share of participatory budgeting investments in the total budget (percent)

Budget Category	Porto Alegre	Belo Horizonte
Participatory budgeting investments in the first year	3.59	2.68
Maximum of participatory budgeting investments	20.80	5.35
Current participatory budgeting investments	5.98	3.93

Source: Planning secretaries in Porto Alegre and Belo Horizonte.

cal society? Before answering this question, let us look into a third case of participatory budgeting in the city of São Paulo.

São Paulo

São Paulo is politically divided on the issue of participation, as I showed in Chapters 2 and 3. The experience of participation under the Luiza Erundina administration (1989–2002), the first PT mayor, did not boost the idea among the population. The few participatory attempts during this period were considered challenges to the sovereignty of the city council, which killed them.[16] The decision to implement participatory budgeting was made during the electoral campaign; Marta Suplicy's program stated that "in order to boost popular participation . . . [it is important] to implement participatory budgeting and decentralization" (Suplicy, 2000). This represents an interesting evolution from Porto Alegre and Belo Horizonte to São Paulo. In 2000, participatory budgeting was sufficiently consolidated as a PT program that it was made part of the electoral platform. Participatory budgeting was implemented in São Paulo in the first year of Suplicy's administration, and she felt the need to issue a decree because of the contentious nature of city politics. In July 11, 2001, she created participatory budgeting coordination linked to her cabinet.

Participatory budgeting was introduced as a small pilot program in 2001, then fully implemented in 2002 with a structure that resembled Porto Alegre's more than Belo Horizonte's. Still, in its first year participatory budgeting decided only on investments in two areas, health and education. The

16. The city council's and other legislative bodies' positions on forms of participation is so far an underdeveloped area of study. The case of São Paulo is the most complicated because the PT administration faced strong opposition between 1988 and 1992. Couto and Abrúcio, 2003. On the relation between Porto Alegre's COP and city council, see Dias, 2002.

first stage of participation in São Paulo encompassed assemblies in all 96 districts of the 31 regions or sub-*prefeituras*.[17] There were two meetings in the districts, one informational and the other deliberative, leading to the election of delegates and councilors. The procedure for electing delegates was similar to other Brazilian cities, such as Porto Alegre and Belo Horizonte, with incentives for organization and a reduction of the weight in the decision-making process of the already very organized sectors.

The most important innovation of the participatory budgeting process in São Paulo was the composition of its council. São Paulo created a council with representatives of all 96 districts, in addition to representatives of underrepresented groups, such as gays and lesbians and the street population, and specific issue areas. The 2003 participatory budget council had 61 councilors elected by the subregions, 4 councilors elected in each thematic area, plus 2 councilors representing vulnerable groups, including gays and lesbians, blacks, street people, the elderly, and the handicapped. The city had one nonvoting representative for each of the secretaries running social programs. The format of the participatory budget council in São Paulo allowed for more interaction between neighborhood associations and the poor, who are concentrated in the downtown part of the city, and, in this sense, it allowed participatory budgeting to tackle social issues.[18] Participation in the participatory budgeting grew steadily from 34,000 people in the first, pilot year to 55,000 in the second and 82,000 people in 2004, the last year of its operation (Table 5.5).

Thus, São Paulo's participatory budgeting was also a bottom-up form of participation. The process started with open-entry assemblies at the local level and continued with the election of a council. However, unlike Porto Alegre and Belo Horizonte, São Paulo's participatory budgeting has always aroused strong doubts about how deliberative its decisions would be. Although participatory budgeting decided on education and health issues, its decisions overlapped with others made in both participatory and nonparticipatory arenas. In education, participatory budgeting decisions overlapped

17. São Paulo participatory budgeting was linked to the process of decentralization of the city. A decentralization law was approved in 2002, and from 2003 on participatory budgeting deliberations were linked to the organization of the 31 sub-*prefeituras*.

18. This has been one of the sharpest criticisms of participatory budgeting. Investments in Brazilian cities typically involve only public works and leave out what in the Brazilian public accounting system is called *custeio,* or operating expenses. Social policies always involve an increase in operating expenses that are decided outside the participatory budgeting process.

Table 5.5. Participation in participatory budgeting in São Paulo, 2001–2004

Type of Participant	2001	2002	2003	2004
Participants	34,000	55,000	80,000	82,000
Delegates	1,076	1,134	2,131	2,219
Councilors	112	139	216	241
Areas of deliberation	Health and education	Health, education, and a third area	All city policy areas	All city policy areas

Source: Sánchez, 2004.

with the decision of the administration to introduce unified centers of education (CEUs), and in health participatory budgeting decisions overlapped with the health councils' decision to boost the Family Health Program. Therefore, although the elements of a bottom-up institution were in place in São Paulo, they overlapped with the administration's decision not to give full priority to the bottom-up process. In the end, São Paulo's participatory budgeting worked only in selected neighborhoods and areas.

São Paulo's participatory budgeting drew more heavily on associations than did the processes in the other two cities. São Paulo, as I showed in Chapter 2, has two large social movement constituencies—one formed in the late 1970s and early 1980s in the area of healthcare and the other formed in the late 1980s and early 1990s in the area of housing. These movements have created a consolidated leadership in the city with high participation and much experience competing with other social movements for resources (Avritzer, 2004). Participatory budgeting started in São Paulo in the areas of housing and education;[19] the participants later chose a third area, and overwhelmingly again selected housing (Wampler, 2004). Not by chance, two of the areas were themes with heavy concentration of social movement activists. Only in its third year was participatory budgeting expanded to all thematic issues, though without the allocation of adequate resources.

In a survey made of all São Paulo participatory budgeting members in 2003, 69 percent belonged to voluntary associations, by far the highest

19. Education is not an area with a strong tradition of mobilization in the city of São Paulo or in other Brazilian cities. However, there is a local law in São Paulo that requires the city to expend at least 30 percent of its annual budget on education. This law created a leeway for more decisions in the area of education. Eventually, Marta Suplicy's administration created the program of integrated centers for education of poor people that were only partially connected to the participatory budgeting process.

number in Brazil (Criterium, 2003). Thus, the first notable characteristic of São Paulo's participatory budgeting is that it was focused on the city's organized population. The city did not want to put all its bets on participatory budgeting, which was one of at least three high-priority social programs, the other two being minimum income and unified centers of education, which did not involve citizen participation. Since the organized population was targeted, the areas of deliberation had to be restricted to already mobilized sectors, such as healthcare, or easily mobilized sectors, such as housing. All these characteristics distinguish São Paulo from Porto Alegre or Belo Horizonte.

Participatory budgeting in São Paulo faced one main obstacle, namely, the administration's need to deliver fast results in social policy. The PT took over a city in disarray and had to cut many deals at the city council to avoid the paralysis of the Luiza Erundina administration (Couto, 1995). These deals mainly involved appointing other parties' administrators to the sub-*prefeituras* to create a coalition majority[20]—an action that considerably diluted the implementation of participatory budgeting. The most progressive sub-*prefeitos* were highly favorable to participatory budgeting and established a new relation with the delegates and councilors, while some coalition sub-*prefeitos* (regional district mayors) were very clientelistic, preventing participatory budgeting from becoming the only way of claiming public goods, as was the case in Belo Horizonte and Porto Alegre.

Thus, the main characteristic of São Paulo's participatory budgeting was that participation and public deliberation were directed mainly to the already organized sectors of the population and to claims in specific areas. Participants could decide on selected public works in the areas of healthcare, housing, and urban infrastructure, but the rest of the city budget was independent of the process. In terms of the scope of the deliberation, we can note that while Porto Alegre assigned full deliberative prerogatives to its COP and gave it a veto over the city budget with two-thirds of the votes (Santos, 2002), Belo Horizonte gave participatory budgeting assemblies full decision-making capacity over half of district resources, while São Paulo gave it shared prerogatives in healthcare, housing, and some district budgets. Table 5.6 compares the different arrangements.

20. It is more difficult to create a coalition majority to govern in the city of São Paulo than in Belo Horizonte and Porto Alegre. São Paulo's conservative sectors are very well organized and financed and are heavily represented in the city's legislative body. There is no similar form of organization in Belo Horizonte and Porto Alegre. In both cities conservative city councils are less organized and often less willing to negotiate with the city administration.

Table 5.6. Variation in participatory budgeting results according to civil and political society configuration in three Brazilian cities

City	Civil Society Participation	Political Society Will	Nature of the Ruling Coalition
São Paulo	High, but concentrated in a few regions.	PT divided on how comprehensive participatory budgeting should be.	Opposition does not participate in participatory budgeting; coalition names members to sub-*prefeituras* that do not favor participation.
Belo Horizonte	High and initially concentrated in a few regions. Expanded later to all regions.	PT divided, but no group radically against participatory budgeting.	Opposition not radically against participatory budgeting; mayor organizes support at the city council, drawing on other forces.
Porto Alegre	High and initially concentrated in a few regions. Expanded later to all regions.	PT united behind participatory budgeting.	Opposition members reduced during four tenures; PT acquires majority at the city council.

Accounting for Differences across Cities

How can we account for these differences? What kind of deliberative results did they produce? The different configurations of civil and political society in the three cities produced different results in the design and effectiveness of their participatory budgeting processes. Porto Alegre is to this day the case with the strongest deliberative emphasis: participatory budgeting provides the framework for all deliberations on major investments, not only for new public works, but also for health, education, and other public policy areas.[21] This strong deliberative emphasis involves the self-perception of the participants on how much they decided. In a survey conducted in Porto Alegre in 1999, I asked whether participants knew of deals for public works made outside the participatory budgeting process. None of

21. Mayors of Porto Alegre have made two interesting attempts to make deliberations on public works outside the framework of participatory budgeting. The first took place during the Tarso Genro administration and involved the construction of the Terceira Perimetral, a highway to cross the city avoiding its crowded downtown areas. Genro wanted the highway and had World Bank financing for it but had to go to a COP meeting to defended it because it was not part of the deliberations in the regional assemblies. Eventually, Genro managed to get approval for the *perimetral*. A second more complicated case took place during the Raul Pont administration.

them knew of any, making the perceived effectiveness of the participatory institutions very high (Avritzer, 2006). To have such strong deliberative capacity, participatory budgeting must have strong civil society participation and firm support within political society as a whole, not only the PT but also other parties represented in the city council. These two contextual conditions are central to the operation of a more radical design.

Belo Horizonte also shows strong deliberative elements, though they are not as strong as in Porto Alegre. The initial design made participatory budgeting a significant institution concerning budget issues, without giving it exclusive prerogatives. In Belo Horizonte half of the regional investment decisions are made within the participatory budgeting process, but it does not decide major city social policies in areas such as health and education. The self-understanding of the participants is that there are public works being decided outside participatory budgeting. In a survey on that issue in Belo Horizonte, 8 percent of the respondents made this claim (Avritzer, 2006). The smaller role of neighborhood associations in city politics and the less consensual nature of participatory budgeting within the city administration are responsible for the smaller deliberative prerogatives in Belo Horizonte, compared with Porto Alegre. Yet, those deliberative prerogatives are not inconsequential: close to 1,000 new public works have been completed in the Belo Horizonte region as a result of participatory budgeting deliberations.

São Paulo is the most complicated case because of the complexity of its politics. Participatory budgeting has been deliberative in a very limited sense in the city of São Paulo, as one of the devices to deliberate on public works in the well-organized areas of the city where mobilization is strong. Participatory budgeting has not been the most important device for deciding public policy: minimum income programs and unified education centers have played a stronger role in Marta Suplicy's policies. The self-understanding of the actors corroborates this analysis. Wampler asked delegates of São Paulo's participatory budgeting forums how they saw their authority to stop government, select projects, and monitor projects. More than half (53 percent) of the respondents answered that they could never stop government, whereas 8 percent answered that they could always do so; 56 percent answered that they could always or almost always select specific participatory budgeting policies (Wampler, 2004). Thus, it is clear that delegates and councilors in São Paulo understood their partial role in deciding city policies.

The reasons for the weak form of participatory budgeting introduced in São Paulo lay both in civil and political society. Neighborhood association actors were unevenly organized in the city's regions. Unlike in Porto Alegre and Belo Horizonte, the city administration was not willing to wait for the change of social leadership at the local level, mostly because it knew that the contentious nature of city politics would not give them time. At the same time, São Paulo's PT was less inclined toward participation than other state branches; inside Marta Suplicy's administration there were groups in favor and against broad participation. In the end, participatory budgeting was in the hands of a leftist group within the administration, with more mainstream groups concentrated in other secretaries. This never happened in Porto Alegre, where the coordination of participatory budgeting is highly disputed by all groups within the PT. Thus, the three cases show that success is not determined only by design, as some authors have claimed (Fung and Wright, 2003); it is rather an interaction between design and civil and political context. What are the distributive effects of participatory budgeting in each of these contexts?

The Distributive Impact of Participatory Budgeting

The impact of participatory budgeting on redistributing access to public goods is not a completely settled issue. This is first of all because it is very difficult to measure distributive impact in the short term, and there are very few cases of participatory budgeting over more than two consecutive administrations. One solution to this methodological problem is to measure how participatory budgeting affected the poor population in the three cities without dealing with public goods stocks. Stocks of public goods in large Brazilian cities have been accumulated over more than 100 years; tracing the impact of short-term changes on them would be almost impossible. We can, however, follow short-term changes in the way access to public goods is distributed among the poor and the wealthy populations of the three cities.

Porto Alegre

Again, the case of Porto Alegre is the most interesting because of its clear distributive implications. Marquetti (2003) sorted Porto Alegre's 16 regions according to the average income—low, low-average, medium, and high—and correlated investments through participatory budgeting works (Table 5.7). The four low-income regions, he found, Extremo Sul, Nordeste, Lomba do Pinheiro,and Restinga, received the highest average investment per person: between 4 and 16 times higher than the investments in the wealthier regions (up to R$1,650 in Extremo Sul compared with R$100 in the Centro District).

Table 5.7. Per capita investments resulting from Porto Alegre's participatory budgeting, by district

Region	Investment per Capita (in R$)	No. of Projects per 1,000 Inhabitants	Income
Extremo Sul	1,650	less than 3.8	Low
Nordeste	1,200	less than 3.8	Low
Lomba do Pinheiro	900	3.2 to 3.8	Low
Restinga	650	3.2 to 3.8	Low
Partenon	250	0 to 2	Low-medium
Eixo da Baltazar	350	3.2 to 3.8	Medium
Norte	500	2 to 3	Medium
Glória	600	less than 3.8	Medium
Centro-Sul	500	0 to 2	Medium
Cruzeiro	500	2 to 3	Medium
Humaitá	450	less than 3.8	Medium
Cristal	750	3.2 to 3.8	Medium
Centro	100	0 to 2	High
Noroeste	200	0 to 2	High
Sul	350	2 to 3	High
Leste	400	2 to 3	High

Source: Marquetti, 2003.

We can also note the greater number of public works implemented in the poor regions, showing that several groups in these regions benefited from public works. Even among the low-medium and medium income groups, we still see a strong distributive effect. Norte and Gloria received high per capita investments of between R$500 and R$600, respectively, although the correlation between income and public works is not as direct in Partenon and Eixo da Baltazar. It is important to note that even if Partenon and Eixo da Baltazar did not receive the same share as other low-medium- or medium-income regions, they still received between 2.5 and 3.5 times more than Centro. The regions at the higher end of the medium-income range (Cruzeiro and Cristal, for example) received R$500 and R$750, respectively. Thus, in Porto Alegre's participatory budgeting the poorest regions of the city received as least double the per capita investments of other regions, showing that participatory budgeting has improved the mid-term access of the population to public goods.

Belo Horizonte

A similar point can be made about the distributive effects of participatory budgeting in Belo Horizonte, in spite of the smaller amount of investments per capita going through Belo Horizonte's process. Belo Horizonte has a way of reversing previous investment priorities that differs from Porto Alegre's. Belo Horizonte uses its IQVU index to integrate socioeconomic measures, such as employment and income, with environmental and cultural dimensions, such as the amount of green space and number of cinemas, theaters, and other cultural facilities in a neighborhood.[22] Using the IQVU, Pires (2001) produced a study similar to Marquetti's in Porto Alegre, measuring the participatory budgeting investment in the city's planning units.[23] He identified six regions according to their IQVU and established a correlation between IQVU levels and city investments made through participatory budgeting. He found that the amount of participatory budgeting investment, as well as the number of investments, were concentrated in the areas with lower IQVUs (Table 5.8). It is important to keep in mind that these are not only the poorest regions in the city, but also those with the highest population density and that there is also a correlation between the amount of investments and these areas' populations. Per capita investments in wealthy regions are very low in Belo Horizonte, lower than in Porto Alegre—around R$5 per inhabitant in regions such as Mangabeira and Savassi.[24] Investments in the next-wealthiest region are also very low, an average of R$12. Middle-class neighborhoods, such as Barrroca or Santo Antonio also receive very little investment from the city. In lower-middle-income areas, the level of investment increases dramatically to R$36 per capita, and in low-income areas it reaches to R$44 per capita. These are working-class neighborhoods with low to average urban infrastructure. The largest investment is in some of the poorest areas in the city, such as Aglomerado da Serra and Aglomerado Santa Lucia, which receive nearly R$90 per resident, 40 times

22. It is interesting to point out that almost all kinds of public equipment are unevenly distributed in large Brazilian cities, from hospitals and theaters to pavement and schools. For results of Sposati's survey of the availability of public equipment in the city of São Paulo, see *Folha de São Paulo,* 2000.

23. Because of the way most Brazilian cities are organized, with wealthy and poor inhabitants sometimes living in the same region, it is not sufficient to make investments in poor regions or not to make investments in wealthy regions. The largest *favela* in the city of São Paulo, Paraisopolis, is located in Morumbi, one of the wealthiest regions of the city. The largest *favelas* in Belo Horizonte, Morro Santa Lucia, is located in the center-south, the wealthiest region in the city. Belo Horizonte administration introduced the IQVU in order to be able to invest in smaller areas of the city that are pockets of poverty and are located in well-off neighborhoods.

24. This is not the total amount of money that wealthy inhabitants will receive from the city. Every Brazilian city spends lot of resources in the maintenance of the already constructed infrastructure. The center-south region of Belo Horizonte already has its infrastructure constructed, and the city spends money in its maintenance, which is above the maintenance costs in poorest regions of the city.

Table 5.8. Distributive effects of Belo Horizonte's participatory budgeting in selected regions, 2002

Region	Number of planning units in the region	IQVU range	Average population	Average investment (in R$)	Average number of public works in participatory budgeting per region
Mangabeiras Savassi	6	0570–0645	18,677	93,374.20	0.50
Padre Eustaquio Barroca	19	0491–0550	24,985	307,255.16	0.84
Barreiro de Baixo Cachoeirinha	12	0463–0488	35,027	1,185,151.05	2.08
Lindeia Ribeiro de Abreu	18	0423–0456	30,102	1,075,192.75	2.44
Ribeiro de Abreu Sarandi Jatoba	15	0384–0415	26,109	1,149,208.66	1.73
Aglomerado da Serra Barragem Taquaril	11	0328–0368	13,709	1,221,302.76	1.82

Source: Pires, 2001.

higher than in the richest neighborhoods. Again, we see the strong distributive impact of participatory budgeting for the poor of Belo Horizonte, in spite of a ceiling of distribution almost ten times lower than in Porto Alegre.

Although Porto Alegre's participatory budgeting has stronger deliberative elements and makes larger transfers per capita to the poor than Belo Horizonte's, both cities show strong distributive results in terms of the inversion of access to public goods. Porto Alegre and Belo Horizonte also demonstrate together that the rules for distributing public goods introduced by the participatory budgeting have a strong influence on the results. Here, too, the deliberative process in São Paulo provides an interesting third case.

São Paulo

Participatory budgeting in São Paulo in early 2003 concerned investment planning in the sub-*prefeituras* in education, health, and a third area chosen by the local population. Investments made through the participatory budgeting process, as shown in Table 5.9, were focused on poor areas, though they represented only a small share of the city's investments as a whole (R$966 million over two years, as against a total annual budget of close to R$11 billion).[25]

25. Not all planned investments shown in Table 5.9 have been implemented, and the data for implementation vary. *Folha de São Paulo* ran a piece on São Paulo participa-

Table 5.9. Investments in selected regions of the city as a result of São Paulo's participatory budgeting (in thousands of R$)

Sub-prefeitura in rising income order	Investment in education	Investment in healthcare	Family health program	Third area	Total investment
Cidade Tirad.	22,400	6,936	5,911	6,200	41,477
Guaianases	19,044	972	6,939	—	26,956
M'Boi Mirim	17,907	17,746	27,242	2,126	65,000
Parelheiros	4,394	3,862	3,598	—	11,855
São Mateus	37,000	8,085	4112	8,700	57,897
São Miguel	19,550	10,760	7,710	—	38,021
Campo Limpo	25,732	23,168	19,789	1,890	70,579
Perus	21,000	6,826	2,048	—	29,875
Itaquera	18,506	14,481	3,341	1,653	37,981
Jabaquara	6,000	400	2,056	230,00	8,686
Socorro	50,400	12,496	5,397	—	68,294
Penha	8,250	4,991	3,341	—	16,582
Butantã	19,738	5,199	1,799	—	26,737
Sé	8,155	1,876	3,084	—	13,076
Mooca	8,050	11,066	2,056	—	21,173
Lapa	4,337	3,528	2,570	1,733	12,168
Pinheiros	559	4,188	771	946	5,519
Total	541,201	209,257	177,252	38,508	966,219

Source: Sanchez, 2004.

Two important differences between São Paulo and the two other cities should be pointed out. First of all, São Paulo investments are lower in reais per person than the investments of the two other cities. Even if we take into account poor regions of the city, such as M'Boi Mirim, which received R$65 million over two years, São Mateus, which received R$58 million, or Campo Limpo, which received R$70 million, the per capita investments in São Paulo are still below those in Belo Horizonte and Porto Alegre. On a per capita basis,[26] these investments represent roughly 10 percent of the per capita investment made by Porto Alegre and close to the ceiling of Belo Horizonte's investments in poor neighborhoods.

Even though the amount of resources transferred to the poor may be equivalent to the transfers in Belo Horizonte, São Paulo's participatory budgeting follows a very different deliberative method. In M'Boi Mirim,

---

tory budgeting claiming that only 37 percent of the decisions were implemented, an estimate provided by the opposition to Suplicy's administration. Though the effective estimate should be higher, the implementation rate in São Paulo was much lower than in Porto Alegre and Belo Horizonte. See *Folha de São Paulo,* 2004.

26. For example, in M'Boi Mirim investment was around R$190 per capita over two years, in São Mateus close to R$200 per capita, and in Campo Limpo R$180.

for example, among the R$65 million received by the region, R$44 million came from other programs, such as the unified centers of education or family health program, and were only reratified by participatory budgeting assemblies. If we analyze the deliberations taken only by participatory budgeting regional assemblies, investments amount to R$20 million, or around R$60 per capita over two years. Thus, although the distribution by neighborhood followed the same pattern of Belo Horizonte and Porto Alegre, the exclusive investment through participatory budgeting in São Paulo was much lower. Participatory budgeting in São Paulo became a method of mobilization to corroborate decisions made by the administration in areas of health and education.

A second observation is that not all the resources invested during the Marta Suplicy administration were made through participatory budgeting. Minimum income programs had more resources and more beneficiaries in very poor neighborhoods of the southern zone of São Paulo, such as Campo Limpo and M'Boi Mirim (Pochman, 2003). This shows that the deliberation on the scope of the participatory budgeting is a key factor for its distributive results. As explained above, São Paulo's administration decided to place limited emphasis on participatory budgeting in order to deliver public policies quickly and craft a broad coalition. Participatory budgeting is the worst possible program when the concern is to craft a coalition at the center, since social actors used to public deliberation tend to challenge clientelist relations. Public programs, such as minimum income or family health program are more prone to appropriation by politicians at the center because they do not empower constituencies.

Accounting for Differences across Cities

This discussion of deliberative and distributive effects allows us to propose a typology based on three categories: civil society strength, political society composition, and institutional design. Porto Alegre stands out by its singular configurations of civil and political society. Civil society organizations in Porto Alegre are strong, and well-organized associations have had a positive effect on the weaker organizations, creating a favorable environment for state–civil society interaction (Baiocchi, 2005). However, it is clear from other cases that civil society's organizations cannot be expanded by participatory budgeting in a similar fashion (Silva, 2003). Political society in Porto Alegre also stands out. First of all, within the local PT there is general consensus on the importance of participation, with different parties contending for control over the participatory process.[27] In addition, the opposition in Porto Alegre did not oppose the participatory budgeting, but rather stressed its importance. There was only one major law suit against participatory budgeting in Porto Alegre, and it was defeated (Vitale, 2004). Thus, in Porto Alegre there has been a concerted effort behind participatory budgeting, with clear deliberative and distributive effects: the influence of the COP in city politics, on the one hand, and the investment of up to R$1,000 per resident in the city's four poorest neighborhoods, on the other. Porto Alegre's context and achievements are contrasted with the other two cases in Table 5.10.

In Belo Horizonte civil society associations are not as influential or as confrontational as in Porto Alegre, but they are strong and have been able to expand throughout the city. Participatory budgeting does not enjoy nearly the consensus in Belo Horizonte's political society that it does in Porto Alegre. The first mayor, Patrus Ananias, favored participation and invested heavily in expanding it to all areas of the city. His PSB successor also strongly favored participatory budgeting, while PT mayor Fernando Pimentel's limited support for participation derailed some participatory policies. Thus, Belo Horizonte's participatory budgeting is also strongly deliberative, though different from Porto Alegre's. It deliberates on half of the city's investments in the regions, but has no say in other social policies. Its distributive effects are strong, but less so than in Porto Alegre. The four poorest regions of Porto Alegre, with a total population of 150,000 people, close to 12 percent of the population, received average investments of R$1,100 per person. The 11 poorest planning units in Belo Horizonte, with a combined population of 140, 000, close to 5 percent of the population, received an average investment of R$90 per person. Thus, there is a difference in deliberation and distribution effects, despite the fact that Belo Horizonte is also clearly a successful case. Belo Horizonte shows that the presence of a strong civil society, its expansion to all regions, and the lack of opposition within political society are sufficient conditions for the success of participatory budgeting.

27. Representatives of the different PT groups were involved in the organization of participatory budgeting in Porto Alegre. Iria Charao from the Olivio Dutra group played an important role in the first four years of participatory budgeting. Ubiratan de Sousa and Gildo Lima played an important role in the Tarso Genro administration. Luciano Brunet played an important role during the Raul Pont administration. Thus, in each administration, key people very close to the mayor coordinated the participatory budgeting.

Table 5.10. *Relationship between council and political society configuration and participatory budgeting effectiveness in three Brazilian cities*

City	Civil Society	Political Society	Nature of the Political Coalition	Deliberative Effects	Distributive Effects
Porto Alegre	Well organized in a few regions. Participatory budgeting helped to expand civil society organization.	PT unified behind participatory budgeting, and the opposition did not make an effort to oppose it.	Consensually in favor of the participatory process.	Strong. Participatory budgeting council influences city politics. Participatory budgeting council deliberates on all city investments.	Strong in the city as a whole. Particularly strong in poor neighborhoods.
Belo Horizonte	Well organized in a few regions. Participatory budgeting helped to expand civil society organization.	PT is not completely unified behind participatory budgeting. Celio de Castro, the PSB mayor, strongly favored participatory budgeting.	Consensually in favor of participatory budgeting, yet withholding some of its deliberative aspects, such as the participatory budget council.	Strong.	Strong in the city as a whole. Particularly strong in poor neighborhoods.
São Paulo	Well organized in a few regions. Participatory budgeting could not help its expansion.	PT chooses not to unify itself behind participatory budgeting and leaves it in the hands of leftist groups.	Divided on the need for participatory budgeting since allies in the sub-*prefeitura* choose not to carry it.	Medium-strong.	Medium. Targeted poor neighborhoods with little resources.

São Paulo differs in all respects. In 2001, São Paulo's civil society was at least as strong as Belo Horizonte's and Porto Alegre's at the beginning of their participatory processes. As was the case in the other two cities, the administration could have acted to strengthen it across the city. The problem the Marta Suplicy administration faced was the lack of time to do so and the need for alliances in the city's south, where civil society associations are weaker (Avritzer, 2004). Hence, the Suplicy administration introduced public policies other than participatory budgeting that could expand the administration's influence over sectors of the poor population. Marta Suplicy was more successful than her predecessor Luiza Erundina in getting city council support, but to do so she had to ally with more conservative sectors in the sub-*prefeituras*. Suplicy made this alliance at the end of the second year of her administration, because of her concern that the 38 percent of the votes that she received would not be enough to sponsor a participatory process. The possibility of a broad coalition against the PT and middle-class opposition to her administration moved Suplicy toward a center-right coalition.

These decisions to introduce other types of public programs and to ally with more conservative elements together sealed the fate of participatory budgeting in São Paulo. It was not the priority social policy in the city, nor were the deliberative drives introduced by participatory budgeting put in place everywhere. However, even in such a difficult situation, participatory budgeting had deliberative and distributive effects, though they were more limited.

Thus, it is possible to say that participatory budgeting has deliberative and distributive impacts whose scope depends on the specific configurations of civil and political society. Its design alone cannot automatically produce the deliberative and distributive results seen in Porto Alegre. When the design meets with a favorable context, as Belo Horizonte's case shows, strong deliberative and distributive results follow. São Paulo's case also shows that in cases in which bottom-up designs face implementation problems their deliberative and distributive effectiveness sharply decreases.

The Variation in Bottom-up Designs

The cases of Porto Alegre, Belo Horizonte, and São Paulo show how the civil and political society elements proposed in our analysis emerge and vary in effectiveness according to context. In the discussion on participatory design in Chapter 4, I proposed an analysis of design according to two broad categories, namely, power and access to resources. I also argued that the way civil and political societies operate in the emergence and expansion of a specific participatory design influenced the distribution of power and resources.

Participatory budgeting is the participatory design that most radically re-allocates power and resources. It reallocates power by substituting open-entry assemblies for elections as a form of authorization. It also reallocates access to resources by creating a mechanism for the inversion of access to public goods, from rich to poor. I have shown that in the case of Porto Alegre the success of participatory budgeting is expressed in the effectiveness with which power and access can be redistributed to grassroots poor population This statement, although corroborated by new data, is not completely new (Avritzer, 2002; Baiocchi, 2005). What is new is the way I showed in the Belo Horizonte and mainly in the São Paulo case that the effectiveness of the redistribution depends upon the political context in which the participatory design is implemented.

The cases presented on participatory budgeting in Belo Horizonte and São Paulo show very well that the effectiveness of bottom-up designs varies sharply according to the political will of the governing party and the capacity of civil society actors to carry out through the participatory process the distribution of public goods. Porto Alegre has a much more intense bottom-up participatory institution than Belo Horizonte or São Paulo, because (a) Porto Alegre's administration made a long-term commitment to carry out the participatory process and (b) its civil and political cultures cooperated to make the participatory process sustainable. The two together explain the high amount of resources involved in Porto Alegre's participatory budgeting.

Nonetheless, design is not a recipe to be repeated, but a practice whose effectiveness has many preconditions. We analyzed, in this chapter, two other participatory experiences based on Porto Alegre's design, the cases of Belo Horizonte and São Paulo. Belo Horizonte proved successful in spite of the fact that both power and public goods are distributed in a less effective way than in Porto Alegre. In Belo Horizonte there has never been a council to integrate all participatory proposals that emerged in the regional assemblies. In Belo Horizonte the ceiling of participatory budgeting distributive capacity is close to 100 reais, whereas in Porto Alegre it is ten times higher. However, the two experiences can both be considered successful because of the capacity of the administration to release power to the grassroots and the capacity of the grassroots to deliver goods to the poor through the participatory process.

São Paulo, in contrast, illustrates the limits of a bottom-up participatory institution. São Paulo can be considered an almost unsuccessful case for two reasons. The first is that the participatory process generated mixed deliberations that did not strengthen the participants' perceptions of their ability to decide on the distribution of public goods. In this sense, the release of power by the administration that empowers social actors at the bottom was not fully accomplished. The second reason is that the redistribution process also generated mixed results, because participatory budgeting actors had very little prerogative to decide on issues such as healthcare and education. Their deliberations were always intertwined with deliberation taken in other instances, such as the health and educations ministries and the health councils. Thus, São Paulo's experience poses a fundamental question: is it worthwhile to try to institute a bottom-up participatory process with very limited deliberative prerogatives? My answer is negative. As I show in Chapters 6 and 7, mandatory designs, such as power-sharing and ratification, are more effective in a divided political society.

6

Health Councils

Health councils, the most widespread participatory institution in Brazil, arose from the struggle of two social movements in Brazil, the popular health movement (MOPS) and the *sanitarista* movement (public health professionals' movement), to improve public health and expand access to healthcare for all Brazilians. The councils were codified in the 1988 Constitution's chapter on health and the infraconstitutional legislation[1] that emerged in 1990 through the Healthcare Statute (*Lei Orgânica da Saúde,* or LOS). During the 1990s, more than 5,000 health councils were formed in Brazil, and today there are health councils in 98 percent of Brazilian cities (IBGE, 2002).

Health councils are based on an institutional design that I call power-sharing. In a power-sharing design, bottom-up participation meets state actors. The encounter between the two generates mandatory negotiation and deliberation. In the power-sharing on health issues, local administrations are required to bring health issues to health councils for discussion and action. This participatory design creates new forms of accountability, as well as new forms of joint deliberation.

This chapter begins by describing the ill condition of Brazil's healthcare system before democratization and shows how the poor quality and lack of access to services prompted two different movements, one professional and

1. Brazilian law does not allow for constitutional precepts to be applied without further legislation at the infraconstitutional level. In the case of the Constitution chapter on health, it was specified by Laws 8,080 and 8,142 of December 1990. The latter one was the law that incorporated conferences and councils in the organization of the healthcare system in Brazil.

the other popular, to come together to establish a participatory and inclusive agenda for healthcare reform in democratic Brazil. I show how a new participatory health system emerged from legislation created during the Constituent Assembly, and I analyze the system's characteristics as a power-sharing design. Then I describe the specific operation of health councils created in São Paulo, Porto Alegre, Belo Horizonte, and Salvador. Finally, I show their results in terms of social inclusion, comparing the operation of power-sharing institutions in the four cases.

Healthcare Conditions in Brazil

Access to state-sponsored healthcare was not a universal right in Brazil until 1988, following the country's democratization. At that time, Brazil was considered to have one of the worst health systems in the developing world (Van Stralen, 1996; Arouca, 2003), with services highly centralized and many people excluded from using them The Vargas regime (1930–45) had introduced state-sponsored health during the 1930s, but tied access to healthcare to work in the formal labor market (Santos, 1979).[2] Urban dwellers and all those who were not registered in the formal labor market—peasants, casual laborers, workers in small companies or self-employed, and the unemployed—were excluded from the healthcare system and stayed outside the coverage provided by the state. The 1937 constitutional chapter on health, as well many other social rights such as vacations or pension, granted broad social rights, but required either the political will of the state or the regulation of professional associations to make those rights effective.

Lack of Access in the Authoritarian Era

The health system in Brazil deteriorated after 1964 as the democratic order was broken by a military coup (Alves, 1988). The authoritarian regime took three measures regarding the organization of the health system, all of which proved disastrous in the long run. The first one was to centralize health and social security in the hands of the federal government, while keeping the

---

2. Brazil always had a formal and a nonformal labor market. The formal was made of state employees and all those who worked for large companies and have had organized trade unions (French, 2004). The nonformal was made of peasants, poor workers and those who worked for small companies.

most important structures of social exclusion. Thus, peasants and poor urban dwellers continued to be excluded from the system, whose resources started to be all handled by the federal government (Escorel et al., 2005: 60).

Second, the authoritarian regime sponsored a huge expansion of private hospitals in large metropolitan regions without giving much importance to preventive health. The result was a shift in the expenses of an already underfunded health system from preventive medicine to hospital expenses. The total budget for healthcare did not surpass 2 percent of GNP, and most indicators of public health, such as infant mortality and life expectancy, were dismal. In 1980 infant mortality in Brazil was 94.3 per 1,000 live births. In the Northeast region it was 144 per 1,000, a rate close to the poorest African countries. These dismal rates were linked to the lack of preventive medicine, as well as the sharp reduction of coverage at the local level.

Third, the regime's emphasis on building hospitals diverted resources from local health centers at a time of great internal migration in Brazil. As millions of people moved from the countryside to growing cities in the postwar, poor peasants without access to health became poor urban dwellers without access to the same rights. Between 1970 and 1981, the city of São Paulo's population increased by 4.6 million, but only four new health centers were created (Jacobi, 1986: 346). It was as a reaction to this situation that the health movement emerged in Brazil.

The Rise of Two Health Movements

The lack of access to healthcare was transformed into a political issue by two movements that emerged during the late 1970s: the *sanitarista* movement — the Public Health Professionals' Movement (Arouca, 2003)—and the MOS, the Popular Movement for Access to Health (Sader, 1988; Doimo and Rodrigues, 2003; Avritzer et al., 2005). Although the *sanitarista* movement can be traced back to the late nineteenth century (Labra, 1985), the modern *sanitarista* movement was formed during the 1970s by doctors, nurses, and residents who criticized the authoritarian regime's disregard for the health conditions of the poor (Escorel, 1998). The *sanitaristas* also criticized the conception of health that guided the regime's actions (Arouca, 2003). For them, the regime spent too much money curing diseases there were preventable or caused by the lack of investment in prevention or basic sanitation. At their origin, the *sanitaristas* were mostly concerned with acquiring a presence inside the state in order to reshape health policy, rather than with sponsoring forms of popular participation. However, in the late 1970s they joined groups of the poor that were organizing to claim a better access to healthcare. One of these first encounters took place in the east zone of São Paulo.

São Paulo's east zone was home to many movements during the democratization period (Kowarick, 1980; Singer and Brant, 1980; Avritzer, 2004). The support of the Catholic Church was the key element for the emergence of these movements. In 1975 the nomination of Dom Angélico Sândalo gave an extra boost to grassroots movements that were already active in the region (Sader, 1988: 263; Sposati and Lobo, 1992). In the case of health, the movement originated in São Mateus and São Miguel Paulista, where the poor population with the help of professionals from the *sanitarista* movement raised the issue of the quality of health services. They took advantage of an old city law mandating committees to oversee the quality of city services. They established a committee for supervising healthcare in eastern São Paulo, leading to the creation of health councils—the first popular councils created during the democratization process (Sader, 1988: 276). This was the beginning of the healthcare movement in Brazil. The movement went national in 1981 with the creation of the MOPS, which proposed during the Constituent Assembly the creation of councils at all levels. Thus, in the area of health, as in that of budgeting (described in Chapter 5) and urban reform (Chapter 7), the new participatory design was not planned out in advance. Health councils emerged in Brazil through the combination of an old law in São Paulo and the actions of two social movements with different conceptions of the state's role in health policy.

The Demand for Participation in Healthcare

The late 1970s and early 1980s were a time of reconstruction for Brazilian civil society. Some scattered, decentralized actions took place in the area of health, particularly in São Paulo, Belo Horizonte, and Porto Alegre. In São Paulo, the encounter between professional healthcare practitioners and popular actors in the eastern zone of the city led to elections for the first popular council to oversee the performance of health centers. After a mobilization in São Mateus, social actors demanded control over health policies in the region. They discovered an old city law that allowed the election of councilors and on March 10, 1979, 8,146 people voted to elect 12 mothers as representatives on Brazil's first embryonic health council (Sader, 1988: 276).

However, it was a long way from the emergence of the health council to the centrality it later acquired in democratic Brazil. The first council in São

Paulo did not have ongoing access to state authorities; its recognition as an institution was contentious. Even the institutional format, with shared deliberation between social and state actors, did not emerge in São Paulo at that point. In its first moment, São Paulo's health council had the format of a bottom-up participatory institution in charge of demanding better services from the state. It would be a long way until health councils would be proposed at the Constituent Assembly and would acquire the elements of a power-sharing institution.

A Critical Series of National Conferences

At the same time that the first health council was being implemented in São Paulo, debates were going on in Belo Horizonte, Rio de Janeiro, and other parts of the Southeast on the reorganization of the medical profession and its role in the improvement of the health conditions of the poor in Brazil. Between 1979 and 1983 there were several national conferences of the healthcare movement. These meetings were attended by public health professionals and university people and were in tune with other civil society actions during the period (Boschi, 1987; Fleury et al., 1989; Dagnino, 2002). At these meetings, the idea of unifying the healthcare system by abolishing the requirement for participation in the formal labor market progressively emerged, as did the idea of integrating newly emerging forms of participation into a national healthcare structure instead of creating a communitarian health system (Escorel, 1999: 185). Two moments were central in the unification of the demands of the healthcare movement: the Fifth National Health Conference in 1975 and the Eighth National Health Conference in 1986. It was during the fifth conference that the contemporary agenda of the healthcare movement gelled around the following issues:

- The abandonment of the idea of community-based medicine separate from the state, which was still strong in the movement. This point was important for the later differentiation of participatory budgeting and health councils, as well for the later emergence of the power-sharing format. The presence of state officials in the elaboration and implementation of health policies emerged at this point.
- The adoption of the council form as the institutional design for this kind of participation.
- The demand for equivalent health services for urban and rural populations.

• The institution of public services in all three levels of government—federal, state, and city (Gerschman, 1995: 74).

A Progressive Agenda of Issues

Thus, we can see the emergence of two logics within the health movement in the mid-1980s at the end of authoritarian period. The first pointed toward the unification of health policies and the transformation of healthcare into a universal right. This logic had both an administrative and a political component, because of the administrative irrationality of the model pursued between 1964 and 1984. The second logic was the integration of civil society associations into the elaboration of public policy. In this regard, the health movement was far ahead of other sectors of Brazilian civil society, which still followed a logic of confronting the state (Weffort, 1989; Dagnino, 1994; Avritzer, 1994). The fifth and the eighth conferences showed the unanticipated elements of the emergent design: power-sharing emerged as an institutional design to accommodate the different conceptions of two social movements.

Brazil has had a tradition of health conferences since the 1930s, when Gustavo Capanema headed the Health and Education Ministry during the Vargas regime. The First National Health Conference took place in 1941, beginning a tradition of convening national conferences at key moments to redefine health policies. The eighth conference, called by the Ministry of Health through Decree 91,466 of July 1985, was one of these moments. The Ministry took a new step by allowing the participation of civil society associations. The conference was composed as follows: 10 percent neighborhood associations dealing with health issues; 20 percent other civil associations dealing with health; 5 percent political party representatives; 30 percent health-worker trade unions; 20 percent health-worker professional associations; 15 percent private health service providers (Nascimento, 1986).[3] President Jose Sarney opened the conference. The MOPS's proposals centered around the autonomy of health movements from the state;

3. This composition shows signs of the presence of the Brazilian Communist Party in the preparation of the conference. The popular health movement that emerged in São Paulo was very strong in neighborhood associations. The Brazilian Communist Party had a strong presence in trade unions linked to health activities—nurses, residents, and in some cities even doctors. The Eighth National Health Conference put together all these actors (Stotz, 2003; Fleury, 1997).

the institutionalization of popular councils in charge of deliberating on and implementing health policies; the decentralization of health policy; the *eta-tization* of health; and universal access of the population to health services (Gerschman, 1995: 78). Though many of these proposals were refashioned, the idea of broad popular participation was integrated into the conference report. The *sanitaristas* already had a more *etatist*[4] profile, and their actions at the conference led to the approval of a unified healthcare system (later known as the SUS) and the formation of a committee to defend their position at the National Constituent Assembly (Cordeiro, 2004: 7).

A Growing Consensus on Participation

Thus, we can see that the emergence of a set of participatory policies on healthcare was the result of different actions that started during the key moment of Brazilian democratization, the late 1970s and early 1980s. Different actions at the grassroots level in 1979 led to the formation of the first health council in Brazil in the eastern zone of São Paulo. Yet, its incorporation into the democratization agenda required several other steps by the *sanitaristas,* the MOPS, and other key actors within the state. The fifth and the eighth conferences were of key importance for the formation of a progressive agenda within civil society and the state, pointing to a cooperative institutional format. Within civil society, the most important consensus reached during the period was to abandon a proposal for a healthcare system independent of the state. Among the few *sanitaristas* within the state, the most important consensus was for a decentralized health system run with the participation of civil society. The health reform movement was stronger than other civil society movements such as the urban reform movement at that point, because of its capacity to organize itself well in advance of the Constituent Assembly and to get the Ministry of Health to sponsor some of its proposals. However, the most important element that emerged in the two health conferences mentioned above was the initial design of the power-sharing format in the area of health. The idea of a state organized system with civil society participation emerged during both the fifth and the eighth conferences. At the same time, the idea of a health system with civil society control organized at the federal, state, and municipal levels also

---

4. The *etatist* profile of the *sanitaristas* did not mean that they favored the complete *etatization* of the Brazilian health system, proposed at the eighth conference by more radical groups within civil society and the PT (Pereira, 1996).

emerged at these conferences. Both would be the basis for the later power-sharing design.

The Emergence of a Participatory Health System

The period 1985–87 was critical for the emergence of participatory institutions in Brazil. The urban reform movement and the Statute of the City discussed in Chapter 7 originated in that period, as did participation in social assistance and environmental policy. All the important institutional changes that would make democratic Brazil more participatory started at the Constituent Assembly, convened in 198 to draft a new democratic Constitution. Brazilian civil society actors proposed participation in different areas by taking advantage of the popular amendment system.

Constitutional Foundation

A popular amendment in the area of health was presented to the Constituent Assembly with fewer than 60,000 signatures (Rodrigues Neto, 2003). Its main elements were obliging the state to be the main health provider in Brazil; creating a unified national healthcare system without preconditions for access; decentralizing the provision of healthcare; and fostering broad popular participation in the elaboration and implementation of health services. The popular amendment on health was defended in the subcommittee on social policy by the well-known public health doctor Sérgio Arouca.[5] Arouca argued for increased health coverage and a democratization of access to it (Arouca, 2003).

In the area of health, however, conservative sectors were also organized (see Chapters 5 and 7). The *centrão,* the broad coalition of conservative sectors in charge of maintaining the status quo, was not well enough organized to propose a different line of reform during the Constituent Assembly (Pereira, 1996: 446). Nevertheless, it managed to insert one device into the Constitu-

---

5. Sérgio Arouca has played a crucial role in the change of the Brazilian health system during democratization. He was a well-known public doctor who occupied a key position in the Health Ministry during the Sarney government. His position in the Health Ministry was important for the calling of the Eighth National Health Conference. He also played a very important role in the extinction of INAMPS, the institution that was in charge of the segmented health assistance for the different professionals. For Arouca's role in the change of the health system, see Cordeiro, 2004.

tion that suited conservative demands: the chapter on the state's exclusive responsibility in health matters was exchanged for the possibility of subcontracting health services to the private sector (Costa, 2002: 54). In spite of the late insertion of subcontracting to the private sector, the healthcare movement was more successful than other civil society actors, such as the urban reform movement, within the Constituent Assembly. The Constitution's Article 198 described health as an integrated system organized according to the following principles: (a) decentralization; (b) unified care with a focus on prevention; and (c) civil society participation in policy deliberation.

It is worth noting the role of political society and the PT in particular in this first phase of the public health reform. The PT's position on healthcare during the 1980s was for full *etatization*. It defended this position during the eighth conference and was defeated, but it entered the Constituent Assembly defending the same position. Inside the Constituent Assembly, however, the PT and other sectors of the left reached the conclusion that full *etatization* would be impossible and decided that the relation between the state and the private sector would be the key issue (Costa, 2002). With this move, the PT started to play a central role in the emergence of the new health legislation (Pereira, 1996: 450).

Infraconstitutional Legislation

The end of the Constitution-making process meant a shift to infraconstitutional legislation in the area of health, as well as urban planning. Conservative interests were more concerned about the effects of constitutional legislation in health than in urban planning because they had suffered parallel administrative defeats on health issues, both in the Constitution and in the creation of the SUDS, a unified health system, in 1987 (Costa, 2002). A legislative and administrative battle between the health movement and conservative sectors had to be fought between 1988 and 1993 before inclusion and participation could be made effective principles of the Brazilian healthcare system.

The elaboration of the Healthcare Statute (*Lei Orgânica da Saúde*, LOS) took almost two years after the completion of the 1988 Constitution, showing how contentious these issues were. After the Constituent Assembly, conservative sectors had two lines of attack. The first was showing the financial nonviability of the new institutional format. Resources for healthcare decreased in Brazil from 1989 to 1992 during the late Sarney and Collor governments. In 1989 the health budget in Brazil was $11.3 billion; in 1992 it was only $6.571 billion. These resources had to cover almost three times more people than had access to healthcare before democratization took place in 1985 (Costa, 2002: 54). Only after Collor's impeachment did the health budget start to grow again.

The second line of attack for the conservatives concerned the organization of the healthcare system. The Healthcare Statute was elaborated in Congress and sent for the approval of President Collor in 1990. Collor vetoed Law 8,080, which sought to institute a unified healthcare system with broad political participation, singling out the articles on participation (Rodrigues and Zauli, 2002). The veto created a stalemate with Congress, generating protests throughout Brazil. Law 8,142 in December of the same year solved the stalemate by regulating participation in the healthcare system by means of the national health conferences and health councils, as described in the following section. According to the law, health councils "will be permanent deliberative institutions composed by representatives of the state, services providers, and representatives of the population. They will act in the elaboration of strategies as well as in the control of the implementation of the health policies at each one of the levels of government" (Brasil, 1990).

Institutionalization of Power-sharing

The insertion of health councils as the key element of the organization of healthcare was the result of at least 12 years of civil society activity and led to the institutionalization of the power-sharing format. Law 8,142 of 1990 included in the organization of healthcare the following institutional devices: (a) the health conference and the health councils; (b) the control by health councils of the expenses in the area through a fund with civil society control; (c) parity between state and civil society as the form of organization of health councils at the three levels of government; (d) sanction in the case of noninstitutionalization of participation (Brasil, 1990). The four mechanisms together instituted a second form of participation in Brazil that is today practiced in many other areas, such as social assistance and the environment.

The emergence of the power-sharing format in the area of health policies required a change in the conceptions of civil society. The original civil society proposal had been very close to a bottom-up format and could have led to a different form of institutionalization. It was in fact the actions of the *sanitarista* movement, which had a much stronger *etatist* orientation, that in the end led to the power-sharing format. The role of the PT was also very important. Inside the Constituent Assembly, the PT changed its position on full *etatization* to a position of a public system with civil society control. In the end, the PT championed the councils, if we have in mind the administrations that first implemented health councils in Brazil as well as the administrations that elaborated their health policies with the participation of the councils (Cohn, 2002). In the next section I discuss the implementation of health councils in São Paulo, Porto Alegre, Belo Horizonte, and Salvador, focusing on how state actors and civil society interacted in implementing participatory policies on healthcare and how participation generated new results in terms of social inclusion. At the end of this chapter I will compare the bottom-up format that emerged in Brazil with the power-sharing format to evaluate their democratization and distributive effects.

Participatory Healthcare in Four Cities

The creation of the popular movement for health (MOPS) and the implementation and consolidation of participatory policies in healthcare had different itineraries in the cities of São Paulo, Belo Horizonte, and Porto Alegre. São Paulo's experience is the best known, though singular case.

The Health Movement in Context

São Paulo

As I pointed out earlier, the health movement originated in the city's east zone in the late 1970s, leading to the emergence of the council form in 1979 (Sader, 1988). In the city's south region, the popular health movement emerged in the late 1980s and had a more institutional conception (Sacardo and Castro, 2002: 14). The dominant form of action that resulted from the São Paulo health movement was anti-institutional, and it prevailed at least until the Constituent Assembly. The movement had strong doubts about whether it should sign the popular amendment on health to be presented at the Constituent Assembly (Doimo, 1995). It the end, it joined the petition not as a movement but on an individual basis. Yet, São Paulo was one of the first cities to establish a participatory infrastructure in the area of health. This occurred under a PT administration from 1989 to 1992. During this period, 165 local councils were created and a municipal council was established (Neder, 1997).

Belo Horizonte

Belo Horizonte's popular health movement was formed later than São Paulo's, in the early 1980s. In Belo Horizonte the *sanitarista* movement was initially stronger than the popular health movement (Avritzer et al., 2005). Doctors, residents, and nurses were at the root of the movement, participating in national meetings such as the Salvador meeting and the eighth conference. The popular health movement emerged in the east zone of Belo Horizonte in the early 1980s and rapidly organized itself in the Barreiro and Venda Nova regions, which saw the best-organized popular participation. Belo Horizonte's health movement has generated important leaders, such as the well-known doctor, Célio De Castro, elected president of the Medical Trade Union, constituent to the Constituent Assembly in 1986, and mayor in 1996. The popular health amendment was strongly supported by healthcare trade unions, psychologists, nurses, and members of popular movements. The most important difference between Belo Horizonte's health movement and São Paulo's was the early presence of the movement activists within political society. Both the PT and other parties of the left, such as the Brazilian Socialist Party and the PC do B, had a strong presence in the movement. Belo Horizonte's participatory infrastructure for healthcare was established in 1991, just before the PT won the city's mayoralty in 1992.

Porto Alegre

Porto Alegre presents a third case because of its consensus of the left on participatory policies. Its popular health movement also emerged in the late 1970s, in tandem with a proliferation of neighborhood associations in the city. A committee for the improvement of health and sanitation was created in 1978, claiming that the precarious health conditions of the population were linked to the lack of sanitation infrastructure (Réos, 2003: 68). The Grande Cruzeiro region created its health and sanitation committee during the same period. In 1984, the last year of authoritarianism in Brazil, an important event occurred in Grande Cruzeiro. After years of demanding the improvement of sanitation in the region, a group of poor residents learned of idle pipes in the Porto Alegre Sewerage Department and decided to seize them and install a sewerage system in the neighborhood. This was the beginning of a health movement that integrated demands for better health conditions with demands for better sewerage and sanitation infrastructure. In 1992, after a long discussion with local health committees, a health council was created.

Salvador

The origin of popular movements in the city differs from the large cities of the Southeast, because of the weakness of both the progressive Catholic

Church and the PT in Salvador. The *sanitaristas* have had a strong presence in the city since the late 1970s. However, the health movement in Salvador did not have a popular branch or a strong presence in the neighborhood associations movement. The PT in the city did not draw in health movement activists, as it had in São Paulo and Belo Horizonte. In addition, Salvador's neighborhood associations were as a whole not very strong. Salvador's health council was created in 1991, with a strong influence of conservative political society.

The Role of Local Civil and Political Society

Analysis of the emergence of participatory institutions in São Paulo, Belo Horizonte, Porto Alegre, and Salvador reveals different trajectories in how civil society and political society have related. São Paulo championed the organization of popular actors in the area of health, and the first popular council emerged in the city. However, popular actors were unevenly concentrated across the city. In addition, São Paulo is a singular case, as I will show below, in the following respect: if it is true that the PT championed the institutionalization of health councils in the city, São Paulo is the only case in which sectors of political society—the *malufismo*—were openly against participation and willing to change an existing law allowing participation. Belo Horizonte differs in two important respects: the health movement was not as strong as in São Paulo and was composed more of professionals than of social actors. However, the greatest difference concerns political society's support for healthcare reform. In Porto Alegre civil society was less present in health matters, but the introduction of participatory health policies was more consensual at the level of political society. Salvador, finally, constitutes a contrasting case insofar as civil society was weak and political society was opposed to popular participation. Table 6.1 synthesizes these different political configurations.

The Creation of Local Health Councils

Participatory legislation emerged in the four cities at almost the same time, but each city took its own path of implementation.

Belo Horizonte

Belo Horizonte's health council was created through Law 5,903, approved by city council in 1991. The bill was debated in city council even before the

Table 6.1. Civil and political society role in the implementation of healthcare participation in four Brazilian cities

City	Civil Society Organization	Political Society Organization	Characteristics of the New Health Legislation
São Paulo	Strong, but territorially uneven.	Divided. PT supported participation, and *Malufismo* was against.	Strongly participatory. The main problem is implementation when the PT is not in power.
Belo Horizonte	Strong, but territorially uneven.	United. Both PT and opposition favored participation.	Strongly participatory. Civil society chairs the city health council since 1998.
Porto Alegre	Strong, but territorially uneven.	United. PT was in favor of participation, but wanted to subordinate it to participatory budgeting.	Strongly participatory. The only city in which private health-care providers are not part of civil society representation.
Salvador	Weak.	Political society united against participation, but wanted to abide by national legislation.	Weakly participatory. Conservative civil society members strongly represented in the council.

national legislation was passed. The council is composed of 9 public and private healthcare providers, 9 representatives of health service professionals, and 18 representatives of users of health services. The council's main roles are to follow the implementation of the decisions of the health conference; to follow the implementation of the unified health system (SUS); to participate in the formulation of municipal health policy in its economic and financial aspects; and to approve and oversee the implementation of the city health plan (Belo Horizonte, Law 7,536). Belo Horizonte's law follows most of the guidelines of the *santarista* and popular health movements. However, this level of consensus was not reached without conflicts between civil society members and the city administration. The most important conflict took place around state representatives' control over the agenda in 1998. The municipal health secretary used to be the council's president in Belo Horizonte, in São Paulo, and in Porto Alegre. In Belo Horizonte, the fact that agenda-setting power was concentrated in the hands of state representatives led to a rebellion at the end of which civil society representatives assumed the presidency of the council in 1998.

Health Councils

Porto Alegre

Porto Alegre's health council was created in 1992 through City Law 277. It is composed of 80 members, 42 health representatives elected by civil society associations, 24 health professionals, 6 private health service providers, and 8 members of the city administration. Compared with the composition of the councils in São Paulo and Belo Horizonte, Porto Alegre seems to be more advanced in at least two respects: civil society association representatives make up more than half the members and, even more important, private health service providers are less represented than in the other two cities. Porto Alegre's health council is charged with defining the city's health priorities, establishing guidelines for the city health plan, overseeing its implementation, and setting criteria for contracts between the state and private health service providers (Porto Alegre, 1997). Here, too, Porto Alegre has gone beyond the other two cities by having the council supervise relations between the state and the private sector (relations between the state and the private sector were incorporated into the constitutional text by conservatives). Thus, we see that Porto Alegre's health council has a more participatory arrangement than in other cities and that its powers are broader than health councils in cities in which civil society is stronger. However, Porto Alegre's health council faces a different challenge: competition from other participatory institutions, in particular participatory budgeting.

São Paulo

In São Paulo, the city health council was created by a decree of Mayor Luíza Erundina in June 1989 (Portaria 1,166). The São Paulo health council is composed of members of the state sector; representatives of service providers, liberal professionals, and health workers; and representatives of the users of health services, who account for half the members (São Paulo, 1998). São Paulo's council has both deliberative and normative attributions. According to its 2001 internal constitution, its main roles are to deliberate on the economic and financial aspects of health policy, to oversee implementation of the unified health system (SUS) at the city level, and to approve the state plan in advance. Both in its composition and in its attributions, the São Paulo health council reflects the key elements demanded by the popular health movement. This was not achieved without conflicts with the state and the *malufismo* in particular. The most important concerned who would represent civil society and how much power civil society representatives would have in relation to other interests.

The initial law approved by the PT administration called for shared representation, but did not detail how civil society would be represented. Both the Maluf and the Pitta administrations (1993–96 and 1997–2000, respectively) manipulated civil society representation in the council by including private providers in civil society quotas, openly manipulating the election of civil society representatives, and even refusing to acknowledge the legal obligation to call the council. The council reacted by further specifying the requirements for civil society representation. The council constitution was rewritten in 2001 to stipulate that, in order to have one of its members elected, a civil society association must have existed for at least a year and must show regular activities in the area during the period. Thus, São Paulo's council embodies the influence of civil society associations in the elaboration of policy, but both an active civil society and further institutional elaboration of the participatory legislation were required to reach this point.

Salvador

The Salvador health council was created in 1991. Its composition differs slightly from those of the other three cities: half of its members are state representatives and the other half are made up, not of users, but of civil society representatives, very loosely defined. The latter include one member of the city diocese, one representative of commerce and industry associations, and one representative of African religions (Salvador, 2003). None of these groups deals directly with health issues. One consequence is the low level of claims made by civil society actors, as I show in the next section. Salvador's health council constitution does not include clear deliberative prerogatives. The council is more to "advise" state representatives than to present claims to the state or to allow joint deliberations between the state and civil society.

Accounting for Differences across Cities

Table 6.2 synthesizes the different components that determined the specific configuration of healthcare participatory institutions in the four capitals.

If we analyze the four cases together, we have three cases of strong civil society in Porto Alegre, São Paulo, and Belo Horizonte, showing that active civil society actors are a key element in the implementation of health councils. In all three cases, civil society actors fought for the deliberative format. Moreover, in the case of São Paulo, where civil society actors perceived the

Table 6.2. Institutional characteristics of health councils in four Brazilian cities

City	Major Characteristic	Major Obstacle to Be Overcome	Institutional Result
Belo Horizonte	Strongly deliberative.	Competition from progressive sectors within political society.	Civil society chairs the council.
Porto Alegre	Strongly deliberative.	Competition from other participatory institutions.	Civil society does not include representatives of the private sector.
São Paulo	Deliberative capacity is contentious.	Resistance from conservative political society.	Council legislation changed several times. Civil society further elaborated its conception of representation.
Salvador	Weakly deliberative.	Resistance from conservative political society.	Civil society is misrepresented by the private sector and conservative churches.

risk of cooptation, they also fought for the very definition of what was civil society participation. Thus, health councils show another feature that differentiates them from participatory budgeting, namely, the prerogatives that civil society actors can assume when political actors are unwilling to implement participatory policies. In the case of health councils, the power-sharing format gave civil society associations the prerogative to fight for the effectiveness of the participatory institution, even for the very definition of participation. As a consequence, the power-sharing format is difficult to disempower, which makes it a more a more effective influence on public policy where political society actors are unwilling to unleash participatory policies. In the next section I analyze the democratizing and the distributive effects of the participatory institutions, showing how power-sharing institutional design generated new forms of social inclusion in democratic Brazil.

The Effects of Participatory Healthcare Institutions

The 1990s saw the consolidation of participatory institutions in the area of healthcare in democratic Brazil. That process changed the operation of health services and profoundly redistributed resources by greatly expanding social inclusion and access to services, especially for the poor.

Social Inclusion

Health councils created in São Paulo, Belo Horizonte, Porto Alegre, and Salvador incorporated under the banner of users (*usuários*), a type of social actor who had not previously had access to deliberative institutions. Studies conducted in São Paulo, Belo Horizonte, and Porto Alegre (Coelho, 2004; Avritzer et al., 2005; Cortes, 2005) show the inclusion of social actors with low income and little education in all three councils. In Belo Horizonte, health council members earn between two and five times the minimum wage. In Belo Horizonte and São Paulo, they have an average of eight years of education. In Porto Alegre data are available for one only subdistrict, Cruzeiro, but show similar indicators (Réos, 2003). No data are available on health councilors' income and education in Salvador, though its composition points to higher income levels. The fact that low-income people participated in these councils represented a break with a longstanding pattern of maldistribution of health services in most cities. A second important inclusionary characteristic of the health councils is their public organization—for example, how open they are to public comment and claims. In all four cases, regular meetings take place once a month, and it is possible to introduce new themes into the meeting. In all four, the agenda is drawn up mainly by the state, but civil society members are informed of it in advance (Coelho, 2004; Avritzer et al., 2005; Cortes, 2002). All council members have the right to speak, though in some of them, such as São Paulo, there is a three-minute time limit. It is interesting to note what kind of claims emerged from the integration of the poor into the healthcare system and to see whether variations in civil society organization affect their ability to present claims. In Belo Horizonte, for example, 34.5 percent of the claims made from 1997 to 2004 were related to the organization of the council itself, and 28 percent to the organization of the city's health policy. In Salvador, where data for 2003 and 2004 are available, the equivalent figures were only 12.4 percent and 15 percent. But the most striking contrast between an active council such as Belo Horizonte's, in which civil society has occupied the council presidency since 1998, and one such as Salvador's, with a very selective civil society presence, is the amount of time each group speaks. Figure 6.1 compares the participation of different groups within the two councils.

Figure 6.1. Percent of users who actively participated in health council meetings in Belo Horizonte and Salvador, 2003–2004

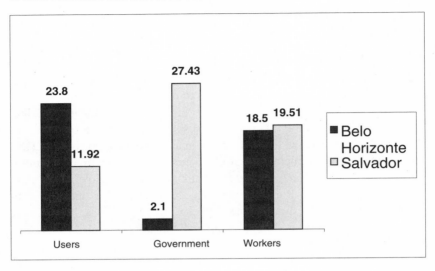

Source: Avritzer, 2006.

A third important form of social inclusion brought by health councils is territorial. The way the legislation selects representatives from the subregions varies in the four cities. In São Paulo the legislation calls for six popular health movement representatives—one from the east, one from the southeast, one from the south, one from the west, one from the north, and one from the center (Decree 38,576). In Belo Horizonte, the legislation provides for one representative from each of the city's nine regions (Law 7,536), while in Porto Alegre it gives local health councils the role of coordinating the decentralized actions of the city council at the regional level (Council Constitution 1997). Of the four cities, only in Salvador is territorial inclusion not provided for.

Thus, inclusionary mechanisms have been created at the regional level in three of the four cities. Two problems do not seem to be resolved. The first is that, even in cities with strong civil society organizations, they are not evenly distributed across regions. Coelho found in São Paulo that regions with prior organization and presence in the area of healthcare are better integrated into the participatory structure than regions where popular associations are more recent (Coelho, 2004). In Belo Horizonte, popular participation is concentrated in three regions of the city, Barreiro, Venda Nova, and Noroeste, two of which have a strong tradition of popular organization.

A second important issue is whether popular actors with less education have deliberative capacity equal to that of state representatives in the councils. As I showed above, the typical participant of health councils in Brazil is a woman over age 40, making between two and ten times the minimum wages[6] and having at least eight years of education. The data show that participants in healthcare institutions have average incomes in their respective cities. However, when we move to state representatives, we see much higher levels of education. Coelho found that five of the eight state representatives on the São Paulo municipal council had graduate studies or more than 15 years of education (Coelho, 2004: 259). A recent survey in Belo Horizonte found that, although 36 percent of the health councilors consider themselves very influential with regard to healthcare decisions (Avritzer et al., 2005: 56), the majority think that the greatest obstacle to being more influential is lack of technical knowledge. Thus, we can note a tension between two elements: the inclusion of poor social actors within a deliberative institution, on the one hand, and their inability to be as influential as state representatives, on the other. In addition, there are cases such as Salvador, where even the power-sharing format does not give civil society representatives effective voice. The question is, how did the new participatory health institutions affect the access of the poor to health services?

Access to Services

The effectiveness of participatory healthcare institutions can be assessed by changes in access to health services brought about by the new participatory design. São Paulo, Belo Horizonte, Porto Alegre, and Salvador show different evidence of improvement in the access to healthcare, as Table 6.3 shows. As in the case of participatory budgeting, Porto Alegre performed best, providing inhabitants each with more than four health appointments per year. Salvador came second with more than three, while Belo Horizonte and São Paulo trailed with two appointments per capita per year. However,

---

6. One interesting exception in terms of income is the city of Curitiba. This city with very high social indicators in Brazil has been governed by the liberal party (PFL). Curitiba council legislation favors the participation of the upper middle class. Fuks found that 33 percent of councilors make 10 times the minimum wage or less and that 22.7 percent of the councilors make more than 20 times the minimum. See Fuks, 2005.

Table 6.3. Health performance in four Brazilian cities, 2000–2001

City	Health Appointments per Capita	Hospital Beds Provided by the City	Amount of Money Spent per Appointment (in R$)	Infant Mortality Due to Gastroenteritis per 1,000
Porto Alegre	4.13	247	6.17	0.67
Belo Horizonte	2.29	333	1.52	1.35
São Paulo	2.27	2,686	7.01	2.61
Salvador	3.54	6.0	1.24	2.23

Source: Datasus, 2002.

number of appointments cannot serve as the sole indicator of health performance (Coelho, 2004). A high number of appointments can be a sign of bad preventive health, so to measure performance we decided to combine it with two other indicators: the amount spent per patient and the number of municipal hospital beds available. Both indicators again show Porto Alegre with very good performance, providing almost the same number of hospital beds per capita as São Paulo. With regard to spending, São Paulo leads with R$7.01 per capita, although it is reasonable to assume a higher cost for medical services in São Paulo. Porto Alegre is second with R$6.17, Belo Horizonte third with R$1.52, and Salvador fourth with R$1.24 (Table 6.3).

Porto Alegre ranks first in two of the four measures. Bearing in mind the higher cost of healthcare in São Paulo, Porto Alegre may be first in the relative value of spending as well in terms of the amount of service provided. Belo Horizonte and São Paulo rank second and third with similar performances in health appointments, although São Paulo spends more than four times more per capita on health than Belo Horizonte. Even so, the indicators in which Belo Horizonte ranks ahead of São Paulo express more qualitative effects, such as infant mortality. Salvador ranks well in one quantitative indicator, the number of appointments per capita, but the city does not make as many hospital beds available as the others. Salvador ranks three or fourth in two key issues, spending per capita and hospital beds. Thus, Salvador's performance lags behind the three other cities in the two most important qualitative criteria. Although it is not possible to show that less civil society strength in the council is responsible for the results, there is at least a strong correlation between the two.

The democratization of health services has had one additional consequence: increased access to healthcare in poor regions. Data by subregion

Table 6.4. Appointments in the public health service in the city of São Paulo, by income quartile, 2001–2004

Sub-prefeituras by Income Quartile		No. of Appointments in 2001		No. of Appointments in 2004		Growth 2001–04 (%)
Quartile	IDH-M	Total	Per User	Total	Per User	
1	0.67	1,557,294	0.87	2,948,353	1.50	72.47
2	0.70	1,966,803	1.19	2,877,234	1.67	40.92
3	0.75	1,803,175	1.23	2,800,854	1.90	54.65
4	0.85	2,140,380	2.83	1,734,367	2.42	−14.51
São Paulo	0.74	7,467,652	1.32	10,360,808	1.78	35.50

Note: Sub-*prefeituras* income quartiles are ranked by their score in the local Human Development Index (IDH-M).
Source: Coelho et al., 2006, reproduced with the author's permission.

are available only for São Paulo (Table 6.4). They show that access is rising in the poorest regions. We should note that regions with the worst index of human development (IDH-M)[7] included those with high levels of social organization, such as Cidade Tiradentes and São Mateus in São Paulo, whose social indicators lag behind wealthy regions. However, when we compare wealthy and poor regions on healthcare, we note an improvement triggered by the participatory institutions. According to Coelho, the number of appointments in the poorest regions increased 72 percent, while the number of appointments in the city as a whole rose 35 percent. She also shows that the number of appointments grew in all regions except those with the best social economic conditions, where the number of appointments was above the international average (2.0 per person) (Coelho, 2005). Thus, we can see that, although there is not a complete equalization of access to healthcare in São Paulo, there was a positive evolution toward this aim. It was not by chance that São Paulo's popular health movement emerged in São Mateus, where health conditions were among the worst in the city and yet civil society was strongly organized.

7. There is too much subregional inequality in Brazilian cities in regard to access to public goods in the areas of health, education, and social assistance. Inequality in the access to public goods results in inequality in such basic health indicators as life expectancy and infant mortality. To differentiate parts of the city according to their different social indicators, the United Nations Development Programme (UNDP) in Brazil introduced the concept of IDH-M, a local version of the UNDP Human Development Index It departs from the city average and recalculates the index for each one of the city subregions. In Belo Horizonte some regions rank close to Scandinavia, whereas other regions rank closer to the poorest regions of Bolivia.

In the case of Belo Horizonte it is possible to see a connection between decentralization and the increase in claiming services in two of the city's nine regions, Nordeste and Venda Nova (Avritzer et al., 2005: 63). Venda Nova had some of the best-organized civil society actors during the 1980s. In Porto Alegre, we see a similar positive evolution of health services in the Grande Cruzeiro region (Réos, 2003: 65). All this attests to the effectiveness of participatory healthcare institutions, an effectiveness that varies with civil society strength and the willingness of political society to implement participatory institutions.

It is possible to evaluate healthcare councils according to the main elements that emerged in the four cases. The first point to bear in mind is that the institutionalization of the power-sharing format gives civil society legal and political prerogatives. In the case of Belo Horizonte's health council the prerogative assumed was to fill the presidency of the health council. In the case of São Paulo, the prerogative assumed was to further define civil society participation. In both cases, as well as in the case of Porto Alegre, these new prerogatives created the capacity to press for a more equitable distribution of health services, as I showed above. Civil society strength was lacking only in the case of Salvador, and homogeneous distributive results were lacking here as well. These four city experiences show the value of a strong civil society for improving social inclusion and access to services, particularly when participation is legally institutionalized and sanctions are imposed for noncompliance. Civil society prerogatives are much stronger in the case of power-sharing formats than in bottom-up institutions, allowing us to clearly differentiate them. Power-sharing formats also makes participatory institutions less dependent upon the political will of administrators.

Comparing Bottom-up and Power-sharing Designs

Based on our examination of the experiences of the four cities, we can draw a few systematic comparisons about health councils as power-sharing institutions and participatory budgeting processes as bottom-up institutions. The first conclusion is that health councils did not emerge according to preconceived institutional strategies. On the contrary, as in the case of participatory budgeting, unanticipated elements are key to the variations in design that made health councils effective. Power-sharing as a design emerged because of the skills, interests, and opportunities of local actors—the presence of doctors and healthcare advocates, as well as mayors and local officials, who understood their own locations and the importance of the state in health issues. Power-sharing, as I pointed out in Chapter 4, also differs from bottom-up designs because it includes sanctions against noncompliance.

The second important comparison between the two designs is based on their deliberative effects. Although participatory budgeting has increased deliberation, even in complicated cases such as São Paulo, its effects have been limited by its perceived lack of effectiveness in the city and its competition with other public policies. The deliberative effects of bottom-up institutions, such as participatory budgeting, are clearly linked to the will of political society to place them at the center of participatory policies. In contrast, the deliberative effect of power-sharing institutions is linked to the institutionalization of civil society participation. Health councils, even in São Paulo, have increased both deliberation and participation, even at less favorable moments, when conservative sectors controlled the city administration and tried to disempower participatory institutions.

The third conclusion concerns the distributive effects of power-sharing and bottom-up designs. Based on the comparison of the four cities, health councils' distributive effects vary, but in a way different from the variation in participatory budgeting. Again, the cases of Porto Alegre and Belo Horizonte seem to be least problematic, though Porto Alegre spends more on health than Belo Horizonte. The case that needs to be analyzed with care is São Paulo. Unlike its participatory budgeting, São Paulo's health councils succeeded in keeping spending high and improving its equitable distribution among poor and wealthy regions. Thus, São Paulo's experience shows the success of power-sharing designs, because it reveals distributive effects even where political society is not clearly willing to implement participatory arrangements. The difference between the least-successful Salvador and São Paulo is not so much the political society's willingness to interfere in the participatory design, since there is evidence of this in both cases. What differentiates Salvador is that civil society was not strong enough to struggle against that interference.

Despite changes in administration between left and right and the enforcement of antiparticipatory policies during the Paulo Maluf and Celso Pitta conservative administrations, São Paulo healthcare actors have taken advantage of the sanction element present in the law to further their interests. Healthcare actors refined the definition of civil society in the law to avoid disempowerment policies by conservative administrations. The healthcare actors also enforced distribution policies during the Marta Suplicy administration, at the same time the participatory budgeting was being financially disempowered. The presence of civil society actors in the approval of health financing has been a key factor in avoiding the disempowerment of the São Paulo health council.

The experiences of the four cities allow us to partially answer the question posed at the outset of this book, namely, what are the conditions required for the introduction of different participatory institutions? The comparison between Porto Alegre and Belo Horizonte, on the one hand, and São Paulo, on the other, points out that in cases of strong civil society and divided political society, power-sharing designs are more likely to succeed than bottom-up designs. Bottom-up designs work well in cases in which civil society and political society gather around the participatory institution. In those supportive circumstances, however, power-sharing designs work at least as well as bottom-up designs. Health councils in both Belo Horizonte and Porto Alegre work as well as participatory budgeting.

The question that remains unanswered is, which kind of participatory policy can be pursued when civil society is weak and political society is opposed to participation? Salvador is the case to be analyzed in order to propose a full typology of participation. Salvador's participatory budgeting was not implemented until 2004, and its health council has been disempowered because civil society has not been able to challenge the antiparticipatory stance of the city's political society. In the next chapter, I analyze the implementation of city master plans in the four cities to show the role that participatory institutions may play in the cases of weak civil society and antiparticipatory political society.

7

City Master Plans

City master plans, required by the 2001 Statute of the City, are the most recent of the new participatory institutions to emerge in democratic Brazil.
These institutions are not based on bottom-up deliberation or power-sharing, but rather on public ratification, a third type of participatory design.
Public ratification requires setting up a participatory body to accept or
reject local administrative policy proposals. Today city master plans are
mandatory in every Brazilian city with more than 20,000 inhabitants, and
the law requires the participation of representative associations in their
elaboration. Public meetings are set up to ratify the plans, and plans proposed without the participation of civil society can be nullified by the courts.

Thus, public ratification as the third type of participatory design has three
main characteristics. First, the initiative to propose a specific public policy
remains in the hands of the administration. Second, public audiences are the
form of participation for civil society. The role of public audiences is to either approve or reject the urban policy proposed by the administration.
Third, the law imposes strong sanctions by the courts in cases of noncompliance. Public ratification is a less deliberative institutional design than
either bottom-up or power-sharing, but as it is implemented in Brazil's city
master plans, it has a much stronger requirement for mandatory compliance
than either participatory budgeting or health councils.

In this chapter, I discuss the emergence of Brazil's urban reform movement, which generated some of the strongest civil society associations during democratization, in particular the MNRU (National Movement for Urban Reform) and FNRU (National Forum for Urban Reform). I focus on
how the relationship between civil society associations and political actors
changed during the struggle for urban reform. Second, I show how urban

141

participation arose and led to reform legislation during the Constitution-making process and after the Constituent Assembly and how the public ratification design emerged. Then, I explore how the Statute of the City requirement of city master plans has been implemented in São Paulo, Belo Horizonte, Porto Alegre, and Salvador. Based on these cases, I propose a typology of the effectiveness of civil society in different contexts, showing how public ratification works well in cities whose political configurations inhibited participatory budgeting or health councils from working effectively.

The Demand for Urban Reform

City master plans are the result of the emergence of a very strong urban reform movement in Brazil, as well as legislation approved both during the Constituent Assembly and following a 13-year battle thereafter that led to the Statute of the City. The urban reform movement initially proposed broad forms of democratic deliberation for urban administration, as it prepared for the Constituent Assembly in 1986–87. However, as the debate on urban reform evolved, it focused on just one institutional form, the public ratification of local administrative changes in city organization. This has been the main result of the struggle for urban reform in Brazil.

The source of the urban reform movement and the new participatory legislation was the deep process of urban development that Brazil experienced from the 1950s through the 1980s. Urban reform was already on the agenda of the Brazilian left and progressive sectors at the end of the previous democratic period (1946–64). In 1963 the first national conference on urban reform took place in Petropolis. But following that conference urban reform would have to wait through 20 years of authoritarianism before returning to the political agenda. The late 1970s and early 1980s, the last years of the authoritarian regime, saw a reconstitution of democratic civil society, especially in the form of popular neighborhood associations (see Chapter 2). In most cities, the issue of the relationship between legal and illegal cities motivated the organization of hundreds of neighborhood associations in the South, Southeast, and parts of the Northeast. A national association, the MNRU (National Movement for Urban Reform) emerged at the beginning of the democratization process and continued to operate throughout the period of urban reform debates (1982–2001). The MNRU became the FNRU (National Forum for Urban Reform) after the 1988 Constitution, effectively reinventing its alliance policy before it finally got the Statute of the City approved in 2001. In the process, it gave up its proposal for broad democratic deliberation and focused on one demand: the public ratification of local government actions.

The Emergence of Urban Participation

The MNRU was formed in 1982 with the aim of elaborating a proposal for urban reform at the Constituent Assembly. It was originally formed by popular movements, neighborhood associations, nongovernmental organizations, and trade unions (Brasil, 2004). The MNRU's composition shows that it was a hybrid between a civil society association and an organized lobby from the very beginning. Like other urban social movements in Brazil during the 1980s, it mobilized and aggregated a broad spectrum of diverse social actors (Doimo, 1995). Yet, since its formation, the MNRU counted on the support of national professional associations of engineers and architects located in Brasília and involved in national politics. The MNRU's composition was atypical of Brazilian civil society in the period, not only in the weight of national professional associations but also in aggregating them with local civil society associations (Table 7.1).

Thus, it included both local institutions, such as FAMERJ, the Federation of Neighborhood Associations in Rio de Janeiro, and the Movement in the Defense of *Favelados,* as well as professional associations such as the FNA (National Federation of Architects) and the FNE (National Federation of Engineers). In addition, the MNRU anticipated the strong presence of nongovernmental organizations in the Brazilian political scene from the 1980s on. Of the small number of influential nongovernmental organizations in Brazil in the 1980s, all were part of the urban reform movement.

Table 7.1. Components of the MNRU (National Movement for Urban Reform)

Type of Organization	Component
Popular movement	MDF(Movement for Defense of *Favelados*)
Neighborhood associations	FAMERJ (Federation of Neighborhood Associations in Rio de Janeiro)
Nongovernmental organizations	FASE (Federation of Associations in charge of Social Assistance), POLIS
Trade unions	FNE (National Federation of Engineers), FNA (National Federation of Architects)
Professional associations	ANSUR (National Coalition on Urban Soil)

Source: Brasil, 2004.

Proposals to the Constituent Assembly

As I showed in Chapter 4, the Brazilian National Constituent Assembly was a congressional assembly that accepted popular amendments. The MNRU proposed an amendment for urban reform based on the following principles:

- *The right to the city.* Its key meaning was a decent living for the urban poor (Saule Júnior, 1995: 23), but it also included the unification of urban struggles in Brazil through the integration of health, transportation, sanitation, and education demands. In the words of a social actor of the period, "urban reform will make viable the unification . . . of the movements for transportation, health, housing, land, allowing them to elaborate a unified platform to reenergize the city" (Teixeira Ferreira, 1988).
- *The subordination of private property to the aims of urban policy.* Brazilian cities before 1988 lacked fiscal instruments to organize real estate interests and actions in large cities. The popular amendment on urban reform envisioned the following instruments: progressive taxation of urban property; taxation on the added value of urban property; state preference in the acquisition of urban land; state prerogatives to expropriate urban land. In the words of another important social actor, urban reform "politicized the debate on planning by bringing to the center of the debate the issue of the social function of property" (Rolnik, 1997).
- *Democratic governance.* The popular amendment envisioned several devices for the exercise of democratic governance, among them public audiences, popular initiatives, popular veto of legislation with the support of 5 percent of the electorate, and the *Ministério Público*[1] empowered to act in case of a legal vacuum. Thus, despite the fact that many forms of democratic deliberation, including bottom-up participation, were included, public ratification was already present in the FNRU's initial proposal. This institutional element, unlike those proposed by the health movement and the UAMPA, would be preserved in the demands of the urban reform movement until the approval of the Statute of the City in 2001.

---

1. *Ministerio Público* is a legal figure in Brazilian law and whose role was completely changed by the 1988 Constitution. Before 1988 the role of the *Ministério Público* was to defend the interest of the federal government and the union. In 1985 the *Ministério Público* acquired other prerogatives, the most important of which was the defense of diffuse interests. The 1988 Constitution consolidated this institutional function through the differentiation of two institutions, the *Advocacia Geral da União* and the *Ministério Público* (Cavalcanti, 2006).

The popular amendment on urban reform was presented to the Constituent Assembly with 131,000 signatures and unleashed a lobbying battle with conservative real estate interests. The thematic Committee on Urban Issues and Transportation did not initially attract many powerful constituents, since conservative sectors had more pressing short-term issues (Arturi, 2001). Charging that the systematization committee had been taken by leftist interests, they constituted a group called Centrão. Centrão was in charge of making amendments to the Constitutional text that would transform it into a conservative charter. Real estate interests inside the Constituent Assembly sought to transfer the final decision on urban issues to another arena outside the Constitution-making process to avoid the automatic application of any new legislation (Saule Júnior, 1995: 28). Most of the subcommittee's proposals on urban issues remained intact, but they were integrated with a requirement that cities have master plans,[2] proposed by Centrão.

Thus, Paragraph 1 of Article 182 of the 1988 Constitution requires a "city master plan approved by City Council as mandatory to all cities with more than 20,000 inhabitants" (Brasil, 1988). All urban reform proposals were made dependent on fulfilling this clause. The MNRU was partially successful in making its proposal for urban reform part of the constitutional text. It was able to incorporate the democratic management of urban policy and the social function of property into the charter as broad principles, but both were subordinated to the requirement of elaborating a city master plan. The consequence of the subordination of the urban reform agenda to master plans was what the Brazilian legal tradition calls a statute or an infra-constitutional process of specifying constitutional law. Thus, a 13-year battle followed the approval of the Constitution.

As with participatory budgeting and health councils, this new institutional format included an element of unanticipated action. In the case of participatory budgeting, no single social actor proposed the design; rather, as I showed in Chapter 5, it resulted from different proposals by progressive civil society associations and the PT. In the case of city master plans, no one envisioned the link between them and participatory public ratification. It emerged through negotiations and clashes between social actors and conservative sectors in the Constituent Assembly and in its aftermath.

---

2. City master plans or *planos diretores* are not inherently conservative devices, although they have been considered conservative by the urban reform movement because of the way they emerged during the Constituent Assembly. Some Brazilian cities, such as Porto Alegre, have had city master plans since the late 1970s. The novelty introduced by the Constituent Assembly was the link between having a city master plan and being able to introduce the other devices approved by the Constitution in its urban chapter.

Civil and Political Society in the Congress

After the Constituent Assembly, the MNRU became the National Forum for Urban Reform (FNRU), with a variety of civil society components (Table 7.2). This change involved an organizational debate on the characteristics of civil society in assuming a legislative battle in Congress.

The struggle for urban reform in the National Congress created a new relationship between civil and political society, allowing us to differentiate between three paths by which participatory institutions emerged in Brazil. In the case of urban reform, mobilization outside Congress did not play a major role. The close relationship between the PT and the FNRU would have never been enough to guarantee the legislation approval. What we see in the case of the Statute of the City is an initial strategy very similar to the one employed in health gradually evolving into an "above-party" strategy.

During the first years after the approval of the Constitution (Grazia, 2001) 16 bills for infraconstitutional legislation were presented in Congress. Already at this point, alignments between civil society actors and leftist parties did not work as well as they had during the Constituent Assembly. The bill that became known as the Statute of the City was Bill 181 of 1990, proposed by Senator Pompeu de Sousa. Pompeu de Sousa was a well-known newsman from Rio de Janeiro had who moved to Brasília in the 1970s, where he became linked to Editora Abril, the largest magazine publisher in Brazil. He was also close to the founders of the University of Brasília, an important project of the Brazilian left during the 1960s. Pompeu de Sousa was not considered a leftist member of parliament. However, his bill incorporated the following elements of the MNRU/FNRU proposals:

- The collective right of urban dwellers to the city (Article 6)
- State coordination of the occupation of urban law (Article 5), though in a lighter form than the FNRU wished
- The social function of private property (Article 7), though in a lighter form than the FNRU wished
- Progressive taxation of urban property (Article 16), though in a lighter form than the FNRU wished
- The requirement that cities with more than 20,000 inhabitants elaborate a city master plan (Article 38).

Yet, the Pompeu de Sousa bill also lagged behind on a few central issues raised by the FNRU, in particular the democratic administration of urban policy. The MNRU's constitutional project had envisioned several instru-

Table 7.2. Composition of the FNRU (National Forum for Urban Reform)

Type of Organization	Component
Popular movement	CMP (Articulation of Popular Movements)
Nongovernmental organization	POLIS, FASE (Federation of Associations in charge of Social Assistance), ANSUR (National Coalition on Urban Soil), INESC (Institute for Social and Economic Studies)
Professional association	FISENGE (Federation of Engineers), FENAE (Federation of *Economiários*), FNA (National Federation of Architects), ANSUR (National Coalition on Urban Soil)

Source: Almeida, 2002.

ments for the democratic administration of urban law, among them popular legislative initiatives, a popular veto of changes in urban law with the support of 5 percent of constituents, and a right to information and control (Silva, 1990). Pompeu de Sousa's bill introduced a far more restrictive formulation for democratic participation: "urban politics would be guided by the following principles: democratic administration (*gestão*) and incentives to popular participation in formulation and implementation of urban development projects" (Article 10).

Pompeu de Sousa's bill was nevertheless highly contentious. Conservatives were not happy at the return of part of the Constituent Assembly agenda, and they targeted local administration prerogatives, such as progressive taxation, the social function of urban property, and preemption prerogatives. Civil society sectors (FNRU), meanwhile, were not happy with some of the bill's formulations, especially the dilution of democratic forms of city administration. Initially the FNRU crafted an alliance with the PT, the Brazilian Communist Party (PC do B), and progressive political actors to propose another bill, the Lourdinha Savignon (PT-ES) Bill. The dispute between civil society actors and conservative sectors in Congress thus revealed important aspects of the strategies employed to create participatory institutions. Initially conservative sectors supported one project and progressive actors another. However, as the legislative process evolved, everyone concentrated on the same bill, Pompeu de Sousa's. For civil society actors (FNRU), the key issue was how to make this bill satisfactory in terms of civil society participation.

The Pompeu de Sousa Bill remained dormant in the Brazilian Congress until 1997, when it was approved in the first subcommittee, the Committee on Economy, Industry and Commerce (CEIC). Then a congressional subcommittee, the Economic Development Committee, issued a very conservative report, eliminating all participatory elements from the bill. The FNRU responded by submitting the Statute of the City to the Committee on Consumer and Environmental Affairs, which was controlled by leftist members of Congress. Many of the breakthroughs that allowed civil society forces (FNRU) to incorporate their agendas into the Pompeu de Sousa Bill took place in this committee (Arruda, 2001), including:

- The right to the city as a conception for the elaboration of urban law, which had been proposed by the FNRU and rejected in the Economic Development Committee
- Local administration preemption prerogatives, which would allow the administration to hold land in areas in which it anticipates expansion.

We thus see how the battle between the FNRU and conservative real estate interests evolved. The Pompeu de Sousa Bill, which became a reference point in the elaboration of the infraconstitutional legislation on urban reform, did not fully incorporate the FNRU agenda. After reinserting these demands, the next step was the Justice and Constitutionality Committee, the most important committee of the Brazilian Congress. The final report on the law issued in 2000 positioned itself on three main items, two of them about participation: how to make the city master plan mandatory and whether the federal government could make local participation mandatory. At a public audience the FNRU defended all instruments for the concession of special housing rights, as well as the principle of the social function of private property. The final challenge was reinserting democratic participation into the final draft of the law. Two PT members of parliament asked the law reporter to listen to representatives of the FNRU on the issue. After that, a new amendment to the law was approved. The amendment called for requiring public audiences in the elaboration of city master plans (Arruda, 2001). Thus, the participatory agenda of civil society was in the end concentrated on the issue of the ratification of local government actions by public audiences. This became a demand that transcended parties and created a new participatory design, the process of ratification. That design, however, was implemented in different ways in the four cities we are examining.

The Implementation of the Statute of the City in Four Cities

Like the previous two chapters, this chapter focuses first on the role of civil and political society in the emergence of the new institution. In this regard, the FNRU's actions were unique in Brazilian civil society. No other national legislation[3] required so much mobilization and lobbying at the national level. Yet, a second dimension also needs to be taken into account to understand the effectiveness of the policy, namely, the implementation of city master plans in different cities. In this section I trace this process in four cities: São Paulo, Belo Horizonte, Porto Alegre, and Salvador. I show that the different characteristics of civil society actions, as well as the different political contexts in each city, generated different results.

Civil and Political Society in the Local Context

Brazilian democratization produced a marked increase in voluntary and independent forms of association, as I showed in Chapter 2. Among our four cities, three experienced an associative boom during the late 1970s and early 1980s, but the cities' different histories and political societies are relevant to understanding the local contexts of civil society associations.

Porto Alegre and Belo Horizonte

These cases are instructive because they involved more continuity in the relationships between leftist sectors, civil society associations, and the city administration. In Porto Alegre, associations that had existed since the 1950s evolved in the 1980s into a new umbrella association, the UAMPA (Avritzer, 2002c). Porto Alegre's tradition of neighborhood mobilization distinguished it from other Brazilian cities throughout this period, as did its strong political left, as I showed in Chapter 3. The moment of redemocratization (1985–88) saw a contest between the left and the right in most Brazilian capitals, but not Porto Alegre, which was disputed by the PDT and the PT—both on the left. After the victory of Olívio Dutra in the 1988 elections, the PT hegemonized the city's left and governed for 16 years. Belo Horizonte, though without such a strong tradition of leftist political parties, was similar because civil society associations and the PT managed to govern the city without creating a left-right divide. As a result, in both Porto Alegre and Belo Horizonte

---

3. The other national legislation on participation that was highly contentious was the health legislation. There has been a battle in 1990 on the participatory format of health policies as the LOS, *Lei Orgânica da Saúde,* was being discussed. Collor vetoed the articles on participation of the LOS triggering a mobilization against the federal government. However, the final format of the LOS with a new law allowing participation emerged in the same year. Thus, in terms of length and mobilization capacity the case of urban reform is more impressive. On health participatory legislation in Brazil, see Chapter 6.

ratification operates smoothly, in a manner similar to bottom-up deliberation. If strong civil society traditions and good relations between civil and political society could be counted on, institutional design would make little difference. However, São Paulo and Salvador point in another direction, namely, to the effects of different participatory designs.

São Paulo

The associated population of São Paulo evolved during the democratic period in intriguing ways. São Paulo has a strong tendency toward informal and religious participation. It has seen ups and downs in the political roles for associations dedicated to public policy. The reason for this variation is that no other city in democratic Brazil has experienced so many changes of administration. Only once in the 20-year period 1985–2005 was an incumbent administration was returned to power. Because of the competition between the PT and the *malufismo,* the city went back and forth between leftist and rightist mayors during the 1990s. Thus, two unique characteristics of São Paulo are expressed in the city's master plans: the strength of civil society and the dispute between left and right within political society. Civil society strength is evident in the city's strong nongovernmental organizations and thematic movements, notably POLIS, (the most important of the nongovernmental organizations that deal with urban politics) and important urban reform leaders. Yet, they alone cannot compensate for the very strong articulation of conservative interests in the city. Precisely this dispute marked the implementation of São Paulo's master plan after the PT came back to power under Marta Suplicy in 2000. Her administration proposed the implementation of a new city master plan according to the recently approved Statute of the City, but the ratification process has twice been annulled by the courts. São Paulo thus allows us to analyze the effect of ratification designs in the face of contentious local politics.

Salvador

Salvador is an interesting fourth case insofar as it has had a much less active civil society since democratization (Boschi, 1999). The number of ethnic associations is very high in the city, almost equal to the number of neighborhood associations. However, these associations do not involve themselves in highly politicized issues, such as urban reform (Fischer and Moura, 1996). Salvadoran political society has been dominated by the PFL, the most stable conservative party in democratic Brazil. In addition, the city is controlled by a family oligarchy, the Magalhães, who have showed a strong antiparticipatory bias. In sum, Salvadoran civil society has historically been weak and divided, while political society has been dominated by conservative sectors. It is the key case for analyzing the operation of ratification designs where civil society is not strong and the organized civil society and state institutions are in opposition.

The Operation of Ratification in City Master Plans

Porto Alegre and Belo Horizonte had similar processes of crafting city master plans. The two cities had institutional participation for a longer period, as well as a long period of partnership between state and civil society actors (Baierle, 1998; Avritzer, 2002b). Although city master plans, health councils, and participatory budgeting operate in similar ways in Porto Alegre and Belo Horizonte, I have also considered more complicated cases in which either civil society is not strong enough to force the implementation of participatory institutions or the political system is strongly against them. Here, Salvador and São Paulo throw more light on the issues involved in the expansion of participatory institutions.

Porto Alegre

Porto Alegre has Brazil's the longest tradition of city planning, going back to 1935. Its first city master plan concerned only traffic, but during the 1950s it already attempted to establish an integrated master plan involving traffic, housing, and the zoning of factories and leisure facilities. Porto Alegre's attempts to produce an integrated city master plan thus date from the authoritarian period. The city's first master plan in 1979 included the separation between urban and rural parts of the city; the differentiation of urban zones according to planning units; and the incorporation of some emerging forms of participation. Porto Alegre was thus introducing elements of urban planning and participation when these discussions were just emerging in other parts of the country.

Porto Alegre's 1979 master plan remained in force for 20 years. During this period, new problems emerged, notably the continuous subdivision of urban land and the impossibility of legalizing occupations of public land. These problems, which were part of the debates in the Constituent Assembly and the elaboration of the Statute of the City, received a differentiated response. Under 16 years of PT administration, the city introduced participatory budgeting and placed on the agenda the issues of subdivision and assigning title to occupants of public land. Several legal instruments for urban planning emerged in Porto Alegre in parallel with debates on urban planning at the federal level. Still, in 1991 the city differentiated its permanent stock of urban land for green areas and urban preservation from occupied lands that could be used to legalize the tenure of the poor. The law also foresaw collective property concessions by the city (Porto Alegre, 1991). In 1994, the city created its urban planning fund, part of which was established by creating and selling city property. Thus, Porto Alegre anticipated legal instruments that most cities would use only after the approval of the Statute of the City, showing how civil and political society together gave it leeway in urban reform that no other city in Brazil had at that point.

What is most interesting, however, is that the courts did not block such attempts. The legal system of the State of Rio Grande do Sul interpreted existing laws in a progressive way, favoring the assignment by the state of lands occupied by poor city dwellers. In 1995, the *Corregedor Geral de Justiça* (Public Overseer of the Legal System) issued a judgment authorizing the legalization of occupied public land. The Justice Tribunal of the Rio Grande do Sul confirmed this judgment, stating that: "parceling of urban land and its registration are not against federal law; they only are not dealt by the law and, due to the peculiarity of the case, registration is a way of guaranteeing property rights" (Tribunal Justiça RGS, 39-1995). The Brazilian Supreme Court then acknowledged the constitutionality of Rio Grande do Sul Court's decision.

Porto Alegre's consensus over a new city master plan emerged in 1993 during the First Congress of the City. The city master plan was crafted in 1995–96 and sent to city hall. In that year, civil society associations demanded more debate and the newly sworn-in administration withdrew the project (Guimaraens, 2001). These debates mainly involved limits on new construction. During 1997 there were new public audiences, and the law returned to city hall, where it was approved two years later on November 5, 1999.

One key advance of Porto Alegre's city master plan over others in large Brazilian capitals was the incorporation of a revision mechanism to be applied according to the city's development. The fact that Porto Alegre has had a master plan since 1979 created an awareness that Brazilian cities change fast and that public administration lacks mechanisms to control growth. Porto Alegre's city master plan transformed the whole city into a single urban area to establish control over this process. It also opened a space to redefine the city's aims for urban planning, creating an alternative between no control and total control of land use. The second major advance was the establishment of a council in charge of continuously revising the city master plan, the Council of Urban and Environmental Development. The new council aims, among other things, to suggest new urban development policies, propose ways of creating new urban land, approve specific land-creation proposals, and deliberate on environmental issues (Porto Alegre, 1999). Thus, Porto Alegre shows two characteristics of ratification designs: in cities with a strong civil society tradition and a solid relation between civic associations and the political system, approval of ratification designs takes place smoothly, while the legal system tends to be integrated into the broad agreement that organizes the interaction between civil society and the state actors.

Belo Horizonte

Elaboration of Belo Horizonte's city master plan was very similar to Porto Alegre's. Belo Horizonte's city master plan was the first to be approved in a large capital in Brazil. When Patrus Ananias from the PT was elected mayor in 1992, he promised to have a city master plan approved in the first six months of his administration. The previous PSDB administration had tried to implement a city master plan, but fell short of approving it. Immediately after his inauguration, Ananias set up a committee, made up mostly of technicians, to work on the plan. Only after the plan was elaborated were the city's most important real estate interests, SINDUSCON (Real Estate Interest Trade-Union) and CMI (Real Estate Market Committee), brought into the debate. There was one public audience in each of Belo Horizonte's nine regions, then the plan was sent to the city council, which held a public audience for the city as a whole (Mendonça, 2006). Most of the devices proposed by the city were approved. However, in Belo Horizonte a delay of six months was allowed to address short-term interests. Thus, real estate interests could adapt themselves to the new law, which was approved on July 1996, but not implemented until the following January. In this sense, negotiation between real estate interests and the administration was internal to the process; it did not reach the courts and did not involve challenging the process. Belo Horizonte and Porto Alegre show that when civil society associations are strong and connected to a secure leftist party in power, most forms of participation work, irrespective of design. However, as I will show for the cases of São Paulo and Salvador, design and legal action become crucial when these conditions change.

São Paulo

The elaboration and approval of São Paulo's master plan expressed the discontinuities in the organization of the city's civil and political society. São Paulo's master plan was elaborated in the first year of Marta Suplicy's administration and sent by the mayor to the city council in May 2002. Its reporter was Nabil Bonduki, a veteran of the urban reform movement. Bonduki had been a professor of urban planning at the University of São Paulo and president of the city's association of architects between 1986 and 1989, when the legislation on participation was proposed at the national level. Bonduki participated in the São Paulo's first PT administration as part of the planning secretary's staff and was elected city councilor in 2000. His presence as reporter shows the strength of civil society actors in the city. However, his actions and the strong conservative lobby would bring him into conflict with the mayor and other councilors.

São Paulo's master plan was approved in two parts, the first establishing parameters for city development and the second involving specific regional plans. The first part set seven main guidelines (*Folha de São Paulo,* 2002):

- Occupying intermediate regions in the process of urban development, to be declared of public interest according to the Statute of the City if their owners did not give them an immediate purpose
- Choosing six new areas on the city's periphery in which occupied public property would be assigned to the poor using the so-called *outorga onerosa* (property concession with onus), an instrument created by the Statute of the City
- Giving incentives for public transportation to reduce the use of cars
- Giving incentives to reoccupy downtown areas to halt the occupation of green space
- Restoring permeability to São Paulo's soil
- Increasing the number of exclusively residential areas
- Creating cultural preservation zones.

The approval of this first part fulfilled the requirements for participation: 26 public meetings were conducted, as well as 15 meetings with nongovernmental organizations and technical personnel. More than 230 organizations participated in the process in August 2002. The most contentious part of the approval process involved delimiting neighborhoods and licensing construction in them, which were essential issues for real estate interests. Huge amounts of money are made in Brazilian cities by changing land designations to make the land available for development. The regional master plan had to be consolidated by the city council; for its approval the administration needed 33 votes. City council representatives made amendments to the plan that took into consideration the specific interests of real estate speculators. The government accepted their amendments and, with their votes, approved the plan. Yet, civil society actors considered the process tainted (Estado de São Paulo, 2002).

The second stage of São Paulo's master plan involved elaborating regional master plans. This proved highly contentious. There were two major conflicts, one concerning access to information and another concerning the status of civil society representatives. The city administration published the relevant information on regional changes in the *City Diary* and called for 31 public audiences in the regions in early November 2003. The audiences attracted three types of actors: members of neighborhood associations who did not want their neighborhoods to change; representatives of real estate speculators, who had limited voice in the meetings; and urban professionals. Real estate interests had two main complaints that ended up in litigation. The first was their lack of complete information. In their case this was important because they could not know exactly whether the law affected their properties. The São Paulo public prosecutor sued the city on this allegation with the claim that "the maps and the attachments [to the law] are incomplete and without that information citizens cannot fully participate in the public audiences" (*Folha de São Paulo,* 2003a). The courts accepted the argument, and the city was required to make public all maps involving changes in construction licensing.

The real estate companies' second complaint concerned their inability to defend their interests, since their representatives were blocked from the assemblies. In fact, the city allowed only individual participation by members of civil society associations. Real estate speculators did not want to go to the meetings themselves; they wanted association lawyers to defend their interests. Neighborhood association members participated normally in the 31 assemblies. Again, the São Paulo prosecutors asked to nullify all 31 assemblies. The courts accepted the claim, saying that "the exclusion of civil associations" violated the Constitution. For Judge Simone Cassoretti, "individual participation is not enough to fulfill the constitutional claim of democratic administration of the city. Representative associations should be granted to the right to participate" (*Folha de São Paulo,* 2003b). Regional master plans were approved in July 2004, after the public audiences were held again.

São Paulo's elaboration of city and regional master plans is very instructive for one main reason: it shows that the interests involved in urban speculation are very strong in the city and need to be offset by political forces. In São Paulo these forces were organized civil society groups, in particular strong nongovernmental organizations such as POLIS and neighborhood associations in neighborhoods faced with unwanted development. Nevertheless, real estate interests organized themselves and were able to nullify several provisions of the city master plan.

The public ratification process of São Paulo's master plan shows the operation of participatory elements: public audiences played the role the FNRU expected them to play—that is, the inclusion of the population in the approval process—as well as a role the FNRU did not expect them to play—namely, the legalization of real estate interests. However, in the end, unlike the laws concerning participatory budgeting and health councils, the law on city master plans established a middle ground, showing the potential of public ratification to mediate between opposing interests. Thus, in a case in which both civil society and real estate interests are strong, the law allowed a compromise between them, with the partial consideration of real estate interests through the city council and the legal system.

Again, it is interesting to compare the process in São Paulo and Porto Alegre. In São Paulo urban controls could not be enacted before the approval of the Statute of the City, despite of the strength of urban civil society movements in the city. Even during the PT's tenure between 1988 and 1992, most urban reform proposals were defeated in city hall or rejected by the courts, as was the case with progressive urban taxation. In Porto Alegre, civil society strength and a PT administration initiative made possible advances in urban legislation, such as the *outorga onerosa* (property concession with onus) even before the approval of the Statute of the City. It is also interesting to note the different role played by the courts. The courts in São Paulo were activated by conservative real estate interests to defend their vested interests, whereas in Porto Alegre the courts anticipated devices of the Statute of the City. Thus, we can conclude that without the Statute of the City most of its new devices would have never been implemented in São Paulo.

Salvador

Salvador is an interesting fourth case. Its city master plan was elaborated between 1999 and 2002. In 1999, the city hired a private consultancy to provide it with a preliminary diagnosis on urban development (Sampaio, 2000). Although not much information is available on what took place at this stage, we know that no civil society associations or urban planning movements participated, allowing the administration to make its own diagnosis based on real estate interests. In 2003, the city set up two public audiences to collect suggestions for its master plan. One audience took place, and the other did not because of a lack of publicity. Even though the law requires more than one public audience during the elaboration of the plan, Salvador Mayor Antônio Imbassay sent the proposed master plan to city hall, ignoring the fact that it failed to meet Statute of the City requirements. Salvador's Federation of Neighborhood Associations and the city section of the Brazilian Bar Association (OAB) asked the city public prosecutor (*ministerio publico*) to file a civil suit against the law (Caribe, 2005). It won on November 12, 2003, annulling the process. A new PDT-led administration inaugurated in 2005 changed the city's approach to public audiences and is currently sponsoring them to elaborate a new plan.

City Master Plans in Comparative Perspective

The comparison of Salvador with São Paulo, Porto Alegre, and Belo Horizonte allows us to propose a typology on the operation of public ratification designs in Brazil (Table 7.3). Porto Alegre and Belo Horizonte are the simpler cases, where the strength of civil society and progressive political actors turned city politics in a progressive direction. Many of the devices that waited for federal law in other cities were already present in Porto Alegre in the early 1990s. Public ratification in Porto Alegre and Belo Horizonte operated effectively, as did power-sharing and bottom-up deliberations. In this sense, we can say that in cities in which civil society associations are strong and well connected to the political system, ratification designs play an auxiliary role alongside other participatory institutions. We can also say in regard to the comparison among different types of participatory designs that in the cases in which bottom-up designs work well, power-sharing and ratification designs also work well.

São Paulo is a completely different case, despite the strength of its urban reform movement. Though Brazil's urban reform movement was born in the city and its most important leaders emerged there, real estate interests were also very strong, and political society was sharply divided. For this reason, São Paulo's city master plan had to wait for a national law, the Statute of the City. Even with the statute, the approval of a new city master

Table 7.3. Ratification designs in four Brazilian cities

City	Civil Society Organization	Political Society Actions	Legal Actions Involved	Result
São Paulo	Strong, an origin of the urban reform movement. However, real estate interests also very well organized.	Divided throughout democratization period. PT administered the city twice, conservative sectors three times.	Legal actions filed by conservative sectors in order to allow real estate interests to be present at public audiences.	City master plan approved after changes made by the courts and city council.
Porto Alegre	Very strong. Participated in the Congress of the City, where the revision of the city master plan was decided.	Hegemonized by the PT and unified around urban reform.	No legal actions taken.	City master plan carried out the reform of urban politics.
Belo Horizonte	Strong. Participated in the proposal of the new city master plan.	PT very strong, had leeway over opposition.	No legal actions taken.	City master plan carried out the reform of urban politics.
Salvador	Weak.	Hegemonized by rightist PFL. Controlled by Magalhães family.	Legal actions taken by civil society and progressive political actors in order to offset real estate interests.	Conservative city master plan curbed by the courts.

plan was contentious. The legal system and city council expressed the conflict over urban politics in the city. Public audiences, attended by civil society associations, were nullified because they failed to incorporate real estate interests, but were ultimately completed successfully with broader representation. São Paulo thus shows that city master plans functioned well in a contentious political environment. Public ratification has the advantage of involving social actors with opposing views in the elaboration of public policies. In the end, when the policy is enforced, it is supported by a whole set of actors. In this sense, public ratification operates better than other participatory institutions in diverse, contentious settings.

São Paulo's case also allows us to compare the democratizing and distributive effect of bottom-up, power-sharing, and ratification designs. Bottom-up designs, as I pointed out in Chapter 5, did not work well in the city because of their high dependency upon the political will of the administration. Power-sharing designs, as I have showed in Chapter 6, worked better because they allowed civil society actors to be more independent in relation to political society. Public ratification designs were the most independent of the three in regard to political will. Ratification's democratizing and distributive effect may be small in the short run, because the design leaves so many regulatory aspects up to the initiatives of the state, but ratification designs may work very well in establishing a long-term consensus around a new way of regulating public policy. In the case of São Paulo, it was also very important that all legal challenges to the new public policy took place throughout the process of implementation of city master plans. In the end, public ratification is the design that is the most efficient in creating consensus around a public policy. It is also the only design that explicitly involves all three levels of government at the local level: the executive, the city council, and the courts.

Salvador is a good contrasting case that allows us to see participatory designs in comparative perspective. None of the other participatory designs that we have discussed so far in the book have been effective there. Participatory budgeting was never introduced in the city until 2004, and health councils were made to avoid civil society participation in health policy. Salvador's city master plan shows that in a context in which both civil society and progressive political society are weak, the Statute of the City has been able to block the actions of conservative sectors. Sanction in this case was enforced not by suspending the transfer of resources, but rather by nullifying the public policy-making process. This sanction also distinguishes public ratification from power-sharing and bottom-up deliberation: public ratification is the design that has the greater capacity to punish noncompliance with participatory requirements. In the conclusion to this book, we look broadly at the limitations and potential of all three institutional designs to increase public participation in policy-making.

Part III

Conclusion

8

The Limits and Potential
of Participatory Institutions

As our survey of experience in four cities has demonstrated, the new participatory institutions of democratic Brazil differ profoundly in the civil and political context in which they have emerged and in the designs they have put into operation. This chapter summarizes and systematizes the relationships among three types of participatory institutions, putting together their differences in context, design, and ultimate effectiveness in increasing social inclusion and redistributing public resources.

This approach suggests some recommendations different from the ones usually made in the mainstream literature on participatory institutions. It places the best-known "success story" of participation—participatory budgeting in Porto Alegre—in perspective through the discussion of two other participatory experiences in Brazil, health councils and city master plans. The discussion of the three experiences in four cities, Porto Alegre, Belo Horizonte, São Paulo, and Salvador, allows us to propose a typology of the circumstances best suited to each type of participatory design. I also show that a strategy of implementing participatory institutions in stages according to context may be a better policy than trying to simply replicate them in different settings.

The Context in Which Institutions Emerge

Drawing on the different experiences of participation in Brazil, we can make three points about the recent debates on introducing participatory institutions where they have not previously existed (Fung and Wright, 2003; Baiocchi, 2005; Dagnino, Olvera, and Panfichi, 2006). The first, developed in Chapters 1 and 2, is that variations in the organization of civil society from place to place can make a critical difference to success. The second point is that civil society associations and political parties tend to be equal partners in the introduction of participatory arrangements. I showed in Chapter 3 that divisions within political parties lead to weak participatory arrangements. The third point is that the designs of participatory institutions should vary in response to the organization of the civil and political society in which they are implemented. The formation of a political coalition in favor of participation should justify changes in the design of a participatory institution. In Chapter 4, I called this process interactive participatory design. The key contextual variables for the introduction of participatory institutions are the local civil and political society.

Civil Society

Several works have showed the importance of civil society organization in the emergence and later success of participatory institutions (Avritzer, 2002a; Dagnino, 2002; Wampler and Avritzer, 2004; Baiocchi, 2005; Bacqué, Rey, and Sintomer, 2005). Other works emphasized the impact of participatory institutions on the strengthening of civil society organization (Abers, 2000; Baiocchi, 2003; Fung and Wright, 2003). Nonetheless, there have been many doubts about the limits that weak civil society organization pose to participatory institutions. I respond to this issue by comparing three cases of participatory budgeting and four cases of participation in health councils.

The comparison of Porto Alegre's participatory budgeting experiences with those of Belo Horizonte and São Paulo showed that participatory budgeting may lead to different results, even in situations in which civil society is strong. Civil society was relatively strong in all three cities at the beginning of the democratization in the late 1970s, when the new mass political party, the PT rose to power. However, differences in the timing of political control and the geographical presence of civil society organizations in various regions of the cities influenced the capacity of the PT administrations in the three cities to carry out participatory policies, as I showed in Chapters 2, 3, and 5.

Political Society

Many observers have focused on the centrality of political parties' initiative in the implementation and later expansion of participatory institutions (Santos, 1998; Abers, 2000; Baiocchi, 2003; Avritzer and Navarro, 2003; Houtzager, Gurza, and Charya, 2003). Still, many doubts remain about the quality of participation in the experiences based uniquely on political parties' initiatives (Silva, 2003; Avritzer and Navarro, 2003). Many of these experiences lack the quality and the intensity of the Porto Alegre's experience. In this book, I have tried to connect civil and political society into one integrated framework to show that the relevant analytical element is how civil and political society interact. This new framework allows me to place the Porto Alegre experience in context and to show successes and failures regarding participatory budgeting, as well as other participatory experiences.

Institutional Designs in Operation

In Chapter 4, I proposed the concept of interactive participatory design to emphasize how participatory designs vary according to the way they allow participation to redefine the distribution of power and material resources. I examined the implementation of three types of participatory designs—bottom-up, power-sharing, and ratification designs—to better understand their limits and potential in different contexts.

The Potential and Limits of Bottom-up Designs

I compared in Chapter 5 three cases of participatory budgeting, Porto Alegre, Belo Horizonte, and São Paulo, to show the relevance of design. Porto Alegre is the classical participatory budgeting case with a strong civil society proposing the democratization of the budget process as early as 1986 (Avritzer, 2002b) and a strong and united PT implementing it from 1990 on (Abers, 2000).

Belo Horizonte's experience differed from Porto Alegre's in at least two ways: Belo Horizonte also had a strong civil society organization and a strong PT presence, but neither was as strong as in Porto Alegre. Belo Horizonte's civil society organization lacked an umbrella organization that could play the integrating role of Porto Alegre's UAMPA, as I showed in Chapter 2. The result was a more moderate experience of participation. Participatory budgeting in Belo Horizonte has been successful in the sense that it has existed for more than 12 years, nearly 1,000 public works have been implemented, and close to R$100 per person has been distributed in the poor regions of the city. However, Belo Horizonte's participatory budgeting has differed from Porto Alegre's in its centrality within public administration, as well as in the value of the investments it allocates. Belo Horizonte's participatory budgeting has not centralized all the city's social policies and has operated in tandem with other participatory policies, as I showed in Chapter 5. The highest investment in Belo Horizonte's participatory budgeting was 5.35 percent of the total budget, while in Porto Alegre it was 20.8 percent. Thus, Porto Alegre and Belo Horizonte's cases show that differences in the configuration of civil and political society led the same participatory institution, participatory budgeting, to distribute power and material resources in different ways.

The most instructive case regarding the expansion of participatory budgeting was São Paulo. São Paulo's civil society was as organized as Porto Alegre's or Belo Horizonte's at the beginning of their participatory processes in the early 1990. In Porto Alegre and Belo Horizonte, civil society generalized itself beyond its original strongholds through the participatory processes. This is precisely what São Paulo's failed to do. Organized civil society became contained in one of the city's regions, the eastern district, hindering the expansion of the process. In the case of political society, the São Paulo PT was less participatory than Porto Alegre's and Belo Horizonte's, making participatory policies more contentious within PT administrations. The result was that São Paulo's PT administration put less priority on participatory budgeting. Investment plans made through participatory budgeting reached less than R$100 per capita in the poor regions of São Paulo, even if we include programs already decided at that level of government, such as the Family Health Programs. Furthermore, only 40 percent of the investment plans were implemented in São Paulo.

The Porto Alegre, Belo Horizonte, and São Paulo's cases demonstrate the variation in the effectiveness of participatory institutions to reallocate power and resources. I called this element the effectiveness of bottom-up designs. Bottom-up designs emerge under very specific conditions. Participatory budgeting first emerged in Porto Alegre, and most likely could only have emerged there. However, our analysis of the expansion of participatory budgeting showed that it could also work well in Belo Horizonte under less favorable conditions. In this sense, distinguishing between conditions of emergence and conditions of expansion can help us understand what differentiates Porto Alegre from Belo Horizonte.

The most important element that this book has showed in relation to bottom-up participatory designs is that they are the most democratic and the most distributive participatory institutions when they work well. However, they are also the most demanding participatory institutions and the ones that pose the largest number of requirements, such as strong civil society and united political society. In addition, bottom-up designs are the most easily disrupted by a hostile political society.

The second important element of participatory budgeting as a bottom-up participatory design is its lack of effectiveness, expressed by low budgetary commitments where political society is less ready to carry it out. São Paulo, with its lack of strong deliberative practices and sanction mechanisms for nonimplementation, shows that effectiveness becomes the main concern in weak cases. This case calls attention to an issue that has often been ignored by advocates of expanding participatory budgeting, namely, that under unfavorable conditions it generates less democratic and distributive results than other participatory institutions, such as health councils. To prove this point, I analyzed four additional cases of health councils focusing on a second element of participatory designs discussed in Chapter 4, namely, power-sharing.

The Limits and Potential of Power-sharing Designs

Health councils are not bottom-up participatory institutions, at least not in the same sense as participatory budgeting. Health councils emerged out of the concern of public health professionals for state action throughout Brazilian democratization, leading to what I called a power-sharing participatory design. Health councils in four cities—São Paulo, Belo Horizonte, Porto Alegre, and Salvador—diverge from participatory budgeting insofar as the willingness of political society to carry out the participatory policy is mandated by the cities' legal obligation to implement the councils.

In the cases of Porto Alegre and Belo Horizonte, there is not much difference between participatory budgeting and health councils. Both institutions emerged very early in the democratization process and did not depend on a strong PT presence in the cities. In Belo Horizonte, health council legislation was approved before a PT mayor was elected. In both cities, health councils have worked well and have produced deliberative and distributive effects. Among the deliberative effects in Belo Horizonte, the chairing of the council by civil society actors and the agenda-setting power of the participants can be singled out. In Porto Alegre the strong civil society presence on the council has led to a strict boundary between civil society and private health service providers. In both cases, the strong presence of the PT and the administrative continuity of the left guaranteed the deliberative elements of the council. Both cities also show the distributive results of participatory health care institutions. Infant mortality in both cities has been very low, and the number of hospital beds has been high, compared with other Brazilian capitals.

In both Porto Alegre and Belo Horizonte, the success of health councils has coincided with the success of participatory budgeting. Thus, we can conclude that power-sharing designs are likely to thrive in circumstances where bottom-up designs are also thriving. However, the other way around is not true, as I showed in the cases of São Paulo and Salvador in Chapters 6 and 7, and this is what brings into our discussion the importance of the sanction element.

São Paulo makes for an instructive comparison because of the problems participatory budgeting faced in the city. However, unlike with participatory budgeting, where the inability of civil society to spread to the city as a whole became the main hindrance to deliberative and distributive effectiveness, São Paulo's health councils were widely considered to be an important form of participation, because of the historical origins of the popular health movement in the city's eastern district. Thus, São Paulo's health council produced both deliberative and distributive effects. The most important democratizing effect was the effort of the councils to define participation and to avoid cooptation. The most important distributive effect was the increased access of the poor to medical appointments, as I showed in Chapter 6.

Thus, the performance of the two participatory institutions in São Paulo reveals the strengths and weaknesses of their different designs: in the case of participatory budgeting, a classic bottom-up design, its dependency on political society undermined its implementation when political support faltered, whereas in the case of health councils, which were based on power-sharing designs, we observed positive democratizing and distributive effects, even under unfavorable administrations. I attribute this difference to two design elements. First, levels of mobilization do not have to be as high for power-sharing institutions as for bottom-up ones. Second, sanctions against state actors for noncompliance with the rules of participation strengthen power-sharing institutions. Thus, civil society organization connected with mandatory sanction in case of noncompliance differentiates power-sharing from bottom-up designs, showing the importance of the concept of interactive participatory designs.

This differentiation of participatory institutions also allows us to make a policy recommendation: in cases in which civil society is strong and political society is not eager to implement participatory policies, a power-sharing design is the most suitable form of participation. The insistence of governments, international institutions, and policy-makers to implement bottom-up design wherever they wish to sponsor participation may lead to participatory policies that are not as effective as they should be.

Nonetheless, Salvador's experience with health councils and city master plans shows that, even where sanctions are present, participatory institutions can still be ineffective. The case of Salvador is the most instructive about the limits and potentials of participatory institutions. Salvador did not implement participatory budgeting until 2005, and its health care movement was not very well organized. Salvador did have a strong presence of *sanitaristas,* but its neighborhood associations were not as active in the area of health because of the overconcentration of civic associations on ethnic issues (Baiocchi, 2007). The long-term political control of liberals (PFL) in the city has led to unusual participatory health legislation. Civil society representatives on Salvador's health councils do not deal directly with health. They are members of the Church and commerce and industry associations. As a result of the weak civil society representation in Salvador's council, its deliberative capacity has also been weak. In Chapter 6, I showed that government representatives in Salvador talked 20 times more in the health council meetings than in Belo Horizonte, while civil society representatives talked less than half as much. In addition, when we look into the distributive results we see that Salvador did not implement key health policies, such as city-funded beds in local hospitals.

The overall result in Salvador compared with São Paulo allows us to further differentiate among participatory designs: if power-sharing designs work better under unfavorable political conditions, as the comparison of participatory budgeting and health councils in São Paulo showed, it is also necessary to point out their main limitation, which is that power-sharing designs require the presence of a strong civil society organization represented in institutions. São Paulo's health associations never gave up in its dispute with the city administration over the composition of the city health council. Salvador does not have a health movement strong enough to play such a role. This difference is expressed in both the deliberative and distributive results of Salvador's participatory healthcare institution. Thus, the strength of civil society is the limit that differentiates the ability of government and international institutions to implement power-sharing participatory designs.

The Limits and Potential of Ratification Designs

City master plans are ratification designs, rather than bottom-up institutions, like participatory budgeting, because the plan emerges within the state administration and is only ratified by public audiences. Nor are they power-sharing institutions, like health councils, because the deliberative process they trigger does not lead to an institution but rather to an overlap between state and civil society on the rules governing urban expansion. In implementing city master plan, two new institutions played a key role, city councils and the judicial system. In Chapter 7, I compared four cases of city master plans—Porto Alegre, Belo Horizonte, São Paulo, and Salvador—to show how variation in design produced results different from participatory budgeting or health councils. The new element of design that I singled out is sanction through the judicial system associated with the blocking of executive branch actions. Though city master plans are the least empowering and the least deliberative among the participatory institutions discussed in the book, the sanction element makes it the participatory institution most enforceable in environments hostile to participation. City master plans are the participatory institution that interferes most with private interests.

Belo Horizonte's city master plan is the oldest of the four cases studied here and was approved in the first year of its PT administration. Belo Horizonte's plan introduced a feature that was emulated in almost all cities: an overlap of broad consultation in the regions and topical negotiations with private interests. The Belo Horizonte plan was approved by city council, a key actor for this kind of institution, but to win approval, the city negotiated a six-month postponement of enforcement, separating short- and long-term enforcement of the new rules.

Porto Alegre's planning process was very similar to Belo Horizonte. The city proposed its master plan as a result of the First Congress of the City. It was elaborated and sent to the city council in 1996. The plan was only approved by the city council after going back to civil society for a broad debate. One feature of the Porto Alegre case that should be singled out is the fact that the courts decided to legalize the occupation of public land by the poor, a kind a legal activism that would not occur elsewhere. The Belo Horizonte and Porto Alegre city master plans were successful for two reasons: (a) both cities managed to contain organized real state interests and approve a more equitable city development plan and (b) both cities managed to integrate different interests into a coalition approved by city council and not challenged by the courts. Indeed, all participatory institutions introduced in democratic Brazil worked well in these two cities.

In this regard, we can conclude that ratification designs, like power-sharing institutions, can be implemented in contexts in which bottom-up institutions have been successful. Porto Alegre and Belo Horizonte provide strong evidence in this direction. The issue that still needs elaboration is, which participatory institutions fit in a situation of strong civil society and a political society hostile to participation? The attempt to answer this question led me to examine the cases of São Paulo and Salvador to differentiate power-sharing institutions from ratification participatory institutions in their effectiveness.

São Paulo is also key to understanding the complexities of different institutional arrangements in the case of city master plans. Its city master plan was proposed by Marta Suplicy a few months after her inauguration and involved negotiations among civil society actors, urban planners, real estate interests, and the city council. The first proposed plan was submitted to public audiences and approved. However, real estate interests challenged the plan in the courts, claiming that their participation had been unduly limited. The courts accepted the claim, and a new round of public meetings followed in which the city master plan was kept intact. In the end, the key negotiation took place within the city council and involved adapting the plan to specific real estate interests in terms of zoning. Yet, in the long term São Paulo's master plan organized the city's expansion, curbed long-term land flipping, and gave the city instruments to pursue the settlement of the poor.

The deliberation of São Paulo's city master plan shows the differences between the three forms of participatory design discussed in the book. Participatory budgeting did not work well in the city because of the lack of a strong civil society across the city or a participatory consensus within political society. São Paulo's health councils faced similar limitations, but were successful after struggles with conservative administrations. Its city master plan seems also to be a positive case: conservative sectors were included in the negotiations, but in the end the city still had a progressive master plan. The difference between power-sharing designs and ratification designs seems to be the greater capacity of ratification to produce citywide deliberation among plural interests. The key element in São Paulo is that it has a strong civil society that can be active in institutions with sanction capacity, which makes ratification and power sharing designs successful.

The last issue that has to be dealt with is identifying the institutions best suited for cases in which civil society is weak and political society hostile to participation. This led me to the case of Salvador. Salvador's city master plan allows us to evaluate the effectiveness of different participatory designs in weak and hostile conditions. Salvador's city master plan was proposed in 1999 and sent to the city council in 2002. Most of the steps required by the legislation and carried out in the other three cities were not taken in Salvador. The diagnosis of the occupation of urban land was made almost in secret, with no urban planning associations being informed of the hiring of an out-of-state private consulting company. When the new plan was proposed, the minimum required number of public audiences was not met. The plan was sent to the city council and challenged in court as not following the requirements mandated by the Statute of the City. In the end, the court cancelled Salvador's plan and required the city to carry out the required public audiences.

Salvador is a limit case because the city had failed to implement participatory budgeting until 2005 and had implemented health councils in a form that departed from the common practices in Brazil and disempowered civil society actors. The difference between city master plans and the other designs in Salvador is that the ratification design punished nonimplementation, which in the two other cases led only to effectiveness problems. In this sense, ratification designs are the least empowering, but the most effective when civil society actors are not strong enough to influence the actions of political society. Ratification design is the only one that can play the role of blocking the action of power-holders when civil society is weak and political society is hostile to participation.

A Typology of Effectiveness
for Participatory Institutions

The 11 cases of participation considered in the book allow us to establish a typology of effectiveness for participatory institutions in different contexts (Table 8.1).

Bottom-up institutions work well with a highly empowered civil society and a pro-participation political society, delivering both deliberative and distributive results. Though this finding is not new (Abers, 2000; Avritzer, 2002a; Baiocchi, 2005), the contribution of this book is to show that when expanded to contexts that do not reproduce these conditions, bottom-up institutions become the less effective.

Power-sharing institutions are distinguished them from bottom-up institutions by two characteristics. First, they are more effective where civil society is weaker. The cases of health councils in São Paulo and Salvador are very instructive in this regard. Whereas participatory budgeting in São Paulo produced very weak deliberative and distributive results, health councils ensured democratic deliberations even under highly unfavorable political conditions, during the conservative Maluf and Pitta administrations. The same was partially true in Salvador. Whereas Salvador could not even have participatory budgeting between 1990 and 2004, it has a health council with limited prerogatives. The difference between Salvador and São Paulo lies in how active political society's opposition to the participatory institution is and how civil society reacts to it. Nevertheless, there is no doubt that bottom-up institutions, when they work well, produce better deliberative and distributive results than power-sharing institutions.

Table 8.1. Context and implementation of participatory institutions in four Brazilian cities

City	Context	Bottom-Up Participatory Institutions	Power Sharing Participatory Institutions	Ratification Participatory Institutions	Which Designs to Implement in Similar Cases?
Porto Alegre and Belo Horizonte	Strong civil society and political society united behind participation.	Strong and effective.	Strong and effective.	Strong and effective.	The three participatory institutions simultaneously.
São Paulo	Strong civil society and divided political society.	Relatively weak and ineffective.	Strong and effective.	Strong and effective.	To implement only power-sharing and ratification institutions.
Salvador	Weak civil society and political society hostile to participation.	Bottom up institutions could not be implemented.	Weak and ineffective.	Relatively weak, but effective in blocking power holders actions.	To implement participation in phases starting from ratification institutions.

The third participatory design discussed in the book is ratification. It has two main characteristics: it operates somewhat well even where civil society is weak and political society is nonparticipatory, and it has strong sanction mechanisms. São Paulo and Salvador express both elements. They also show that the city council and the courts make a huge difference in the implementation of ratification designs. Compared with bottom-up and power-sharing designs, ratification designs produce fewer deliberative effects. However, the fact that small deliberative and distributive effects may be produced under very unfavorable conditions should not be overlooked.

This typology of participatory institutions allows us both to place the Porto Alegre experiment in context and to answer the key questions posed in Chapters 1 and 4, namely, how should the participatory institutions be differentiated and which participatory institutions should be introduced in different contexts? The answer given in this book to the differentiation of participatory institution was to separate the will of power-holders to distribute power and resources from the sanction element incorporated into the operation of participatory institutions. Placing Porto Alegre's experiment in this broader context is not intended to devalue its political impact. On the contrary, it has become clear throughout the book that bottom-up institutions are the most democratic and the most distributive, and this is the reason participatory budgeting have become so popular.

Although this book has made a strong case that most of the attempts to expand Porto Alegre's participatory budgeting without focusing on context are bound to fail, it also has presented alternatives in these cases, which draw upon other institutionalized forms of participation with larger sanction capacity. I showed in Chapters 6 and 7 that these institutions produce better results in less favorable contexts.

Thus, variation in design, integrated to context, is the key variable that generates successful participatory institutions. Neither civil society nor political society alone can account for the success of participatory institutions, but we can see throughout this book that the interaction between civil and political society in the right institutional context can strengthen public deliberation and achieve significant distributional results. The further expansion of these institutions in Brazil, Latin America, and beyond will depend on the ability of the sponsors of participation to leave aside the laudatory phase on the virtues of bottom-up institutions and figure out that the best form of expanding participation is adapting it to the different contexts in which it is carried out.

References

Abers, Rebecca N. 1996. "From ideas to practice: The PT and participatory governance in Brazil." *Latin American Perspectives,* vol. 23, pp. 35–53.

———. 1998. "From clientelism to cooperation: Local government, participatory policy, and civic organizing in Porto Alegre, Brazil." *Politics and Society,* vol. 26, no. 4, pp. 511–37.

———. 2000. *Inventing local democracy: Grassroots politics in Brazil.* Boulder, Colo.: Lynne Rienner.

Abers, Rebecca N., and Keck, Margaret E. 2005. "Muddy waters: Decentralization, coordination and power struggle in the Brazilian water management reform." *International Journal for Urban and Regional Research* (forthcoming).

Aguayo, S. 1996. "A Mexican milestone." *Journal of Democracy,* April, pp. 157–67.

Alegretti, G. O. 2006. "Retorno das caravelas." Centro de Estudos Sociais, Coimbra. Manuscript.

Almanaque Folha. 2006. Available at http://www.uol.com.br/folha/almanaque. Accessed 6 June 2006.

Almeida Silva, Carla. 2002. "Os fóruns temáticos da sociedade civil: um estudo sobre o fórum nacional de reforma urbana." In Dagnino, Evelina, ed. *Sociedade civil e espaços públicos no Brasil.* São Paulo: Paz e Terra, pp. 143–83.

Almond, Gabriel. 1970. *Political development.* Boston: Little, Brown.

Almond, Gabriel, and Verba, Sidney. 1963. *The civic culture: Political attitudes and democracy in five nations.* Princeton, N.J.: Princeton University Press.

———. 1989. *The civic culture revisited.* Thousand Oaks, Calif.: Sage Publications. 376 pp.

Alvarez, Sonia; Dagnino, E.; and Escobar, A. 1998. *Cultures of politics, politics of cultures: Re-visioning Latin American social movements.* Boulder, Colo.: Westview Press.

Alvarez, Sonia E., and Escobar, Arturo. 1992. *The making of social movements in Latin America: Identity, strategy, and democracy.* Boulder, Colo.: Westview Press. 400 pp.

Alves, Maria Helena Moreira. 1988. *State and opposition in military Brazil.* Austin: University of Texas Press.

Ames, Barry. 2002. *The deadlock of democracy in Brazil: Interests, identities, and comparative politics.* Ann Arbor: Michigan University Press. 352 pp.

175

Andrioli, Antônio. 2004. *A reforma agrária e o governo Lula: entre a expectativa e a possibilidade.* Available at http://www.espacoacedemico.com.br. Accessed 8 May 2006.

Antonucci, Denise. 1999. *Plano diretor de São Paulo - 1991 Avanços e permanências.* Universidade de São Paulo. Dissertação (Máster).

Arato, Andrew. 1981. "Civil society against the state: Poland 1980–81." *Telos,* vol. 4 (Spring), pp. 23–47.

Archon, Fung, and Wright, Erik O., eds. 2003. *Deepening democracy: Institutional innovations in empowered participatory governance.* Real Utopias Project. London: Verso Press. 224 pp.

Armony, Ariel C. 2004. *The dubious link: Civic engagement and democratization.* Stanford, Calif.: Stanford University Press. 312 pp.

Arouca, Sergio. 2003. *O dilema preventista: contribuições e crítica da medicina preventiva.* São Paulo: Editora UNESP; Rio de Janeiro: Editora FIOCRUZ. 268 pp.

Arretche, Marta. 2004. "Toward a unified and more equitable system: Health reform in Brazil." In Kaufman, Robert, and Nelson, Joan, eds. *Crucial needs, weak incentives.* Washington/Baltimore/London: Woodrow Wilson Center Press and The Johns Hopkins University Press, pp. 155–88.

Arruda, Inácio. 2001. *Estatuto da cidade uma conquista histórica.* Available at http://www.inacio.com.br/downloads/ESTATUTO_DA_CIDADE_SEPARATA_2001.doc. Accessed 29 May 2006.

———. 2006. *Nota política sobre os vetos do estatuto e as conquistas da reforma urbana.* Available at http://www.camara.gov.br/inaciorarruda/noticias/vetosestatuto .htm. Accessed 20 March 2006.

Arturi, C. S. 2001. "O debate teórico sobre mudança de regime político: O caso brasileiro." *Revista de Sociologia e Política,* vol. 17, pp. 11–31.

Avritzer, Leonardo. 1994. "Modelos de sociedade civil: Uma análise da especificidade do caso brasileiro." In Avritzer, Leonardo, ed. *Sociedade civil e democratização.* Belo Horizonte: Del Rey, pp. 269–303.

———. 1995. "Transition to democracy and political culture: An analysis of the conflict between civil and political society in post-authoritarian Brazil." *Constellations,* vol. 2, no. 2, pp. 242–67.

———. 1996. *A moralidade da democracia.* São Paulo: Perspectiva; Belo Horizonte: Editora da UFMG. 176 pp.

———. 1997. "Um desenho institucional para o novo associativismo." *Lua Nova,* no. 39, pp.148–74.

———. 1999. "The conflict between civil and political societies in post-authoritarian Brazil: An analysis of the impeachment of Collor de Mello." In Rosenn, Keith S., and Downes, Richard, eds. *Corruption and political reform in Brazil: The impact of Collor's impeachment.* Miami: North South Center.

———. 2000. "Democratization and changes in the pattern of association in Brazil." *Journal of Interamerican Studies and World Affairs,* vol. 42, no. 3 (Fall), pp. 59–76.

———. 2002a. *Democracy and the public space in Latin America.* Princeton: Princeton University Press. 205 pp.

———. 2002b. "Orçamento participativo: as experiências de Porto Alegre e Belo Horizonte." In Dagnino, Evelina, ed. *Sociedade civil e espaços públicos no Brasil.* São Paulo: Paz e Terra.

———. 2002c. "Modelos de deliberação democrática: Uma análise do orçamento participativo no Brasil." In Santos, Boaventura de Sousa, ed. *Democratizar a democracia*. Rio de Janeiro: Record, pp. 561–92.

———. 2003. "O orçamento participativo e a teoria democrática: um balanço crítico." In Avritzer, Leonardo, and Navarro, Zander, eds. *A Inovação Democrática no Brasil*. São Paulo: Cortez Editora, pp. 13–60.

———, ed. 2004. *A participação em São Paulo*. São Paulo: Editora UNESP. 470 pp.

———. 2005. "El ascenso del partido de los trabajadores en Brasil: La democracia y la distribucion participativas como alternativas al neoliberalismo." In Garavito, César A. Rodriguez; Barrett, Patrick S.; and Chavez, Daniel, eds. *La nueva izquierda en América Latina: sus orígenes y trayectoria futura*, vol. 1. Bogotá: Norma Editores, pp. 1–460.

———. 2006. "New public spheres in Brazil." *International Journal of Urban Regional Research*, vol. 30, no. 3, pp. 623–37.

———. 2007. *A participação social no nordeste*. Belo Horizonte: Editora UFMG.

Avritzer, Leonardo, et al. 2005. "Reiventando os mecanismos de inclusão e controle social nos conselhos de saúde." Available at http://www.democraciaparticipativa.org/pesquisas. Accessed 10 May 2006.

Avritzer, Leonardo, and Navarro, Zander, eds. 2003. *A inovação democrática no Brasil: O orçamento participativo*. São Paulo: Cortez Editora. 335 pp.

Avritzer, Leonardo, and Pereira, Maria de Lourdes Dolabela. 2005. "Democracia, participação e instituições híbridas." *Teoria and Sociedade* (UFMG), pp. 16–41.

Avritzer, Leonardo, and Pires, Roberto Rocha. 2005. "Orçamento participativo, efeitos distributivos e combate à pobreza." *Teoria and Sociedade* (UFMG), pp. 68–89.

Azevedo, Clovis Bueno. 1995. *A estrela rachada ao meio*. São Paulo: Entrelinhas.

Azevedo, Sérgio, and Prates, Antônio Augusto. 1991. "Planejamento participativo, movimentos sociais e ação coletiva." *Ciências Sociais Hoje*. Rio de Janeiro: Relume Dumará.

Bachrach, Peter, and Baratz, Morton S. 1962. "The two faces of power." *American Political Science Review*, vol. 56, no. 4 (Dec.), pp. 947–52.

———. 1975. "Power and its two faces revisited: A Reply to Geoffrey Debnam." *American Political Science Review*, vol. 69, no. 3 (Sept.), pp. 900–904.

Bacqué, Marie-Hélène; Rey, Henri; and Sintomer, Yves, eds. 2005. *Gestion de proximité et démocratie délibérative: Une perspective comparative*. Paris: La Découverte.

Baierle, S. G. 1998. "The explosion of experience: The emergence of a new ethical-political principle in popular movements in Porto Alegre, Brazil." In Alvarez, S. E.; Dagnino, E.; and Escobar, A., eds. *Cultures of politics, politics of cultures: Re-visioning Latin American social movements*. Boulder, Colo.: Westview Press.

Baiocchi, Gianpaolo. 2002. "Synergizing civil society: State-civil society regimes and democratic decentralization in Porto Alegre, Brazil." *Political Power and Social Theory*, vol. 15, pp. 3–86.

———. 2003. "Participation, activism and politics." In Fung, A., and Wright, E., eds. *Deepening democracy: Institutional innovations in empowered participatory governance*. Real Utopias Project. London: Verso Press.

———. 2005. *Militants and citizens: the politics of participation in Porto Alegre*. Stanford, Calif.: Stanford University Press. 224 pp.

———. 2007. "Uma etnografia sobre sociedade civil, raça e participação: O caso curioso do associativismo étnico em Salvador, Bahia." In Avritzer, Leonardo, ed. *A participação social no Nordeste*. Belo Horizonte: Editora UFMG.

Banfield, Edward. 1959. *The moral basis of a backward society.* Glencoe, Ill.: Free Press.

Baquero, M. 1995. "Matriz histórico-estrutural da cultura política no Rio Grande do Sul e padrões de participação política." In *Cadernos de Ciência Política,* no. 3. Programa de pós-graduação em Ciência Política, Universidade Federal do Rio Grande do Sul, Porto Alegre.

Barbosa, Vivaldo Vieira. 1980. "Law and the authoritarian state: The modern roots of the authoritarian corporative state in Brazil 1930–1945." Cambridge, Mass.: Harvard University. Ph.D. dissertation.

Barnes, M. 1999. "Users as citizens: Collective action and the local governance of welfare." *Social Policy and Administration,* vol. 33, no. 1, pp. 73–90.

Barros, Mauricio Rands. 1999. *Labour relations and the new unionism in contemporary Brazil.* Basingstoke: Palgrave Macmillan. 343 pp.

Barry, Brian. 1970. *Sociologists, economists and democracy.* London: Macmillan.

Bassul, José Roberto. 2005. *Estatuto da cidade: Quem ganhou? Quem perdeu?* Brasília: Senado Federal, Subsecretaria de Edições Técnicas.

Belo Horizonte. 1998. Lei n. 7.536, de 19 de junho de 1998, que dispõe sobre o Regimento Interno do Conselho Municipal de saúde de Belo Horizonte. Available at http://www.pbh.gov.br/smsa/conselho/regimento.doc. Accessed 14 June 2006.

———. 2002. Orçamento Participativo 2001–2002. Revista Planejar BH. Secretária municipal de planejamento, ano. 3, no. 10, pp. 24–25.

Bobbio, Norberto. 1987. *The future of democracy: A defence of the rules of the game.* Mineapolis: University of Minnesota Press. 184 pp.

Boschi, Renato R. 1987. *A arte da associação: Política de base e de democracia no Brasil.* Rio de Janeiro, Vértice/Iuperj.

———. 1999. "Descentralização, clientelismo e capital social na governança urbana: Comparando Belo Horizonte e Salvador." *Dados - Revista de Ciências Sociais,* Rio de Janeiro, vol. 42, no. 4, pp. 655–90.

Bouquat, Aylene; Cohn, Amélia; and Elias, P. E. 2006. "Implementation of the family health program and socio-spatial exclusion in the city of São Paulo, Brazil." Cad. Saúde Pública [online], vol. 22, no. 9, pp. 1935–43. Available at http://www.scielo.br/scielo.php?script=sci_arttext&pid=S0102-311X2006000900025&lng=en&nrm=iso. Accessed 3 April 2008.

Brasil. 1968. Ato Institucional Número 5. Presidência da República.

———. 1988. Constituição da República Federativa do Brasil. Brasília, DF, Senado.

———. 1990. Lei 8.142 de 28 de Dezembro de 1990 que dispõe sobre a participação da comunidade na gestão do Sistema Único de Saúde (SUS) e sobre as transferências intergovernamentais de recursos financeiros na área da saúde. Available at http://www.conselho.saude.gov.br. Accessed 12 May 2006.

———. 2006. Ministério da Saúde. Lei Orgânica da Saúde. Assessoria de Comunicação Social, 2ª ed.

Brasil, Flávia de Paula Duque. 2004. Espaços públicos, participação cidadã e renovação nas políticas urbanas locais nos anos 80. Belo Horizonte: FAFICH/UFMG. Dissertação de Mestrado em sociologia. 247 pp.

Breiner, Peter. 1996. *Max Weber and democratic politics.* Ithaca, N.Y.: Cornell University Press.

Bresser-Pereira, Luiz Carlos. 2004. *Democracy and public management reform: Building the republican state.* New York: Oxford University Press. 317 pp.

Bruneau, Thomas. 1974. *The political transformation of the Brazilian Catholic Church.* Cambridge: Cambridge University Press.

Cabanes, Yves. 2004. *Towards a more inclusive and effective participatory budget in Porto Alegre.* Washington, D.C.: World Bank.

Caldeira, Teresa. 2000. *São Paulo, city of walls.* Berkeley: University of California Press.

Caldeira, Teresa, and Holston, James. 2004. "Estado e espaço urbano no Brasil: Do planejamento modernista às intervenções democráticas." In Avritzer, Leonardo, ed. *A participação em São Paulo.* São Paulo: UNESP, pp. 215–56.

Calhoun, Craig. 1992. *Habermas and the public sphere.* Cambridge, Mass.: MIT Press.

Cammach, P. 1990. "Brazil: The long march to the new republic." *New Left Review,* vol.190, pp. 21–58.

Cardoso, Fernando Henrique. 1989. "Associated-dependent development and democratic theory." In Stepan, A., ed. *Democratizing Brazil: Problems of transition and consolidation.* New York: Oxford University Press. 424 pp.

Caribe, Daniel. 2005. Plano diretor de desenvolvimento urbano de Salvador: Alguns limites para a implementação da participação cidadã na elaboração do projeto. Trabalho de conclusão na disciplina "Governo Local e Cidadania," Mestrado em Administração, UFBA. Manuscript..

Carvalho, Antonio Ivo de. 1995. *Conselhos de saúde no Brasil: Participação cidadã e controle social.* Rio de Janeiro: FASE/IBAM.

Carvalho, J. M. 1998. *Pontos e bordados: Escritos de história e política.* Belo Horizonte: Editora UFMG. 457 pp.

Carvalho, José Murilo. 2001. *Cidadania no Brasil: O longo caminho,* vol. 1. Rio de Janeiro: Civilização Brasileira. 236 pp.

Casanova, José. 1994. *Public religions in the modern world.* Chicago: University of Chicago Press.

Cavalcante Fadul, E. M., and Silva, Mônica de Aguiar Macallister da. 2005. "Plano diretor de desenvolvimento urbano de Salvador." Manuscript.

Cavalcanti, Bianor Scelza. 2006. "A gerência equalizadora: Estratégias de gestão no setor público." In Martins, Paulo Emílio Matos, and Pieranti, Octavio Penna, eds. *Estado e Gestão Pública: Visões do Brasil Contemporâneo.* Editora FGV, pp. 277–312.

Cavarozzi, Marcelo.1992. "Beyond transitions to democracy." *Journal of Latin American Studies,* vol. 24, no. 3, pp. 665–84.

Cidade (Centro de Assessoria e Estudos Urbanos). 1999. "Orçamento participativo– Quem é a população que participa e que pensa do processo" (The Participatory budget: Who participates and what they think of the process). Porto Alegre, Brasil.

Chilcote, R. H. 1982. *Partido comunista brasileiro: Conflito e integração.* Rio de Janeiro: Graal.

Coelho, V. S. R. P. 2004. "Conselhos de saúde enquanto instituições políticas: O que está faltando?" In Coelho, Vera Schattan R. P., and Nobre, Nobre, eds. *Participação e deliberação.* São Paulo: 34 Letras, pp. 255–69.

Coelho, V. S. R. P. et al. 2006. *Projeto – Participação e distribuição de serviços públicos de saúde no município de São Paulo.* Research report. São Paulo: Cebrap.

Coelho, V. S. R. P., and Veríssimo, José. 2004. "Considerações sobre o processo de escolha dos representantes da sociedade civil nos conselhos de saúde em São Paulo."

In Avritzer, Leonardo, ed. *Participação em São Paulo.* São Paulo: Editora UNESP, pp.105–22.

Cohen, Jean L. 1985. "Strategy or identity: New theoretical paradigms and contemporary social movements." *Social Research,* vol. 52, no. 4, pp. 663–716.

———. 1996. "The public sphere, the media and civil society." In Sajo, Andras, ed. *Rights of access to the media.* The Hague: Kluwer.

———. 1997. "Procedure and substance in deliberative democracy." In Bohman, J., and Regh, W. *Deliberative democracy.* Cambridge, Mass.: MIT Press.

Cohen, Jean L., and Arato, Andrew. 1992. *Civil society and political theory.* Cambridge, Mass.: MIT Press.

Cohen, Joshua, and Rogers, Joel. 1995. *Associations and democracy.* London: Verso Press.

———. 2003. "Power and reason." In Fung, A. and Wright, E. O., eds. *Deepening democracy.* London: Verso Press.

Cohn, Amélia. 2002. Equidade e reformas na saúde nos anos 90, vol. 18. Rio de Janeiro: Cadernos de Saúde Pública.

Conniff, Michel. 1975. "Voluntary association in Rio: 1870–1945." *Journal of Interamerican Studies and World Affairs,* vol. 17, no. 1, pp. 64–82.

Copp, David, ed. 1995. *The idea of democracy.* Cambridge: Cambridge University Press. 461 pp.

Cordeiro, Hésio. 2004. "The institute of social medicine and the health reform struggle: A contribution to the history of the unified national health system in Brazil." *Physis,* vol. 14, no. 2, pp. 343–62.

Cornwall, A., and Brock, K. 2005. "What do buzzwords do for development policy? A critical look at 'participation', 'empowerment' and 'poverty reduction.'" *Third World Quarterly,* vol. 26, no. 7, pp. 1043–60.

Cornwall, Andréa, and Coelho, V. S. R. P. 2007. *Spaces for change? The politics of citizen participation in new democratic arenas,* vol. 1. London: Zed Books. 270 pp.

Cortes, S. M. V. 2002. "Construindo a possibilidade da participação dos usuários: conselhos e conferências no Sistema Único de Saúde." *Sociologias,* Porto Alegre, vol. 7, pp. 18–49.

———. 2005. "Arcabouço histórico-institucional e a conformação de conselhos municipais de políticas públicas." *Educar em revista,* Curitiba, vol. 25, pp. 143–74.

Costa, Ricardo Cesar Rocha da. 2002. "Descentralização, financiamento e regulação: A reforma do sistema público de saúde no Brasil durante a década de 1990." *Rev. Sociol. Polit.* no. 18, pp. 49–71.

Costa, Sergio. 1997. "Movimentos sociais, democratização e construção de esferas públicas locais." *Revista Brasileira de Ciências Sociais,* São Paulo, vol.12, no. 35, pp.121–34.

Couto, Cláudio G. 1995. *O desafio de ser governo: o PT na prefeitura de São Paulo (1989–1992).* Rio de Janeiro: Paz e Terra. 264 pp.

Couto, Cláudio G., and Abrucio, Fernando Luiz. 2003. "O segundo governo FHC: Coalizões, agendas e instituições." *Revista Tempo Social,* São Paulo, vol. 15, no. 2, pp. 269–301.

Criterium (Criterium Pesquisas de Opinião e Avaliação de Políticas Públicas). 2003. *Expectativa governo Lula.* São Paulo.

Cunha, Eleonora S. M. 2004. *Aprofundando a democracia: O potencial de conselhos de políticas e orçamentos participativos.* Departamento de Ciência Política, Faculdade de Filosofia e Ciência Humanas, Universidade Federal de Minas Gerais, Belo Horizonte. Dissertação (Mestrado).

Dahl, Robert. 1990. *Democracy and its critics.* New Haven: Yale University Press.

Dagnino, Evelina, ed. 1994. *Anos 90: Política e sociedade no Brasil.* São Paulo: Brasiliense. 172 pp.

————, ed. 2002. *Sociedade civil e espaços públicos no Brasil.* São Paulo: Paz e Terra/ Unicamp. 364 pp.

Dagnino, Evelina, and Teixeira, Ana Cláudia. 1998. "Cultura democrática e cidadania." *Opinião Pública,* vol. 5, no. 1, pp. 11–43.

Dagnino, Evelina; Olvera, Alberto J.; and Panfichi, Aldo, eds. 2006. *A disputa pela construção democrática na América Latina.* São Paulo: Paz e Terra. 501 pp.

DaMatta, Roberto. 1979. *Carnavais, malandros e heróis: Para uma sociologia do dilema brasileiro.* Rio de Janeiro: Zahar Editores.

————. 1985. *A casa and a rua: Espaço, cidadania, mulher e morte no Brasil.* São Paulo: Brasiliense.

Datasus. 2002. *Brasil,* Ministério da Saúde. Indicadores básicos de saúde no Brasil: conceitos e aplicações [texto na Internet]. Brasília. Available at http://tabnet.datasus .gov.br/cgi/idb2005/public.htm. Accessed 11 November 2005.

Diamond, Larry. 1989. *Democracy in developing countries.* Boulder, Colo.: Lynne Rienner.

————. 1994. "Toward democratic consolidation." *Journal of Democracy,* vol. 5, no. 3 (July), pp. 4–17

Diamond, Larry, and Gunter, Richard, eds. 2001. *Political parties and democracy.* Baltimore: The Johns Hopkins University Press and National Endowment for Democracy. 392 pp.

Dias, Márcia R. 2002. *Sob o signo da vontade popular: O orçamento participativo e o dilema da Câmara Municipal de Porto Alegre.* Belo Horizonte: Editora UFMG. 305 pp.

Doimo, Ana Maria. 1995. *A vez e a voz do popular: Movimentos sociais e a participação política no Brasil pós-70.* Rio de Janeiro: Relume-Dumará, ANPOCS.

————. 2004. "Pluralidade religiosa à brasileira, associativismo e movimentos sociais em São Paulo." In Avritzer, Leonardo, ed. *A participação em São Paulo.* São Paulo: Editora UNESP, pp. 123–96.

Doimo, A. M., and Rodrigues, M. M. A. 2003. "A formulação da nova política de saúde no Brasil em tempos de democratização: Entre uma conduta estadista e uma concepção societal da atuação política." *Política and Sociedade,* Florianópolis, Santa Catarina, vol. 1, no. 3, pp. 95–115.

Domingues, Jose Maurício. 2006. *Modernity reconstructed.* Cardiff: University of Wales Press.

Douglas, M. 1986. *How institutions think.* Syracuse, N.Y.: Syracuse University Press. 146 pp.

Draibe, Sonia. 2002. "Social policies in the nineties." In Baumann, Renato, ed. *Brazil in the 1990s: An economy in transition.* Basingstoke: Palgrave Macmillan.

Dryzek, J. S. 2002. *Deliberative democracy and beyond: Liberals, critics, contestations.* New York: Oxford University Press. 208 pp.

Duverger, Maurice. 1951. *Les partis politiques.* Paris: Librairie Armand Colin.

————.1964. *Political parties: Their organization and activity in the modern state.* London: Routledge and Kegan Paul. 439 pp.

Elias, Paulo Eduardo.1999. "PAS: Um perfil neoliberal de gestão de sistema público de saúde." *Estud. av,* vol. 13, no. 35, pp.125–37.

Erickson, Kenneth Paul. 1977. *The Brazilian corporative state and working-class politics.* Berkeley: University of California Press. 255 pp.

Escobar, Arturo, and Alvarez, Sonia E. 1992. *The making of new social movements in Latin America: Identity, strategy, and democracy.* Boulder, Colo.: Westview Press. 400 pp.

Escorel, Sarah. 1998. *Reviravolta na saúde: Origem e articulação do movimento sanitário.* Rio de Janeiro: Editora FIOCRUZ.

————. 1999. *"Vidas ao Léu – trajetórias de exclusão social."* Rio de Janeiro: Editora FIOCRUZ.

Escorel, Sarah et al. 2005. "As origens da reforma sanitária e do SUS." In Lima, E. M., et al., eds. *Saúde e democracia: história e perspectivas do SUS.* Rio de Janeiro: Editora FIOCRUZ, pp. 59–81.

Esping-Andersen, Gøsta. 1990. *The three worlds of welfare capitalism.* Princeton, N.J.: Princeton University Press. 260 pp.

————. 1996. "After the golden age? Welfare state dilemmas in a global economy." In Esping-Andersen, Gøsta, ed. *Welfare states in transition, national adaptations in global economies.* Thousand Oaks, Calif.: Sage Publications Ltd.

Estado de São Paulo. 2002. "Plano diretor aprovado inclui mudanças em zonas residenciais." 23 de agosto. Available at http://www.estadao.com.br/agestado/ noticias/ 2002/ago/23/305.htm. Accessed 20 May 2006.

Evers, Tilman. 1985. "Identity: The hidden side of new social movements in Latin America." In Slater, David, ed. *New social movements and the state in Latin America.* Amsterdam: CEDLA, pp. 43–71.

Faria, Cláudia Feres. 2005. O estado em movimento: Complexidade social e participação política no Rio Grande do Sul. Fafich–UFMG, Belo Horizonte. Tese de Doutorado. Doutorado em Ciências Humanas: Sociologia e Política.

Fernandes, Edésio. 1998. "A regularização de favelas no Brasil: O caso de Belo Horizonte." In Fernandes, Edésio, ed. *Direito Urbanístico.* Belo Horizonte: Del Rey, pp.133–67.

————. 2001. "Direito urbanístico e política urbana no Brasil: Uma introdução." In Fernandes, Edésio, ed. *Direito urbanístico e política urbana no Brasil.* Belo Horizonte: Del Rey, pp. 11–54.

————. 2002. "Do código civil de 1916 ao estatuto da cidade: Algumas notas sobre a trajetória do direito urbanístico no Brasil." In Mattos, Liana Portilho, ed. *Estatuto da cidade comentado.* Belo Horizonte: Mandamentos, pp. 31–64.

Ferreira, M. 1999. "Associativismo e contato político nas regiões metropolitanas do Brasil: 1988–1996. Revisitando o problema da participação." *Revista Brasileira de Ciências Sociais,* vol. 14, no. 41, pp. 90–102.

Fischer, Tânia, and Moura, S. 1996. "De Pelourinho: A shopping cultural." *Revista de Administração de Empresas,* Rio de Janeiro, vol. 33, no. 2, pp. 90–99.

Fleury, Sonia, ed. 1997. *Saúde e democracia: a luta do CEBES.* São Paulo: Editora Lemos.

Fleury, Sonia; Berlinguer, Giovanni; and Campos, Gastão. 1989. *Reforma sanitária: Brasil e Italia.* São Paulo: HUCITEC/CEBES.

Flynn, Peter. 2005. "Brazil and Lula, 2005: Crisis, corruption and change in political perspective." *Third World Quarterly,* vol. 26, no. 8, pp. 1221–67.

Folha de São Paulo. 2000. "30 mil podem ficar fora de pré-escola." 29 September 2000, p. C7.

———. 2002. "Moradores e construtoras duelam na Vila Mariana." 29 September 2002, p. C2.

———. 2003a. "Entidades criticam planos diretores." 13 November 2003, p. C10.

———. 2003b. "Planos regionais terão de voltar à discussão." 20 December 2003, p. C3.

———. 2004. "Tucanos vão atacar ação na saúde." 8 April 2004, p. C4.

———. 2005a. "Chegada ao poder matou Campo, diz analista." 2 September 2005, p. A 15.

———. 2005b. "Por que não mais PT?" 27 September 2005, p. A 3.

Fox, Jonathan A. 1994. "The difficult transition from clientelism to citizenship: Lessons from Mexico." *World Politics,* vol. 46, no. 2 (Jan.), pp. 151–84.

———. 1996. "How does civil society thicken? The political construction of social capital in rural Mexico." *World Development,* vol. 24, no. 6, pp. 1086–1103.

———. 1998. *The Struggle for accountability: The World Bank, NGOs, and grassroots movements.* Cambridge, Mass.: MIT Press.

———. 2005. "Unpacking transnational citizenship." *Center for Global, International and Regional Studies. Annual Review of Political Science,* vol. 8, pp. 171–201.

Fraser, Nancy. 2003. "Social justice in the age of identity politics: Redistribution, recognition, and participation." In Fraser, Nancy, and Honneth, Axel, eds. *Redistribution or recognition? A political-philosophical exchange.* London: Verso Press.

French, John D. 1992. *The Brazilian workers' ABC: Class conflict and alliances in modern São Paulo.* Chapel Hill: University of North Carolina Press.

———. 2004. *Drowning in laws: Labor law and Brazilian political culture.* Chapel Hill: University of North Carolina Press.

Fuks, Mário. 2005. "Participação e influência política no Conselho Municipal de Saúde de Curitiba." *Revista de Sociologia e Política,* Curitiba, no. 25 (Nov.), pp. 47–61.

Fukuyama, F. 1995. *Trust: The social virtues and creation of prosperity.* New York: Free Press.

Fung, Archon, and Wright, Erik O., eds. 2003. *Deepening democracy: Institutional innovations in empowered participatory governance.* Real Utopias Project. London: Verso Press. 224 pp.

Gaspari, Helio. 2003. *A ditadura derrotada.* São Paulo: Companhia das Letras.

Gay, Robert. 1994. *Popular organization and democracy in Rio de Janeiro.* Philadelphia, Pa.: Temple University Press.

Gerschman, S. 1995. *A democracia inconclusa: Um estudo da reforma sanitária brasileira.* Rio de Janeiro: Editora FIOCRUZ.

Giddens, Anthony. 1984. *The constitution of society.* Berkeley: University of California Press.

———. 1991. *Modernity and self-identity: Self and society in the late modern age.* Stanford, Calif.: Stanford University Press. 256 pp.

Gohn, M. G. M. 1991. *Movimentos sociais e lutas pela moradia.* São Paulo: Edições Loyola.

Goldfrank, Benjamin. 2001. *Quem vai participar do OP quando todas as ruas estiverem pavimentadas?* Berkeley: University of California Press.

———. 2005. "The Politics of deepening local democracy: Decentralization, party institutionalization, and participation," Midwest Political Science Association Conference, Chicago, April.

Grazia, Grazia de. 2001. "Reforma urbana e o estatuto da cidade." In *Fundação João Pinheiro: Gestão urbana e de cidades.* Belo Horizonte: Fundação João Pinheiro/ Lincoln Institute of Land Policy.

Grazia, Grazia de, and Ribeiro, Ana Clara T. 2003. *Experiências do orçamento participativo no Brasil: Período de 1997 a 2000.* Petrópolis: Editora Vozes. 120 pp.

Gret, M., and Sintomer, Y. 2002. *Porto Alegre: L'espoir d'une autre démocratie.* Paris: La Découverte.

Gugliano, Alfredo. 2007. *Sobre o ato ou efeito de participar: O caso da descentralização participativa de Montevidéu.* Seminário Arranjos Participativos no Mercosul. Belo Horizonte, MG, Projeto Democracia Participativa, UFMG. Available at http:// www.democraciaparticipativa.org. Accessed 2 April 2007.

Guimaraens, Maria Etelvina. 2001. *O plano diretor de desenvolvimento urbano ambiental.* Porto Alegre. Manuscript.

Guimarães, Juarez. 2004. *A esperança equilibrista: O governo Lula em tempos de transição.* Fundação Perseu Abramo. 168 pp.

Gunther, R.; Montero, J. R.; and Linz, J., eds. 2002. *Political parties: Old concepts and new challenges.* Oxford: Oxford University Press. 384 pp.

Gutmann, Amy, and Thompson, Dennis. 1996. *Democracy and disagreement.* London: Belknap Press of Harvard University Press.

———. 2003. "Deliberative democracy." In Hess, Andreas, ed. *American social and political thought.* New York: New York University Press, pp. 256–62.

Habermas, Jurgen. 1984. *Theory of communicative action.* Translated by Thomas McCarthy. Boston: Beacon Press.

———. 1989. *The structural transformation of the public sphere.* Cambridge: Mass.: MIT Press.

———. 1992. "Further reflections on the public sphere." In Calhoun, C., ed. *Habermas and the public sphere.* Cambridge, Mass.: MIT Press.

———. 1994. "Three normative models of democracy." *Constellations: An International Journal of Critical and Democratic Theory,* vol. 1, no. 1, pp. 1–10.

———. 1995. *Between facts and norms.* Translated by William Regh. Cambridge, Mass.: MIT Press.

Hagopian, Frances. 1996. *Traditional politics and regime change in Brazil.* Cambridge: Cambridge University Press.

Hall, P. A., and Taylor, R.C.R. 1996. "Political science and the three new institutionalisms." *Political Studies,* no. 44, pp. 936–57.

Held, David. 1989. *Political theory and the modern state.* Cambridge: Polity Press. 276 pp.

Heller, P., and Isaac, T. M. T. 2006. "The politics and institutional design of participatory democracy: Lessons from Kerala, India." In de Sousa, Santos B., ed. *Democratizing democracy: Beyond the liberal democratic canon.* London: Verso Press, pp. 405–46.

Hobsbawm, Eric J. 1996. *The age of extremes: A history of the world, 1914–1991.* New York: Vintage Books. 672 pp.

Hollanda, Sergio Buarque de. 1937. *Raízes do Brasil.* Rio de Janeiro: José Olympio.

Holston, J. 1993. "Legalizando o ilegal: Propriedade e usurpação no Brasil." *Revista Brasileira de Ciências Sociais,* vol. 8, no. 21, pp. 68–98.

Houtzager, P.; Gurza, Lavalle; and Charya, A. 2003. "Who participates? Civil society and the new democratic politics in São Paulo, Brasil." *Institute of Development Studies: Working Papers,* Sussex, vol. 210, pp. 1–72.

Humphrey, John. 1982. *Capitalist control and workers' struggle in the Brazilian auto industry.* Princeton, N.J.: Princeton University Press. 258 pp.

Hunter, Wendy. 2006. "The normalization of an anomaly: The workers' party in Brazil." Paper presented at XXVI *International Congress of the Latin American Studies Association* (LASA), March, San Juan.

Huntington, Samuel P. 1993. *The third wave: Democratization in the late twentieth century.* Revised ed. Norman: University of Oklahoma Press. 384 pp.

Huntington, Samuel. 1996. *The clash of civilizations and the remaking of world order.* New York: Simon and Schuster.

Inglehart, Ronald. 1989. *Culture shift in advanced industrial society.* Princeton, N.J.: Princeton University Press. 504 pp.

———. 1997. *Modernization and post-modernization.* Princeton, N.J.: Princeton University Press. 440 pp.

IBGE (Instituto Brasileiro de Geografia e Estatística). 1996. Pesquisa Nacional de Emprego (PNE). Pesquisa Suplementar Associativismo, representação de interesses e intermediação política. Available at http://www.ibge.gov.br. Accessed 5 May 2003.

———. 1998. Base de dados metodologia: micro dados da PNAD 1998. Rio de Janeiro: IBGE. Available at http://.ibge.gov.br. Accessed 12 May 2003.

———. 2002. *Perfil dos municípios brasileiros: Gestão pública 2001.* Coordenação de População e Indicadores Sociais. Rio de Janeiro. 245 pp. Available at http://www .ibge.gov.br/home/estatistica/economia/perfilmunic/2001/munic2001.pdf. Accessed 1 June 2006.

Ireland, Rowan. 1999. "Popular religions and the building of democracy in Latin America: Saving the Tocquevillian parallel." *Journal of Interamerican Studies and World Affairs,* vol. 41, no. 4 (Special Issue: Religion in America: Churches, Globalization, and Democratization, Winter), pp. 111–36.

Jacobi, P. 1986. Políticas públicas de saneamento básico e reivindicações sociais no município de São Paulo. 1974–1984. Faculdade de Filosofia, Letras e Ciências Humanas, Universidade de São Paulo. São Paulo: Cortez Editora. Tese de Doutorado.

Jelin, Elizabeth, and Hershberg, Eric. 1996. *Constructing democracy: Human rights, citizenship and society in Latin America.* Boulder, Colo.: Westview Press.

Jeperson, R. L. 1991. "Institutions, institutional effects and institutionalism." In Powell, Walter W., and DiMaggio, Paul J., eds. *The new institutionalism in organizational analysis.* Chicago: University of Chicago Press.

Kaase, Max, and Newton, Kenneth. 1995. *Beliefs in government.* New York: Oxford University Press.

Kaldor, Mary. 1995. "European institutions, nation-states and nationalism." In Archibugi, Daniele, and Held, David, eds. *Cosmopolitan Democracy.* Cambridge: Polity Press.

Keck, Margaret E. 1989. "The new unionism in the Brazilian transition." In *Democratizing Brazil.* New York: Oxford University Press.

———. 1991. *A lógica da diferença.* São Paulo: Editora Ática.

———. 1992. *The workers party and democratization in Brazil.* New Haven: Yale University Press.

Keck, Margareth E., and Abers, Rebecca N. 2006. "Muddy waters: Decentralization, coordination and power struggle in the Brazilian water management reform." *International Journal for Urban and Regional Research,* vol. 30, no. 3, pp. 601–22.

Kinzo, Maria D'Alva G. 1988. *Legal opposition politics under authoritarian rule in Brazil: The case of the MDB, 1966–79.* Basingstoke: Palgrave Macmillan. 284 pp.

Kitschelt, H. 2000. "Linkages between citizens and politicians in democratic polities." *Comparative Political Studies,* vol. 33, no. 6/7, pp. 845–79.

Kowarick, Lúcio. 1980. *A espoliação urbana.* Rio de Janeiro: Paz e Terra.

Krishna, Anirudh. 2002. *Active social capital.* New York: Columbia University Press. 192 pp.

Labra, Maria Eliana. 1985. *O movimento sanitarista nos anos 20, da "conexão sanitária internaciona" à especialização em saúde pública no Brasil.* Dissertação de Mestrado apresentada à Escola Brasileira de Administração Pública/FGV, September. 410 pp.

Laclau, Ernesto. 1985. "New social movements and the plurality of the social." In Slater, David, ed. *New social movements and the state in Latin America.* Amsterdam: CEDLA, pp. 27–42.

Ladrech, R. 1999. "Political parties and the problem of legitimacy in the European Union." In Banchoff, T. F., and Mitchell, P. S., eds. *Legitimacy and the European Union.* London: Routledge.

Lamounier, B.; Weffort, F.; and Benevides, M. V., eds. 1981. *Direito, cidadania e participação.* São Paulo: T. Queiroz.

Latin America Weekly Report. 1990. "Debate over taking more IMF medicine." 1 February 1990.

Leal, Victor Nunes. 1977. *Coronelismo: The municipality and representative government in Brazil.* Cambridge: Cambridge University Press. 200 pp.

Lievesley, Geraldine. 2005. "The Latin American left: The difficult relationship between electoral ambition and popular empowerment." *Contemporary Politics,* vol. 11, no. 1 (March), pp. 3–18.

Lima, Eduardo Martins de. 1988. PT origem e proposta, estudo sobre a novidade histórica representada pelo Partido dos Trabalhadores no quadro partidário brasileiro pós-45. Universidade Federal de Minas Gerais. Dissertação (mestrado).

Linz, Juan, and Stepan, Alfred. 1996. *Problems of democratic transition and consolidation.* Baltimore: The Johns Hopkins University Press.

Locke, R. M. 1995. *Remaking the Italian economy.* Ithaca, N.Y.: Cornell University Press.

Love, Joseph. L. 1971. *Rio Grande do Sul and Brazilian federalism 1882–1930.* Stanford, Calif.: Stanford University Press.

Lowi, Theodor J. 1979. *The end of liberalism: The second republic of the United States.* New York: W. W. Norton. 331 pp.

Macaulay, Fiona. 1996. "Governing for everyone: The Workers Party administration in São Paulo, 1989–1992." *Bulletin of Latin American Research,* vol.15, no. 2, pp. 211–29.

Mainwaring, Scott P. 1999. *Rethinking party systems in the third wave of democratization: The case of Brazil.* Stanford, Calif.: Stanford University Press.

Mainwaring, Scott, and Scully, Timothy, eds. 1995. *Building democratic institutions: Party systems in Latin America.* Stanford, Calif.: Stanford University Press. 578 pp.

Mainwaring, Scott, and Viola, Eduardo. 1986. "New social movements, political culture and democracy: Brazil and Argentina in the 80's." *Telos,* vol. 61 (Fall), pp. 17–52

Manin, Bernard. 1987. "On legitimacy and political deliberation." *Political Theory,* vol. 15, no. 3 (Aug.), pp. 338–68.

Marquetti, Adalmir. 2003. "Participação e redistribuição: O orçamento participativo em

Porto Alegre." In Avritzer, Leonardo, and Navarro, Zander. *A inovação democrática no Brasil.* São Paulo: Cortez Editora, pp. 129–56.

Marshall, T. H. 1973. *Class, citizenship and social development.* Westport, Conn.: Greenwood Press.

Martins, Carlos Estevam, and Velasco e Cruz, Sebastião. 1983. "De Castello a Figueiredo: Uma incursão na pré-história da 'Abertura'." In *Sociedade e política no Brasil pós-64.* São Paulo: Editora Brasiliense, Coleção Leituras Afins, pp. 13–61.

Melucci, Alberto. 1980. "New social movements: A theoretical approach." *Social Science Information,* vol. 19, no. 2, pp. 199–226.

———. 1985. "The symbolic challenge of contemporary movements." *Social Research,* no. 52, pp. 789–816.

———. 1989. *Nomads of the present.* Philadelphia, Pa.: Temple University Press.

———. 1996. *Challenging codes.* Cambridge: Cambridge University Press.

Mendez, Juan; O'Donnell, Guillermo; and Pinheiro, Paulo Sérgio, eds. 1999. *The rule of law and the underprivileged in Latin America.* Notre Dame, Ind.: University of Notre Dame Press.

Mendonça, Jupira. 2006. Interview given to Claudia Feres on the local city master plan.

Menegello, R. 1989. *PT: A formação de um partido: 1979–1982.* Rio de Janeiro: Paz e Terra.

Milani, Carlos R. S. 2006. "Políticas públicas locais e participação na Bahia: O dilema gestão *versus* política." *Sociologias,* no. 16, pp. 180–214. Available at http://www.scielo.br/scielo.php?script=sci_arttext&pid=S1517-45222006000200008&lng=en&nrm=iso. Accessed 10 May 2008.

Moisés, José Álvaro. 1975. "Associações voluntárias e participação política." *Cadernos Noel Nütels,* Rio de Janeiro, vol. 1, pp. 1–23.

———. 1993. "Elections, political parties and political culture in Brazil: Changes and continuities." *Journal of Latin American Studies,* vol. 25, no. 4, pp. 575–611.

———. 1995. *Os Brasileiros e a democracia:* São Paulo: Ática.

———. 2005. "Cidadania, confiança e instituições democráticas." *Revista Lua Nova,* no. 65, pp. 71–94. São Paulo: CEDEC.

Morse, R. M. 1982. *El espejo de próspero: Un estudio de la dialéctica del Nuevo Mundo.* Mexico City: Siglo veintiuno.

Muller, Edward N., and Seligman, Mitchell A. 1994. "Civic culture and democracy: The question of causal relationships." *American Political Science Review,* vol. 88, pp. 635–52.

Nascimento, Álvaro. 1986. Available at http://www.fameca.br/caer/esq_artigos/04.htm.

Navarro, Zander. 1998. "Affirmative democracy and re-distributive development: The case of participatory budgeting in Porto Alegre." Cartagena: World Bank.

———. 2005. "PT à deriva." Available at http://www.democraciaparticipativa.org/. Accessed 2 June 2006.

Neder, Ricardo T. 1997. Figuras do espaço público contemporâneo: Associações civis, ONGs no Brasil. 1ª versão, Campinas IFCH, Unicamp.

Nunes, Edson de Oliveira.1984. "Bureaucratic insulation and clientelism in contempory Brazil: Uneven state building and the taming of modernity." University of California, Berkeley, Deparatament of Political Science. Ph.D. dissertation.

Nylen, William R. 2003. *Participatory democracy versus elitist democracy: Lessons from Brazil.* Basingstoke: Palgrave Macmillian.

O'Donnell, G. 1996. *Another institutionalization: Latin America and elsewhere.* Notre Dame, Ind., Helen Kellogg Institute for International Studies.

O'Donnell, Guillermo, ed. 1986. *Transitions from authoritarian rule.* Baltimore: The Johns Hopkins University Press. 208 pp.

O'Donnell, Guillermo A. 1992. "Transitions, continuities, and paradoxes." In Mainwaring S.; O'Donnell, G. A.; and Valenzuela, J. S., eds. *Issues in democratic consolidation: The new South American democracies in comparative perspective.* Notre Dame, Ind.: University of Notre Dame Press, pp. 17–56.

O'Donnell, Guillermo A.; Cullell, Jorge Vargas; and Iazzetta, Osvaldo M., eds. 2004. *The quality of democracy: Theory and applications.* From the Helen Kellogg Institute for International Studies. Notre Dame, Ind.: University of Notre Dame Press. 274 pp.

Oda, Leila Macedo, ed. 2000. "Análise de riscos em laboratórios de saúde pública no Brasil." *Cadernos de Saúde Pública* - ENSP/FIOCRUZ, Rio de Janeiro.

Offe, Claus.1974. "Structural problems of the capitalist state. On the selectiveness of political institutions." *German Political Studies,* no. 1, pp. 31–57.

———.1984. *Contradictions of the welfare state.* Cambridge, Mass.: MIT Press. 304 pp.

———. 1996. *Modernity and the state: East, west.* Cambridge, Mass.: MIT Press. 288 pp.

Oliveira, Francisco. 2003. *Crítica à razão dualista/O ornitorrinco.* São Paulo: Boitempo. 150 pp.

Olson, Mancur. 1971. *The logic of collective action: Public goods and the theory of groups.* Revised ed. Cambridge, Mass.: Harvard University Press. 192 pp.

Olvera, A. 1995. *Regime transition, Democratization and civil society in Mexico.* New York: New School for Social Research.

Olvera, Alberto. 1994. *A sociedade civil no México: A realidade, o projeto e o mito.* In Avritzer, Leonardo. *Sociedade civil e democratização.* Belo Horizonte: Del Rey.

———. 1997. "Civil Society and political transition in Mexico." *Constellations,* vol. 4, no. 1, pp. 105–23.

———. 2003. *Sociedade civil, esfera publica y democratizacion en America Latina.* Mexico. Fondo de Cultura Económica.

Ostrom, Elinor, 2005. *Understanding institutional diversity.* Princeton, N.J.: Princeton University Press.

Oxhorn, Phillip. 1995. *Organizing civil society in Chile.* University Park: Penn State Press.

———. 1999. *When democracy isn't all that democratic: Social exclusion and the limits of the public sphere in Latin America.* Atlanta: American Political Science Association.

———. 2006. "Citizenship as consumption or citizenship as agency. Comparing democratizing reforms in Bolivia and Brazil." *Latin American Studies Association (LASA),* March, pp. 15–18.

Pacheco, Eliezer, and Ristoff, Dilvo. 2004. *Educação superior: Democratizando o acesso.* Brasília: Inep.

Paiva, José Maria de. 1987. "Comunidades eclesiais de base." In Pompermayer, Malori José, ed. *Movimentos sociais em Minas Gerais: Emergência e perspectivas.* Belo Horizonte: Editora da UFMG, pp. 141–68.

Pallocci Filho, Antônio. 2003. *Política econômica e reformas estruturais.* Available at http://www.fazenda.gov.br. Accessed 22 April 2006.

Parsons, T. 1971. *The system of modern societies.* Englewood Cliffs, N. J.: Prentice-Hall.

Pateman, C.1970. *Participation and democratic theory.* Cambridge: Cambridge University Press.

Pereira, Carlos. 1996. "A política pública como caixa de Pandora: Organização de interesses, processo decisório e efeitos perversos na reforma sanitária Brasileira 1985–1989." *Dados,* vol. 39, no. 3, pp. 63–84.

Peruzzotti, Enrique. 1997. "Civil society and the modern constitutional complex: The Argentinian experience." *Constellations,* vol. 4, no. 1, pp. 94–104.

———. 2007. "The politics of institutional innovation. The implementation of participatory budgeting in the city of Buenos Aires." Paper presented at Seminário Internacional Arranjos Participativos no Mercosul, organized by Projeto Democracia Participativa, Departamento de Ciência Política, UFMG.

Peruzzotti, Enrique, and Smulovitz, Catalina. 2006. *Enforcing the rule of law.* University Park: Penn State Press.

Pires, Roberto Rocha Coelho. 2001. *Orçamento participativo e planejamento municipal: Uma análise neoinstitucional a partir do caso da Prefeitura de Belo Horizonte.* Monografia (Curso Superior de administração, habilitação em administração pública). Belo Horizonte: Fundação João Pinheiro.

Pitkin, H. 1967. *The concept of representation.* Berkeley: University of California Press.

Pochman, M. 2003. "Gastos sociais, distribuição de renda e cidadania: Uma equação política." *Econômica,* vol. 5, no. 1 (June), pp. 109–13.

Polis (Instituto Polis). 2005. "São Paulo: Considerações sobre a proposta orçamentária para 2006." Available at http://www.polis.org.br/download/106.pdf. Accessed 13 M2006.

Porto Alegre. 1991. Lei Complementar 242. 9 January 1991.

———. 1997. Regimento do Conselho de Saúde de Porto Alegre.

———. 1999. Plano Diretor Municipal (City Master Plan). Lei Complementar 434. 1 December 1999.

Powell, Walter, and Dimaggio, Paul. 1991. *The new institutionalism in organizational analysis.* Chicago, Ill.: University of Chicago Press.

Przeworski, Adam. 1988. "Democracy as a contingent outcome of conflicts." In Przeworski, Adam, and Slagstad, Rune, eds. *Constitutionalism and democracy.* Cambridge: Cambridge University Press.

———. 1991. *Democracy and the market.* New York: New York University Press.

PT (Workers Party). 1979. Declaração Política Aprovada no Encontro de São Bernardo.

———. 1980. Manifesto de Fundação. Colégio Sion. São Paulo.

Putnam, Robert. 1993. *Making democracy work: Civic traditions in modern Italy.* Princeton, N.J.: Princeton University Press. 280 pp.

Rawls, John. 1971. *A theory of justice.* Cambridge, Mass.: Belknap Press of Harvard University Press.

Reis, Elisa. 1995. "Desigualdade e solidariedade: Uma releitura do familismo a-moral de Banfield." *Revista Brasileira de Ciências Sociais,* vol. 10, no. 29, pp. 35–48.

Réos, Janete Cardoso. 2003. *Participação de usuários e responsáveis dos gestores de políticas sociais do município de Porto Alegre.* Universidade Federal do Rio Grande do Sul, Conselho Nacional de Desenvolvimento Científico e Tecnológico. Dissertação (Mestrado em Sociologia).

Rodrigues, Leôncio M. 1987. *Quem é quem na constituinte: Uma análise sócio-política dos partidos e deputados.* São Paulo: OESP-Mahltese.

Rodrigues, M. M. A., and Zauli, E. M. 2002. "Presidentes e congresso nacional no processo decisório da política de saúde no Brasil democrático (1985–1998)." *Dados —Revista de Ciências Sociais,* Rio de Janeiro, vol. 45, no. 3, pp. 387–429.

Rodrigues Neto, Eleutério. 2003. *Saúde: Promessas e limites da constituição.* Rio de Janeiro: FIOCRUZ.

Rolnik, R. 1997. *A Cidade e a lei - legislação, política urbana e territórios na cidade de São Paulo,* vol. 1. São Paulo: Studio Nobel / FAPESP.

————. 2006. Entrevista concedida a Marcos Morais on the Statute of the City.

Romero, Mauricio. "Os trabalhadores bananeros de Uraba: De súbditos a cidadãos?" In Santos, Boaventura de Souza, ed. *Trabalhar o mundo: Os caminhos do novo internacionalismo operário.* Rio de Janeiro: Civilização Brasileira.

Roniger, Luis, and Ayata Ayse, G. 1995. "Democracy, clientelism, and civil society." *Contemporary Sociology,* vol. 24, no. 6 (Nov.), p. 769.

Roniger, Luis, and Waisman, Carlos, eds. 2002. *Globality and multiple modernities: Comparative North American and Latin American perspectives,* vol. 1. Sussex: Sussex Academic Press.

Rosanvallon, Pierre. 1990. "The decline of social visibility." In Keane, John, ed. *Civil society and the state.* London: Verso Press.

————. 1991. *Le sacre du citoyen.* Paris: Gallimard.

Rosenbaum, Walter. 1974. *Political culture.* New York: Praeger.

Rousseau, Jean Jacques. 1997. "Rousseau: 'The Social Contract' and other later political writings." *Cambridge texts in the history of political thought,* Gourevitch, Victor, ed. Cambridge: Cambridge University Press. 398 pp.

Sacardo, G. A., and Castro, I. E. 2002. *Saúde: Conselho municipal.* Observatório dos direitos do Cidadão. São Paulo: Instituto Polis.

Sader, Eder. 1988. *Quando novos personagens entraram em cena: Experiências, falas e lutas dos trabalhadores da Grande São Paulo, 1970–1980.* Rio de Janeiro: Paz e Terra. 327 pp.

Salvador. 2003. Regimento do Conselho de Saúde.

Sampaio, A. H. L. 2000. *Consultoria para atualização do plano diretor de Salvador.* Manuscript.

Sánchez, Félix R. 2004. "O orçamento participativo em São Paulo (2001/2004): Uma inovação democrática." In Avritzer, Leonardo, ed. *A participação em São Paulo.* São Paulo: Editora UNESP, pp. 409–70.

Santos, Boaventura de Sousa. 1977. "The Law of the oppressed: The construction and reproduction of legality in Pasargada." *Law and Society Review,* vol. 12, pp. 5–125.

————. 1998. "Participatory budgeting in Porto Alegre: Toward a redistributive democracy." *Politics and Society,* vol. 4, pp. 461–510.

————. 2002. "Orçamento participativo em Porto Alegre: Para uma democracia distributiva." In Santos, Boaventura de Sousa, ed. *Democratizar a democracia.* Rio de Janeiro: Civilização Brasileira, pp. 455–559.

————. 2006. *Democratizing democracy.* London: Verso Press.

Santos, B. S., and Avritzer, Leonardo. 2006. "Opening up the cannon of democracy." In Santos, Boaventura de Sousa, ed. *Democratizing democracy: Beyond the liberal democratic canon (reinventing social emancipation: Towards new manifestos).* London: Verso Press.

Santos, Wanderley Guilherme dos. 1979. *Cidadania e justiça: A política social na ordem brasileira.* Rio de Janeiro: Forense Universitária.

————. 1993. *Razões da desordem*. Rio de Janeiro: Rocco. 152 pp.

São Paulo. 1989. Portaria n. 1.166, de 29 de junho de 1989. Da Lei Orgânica do Município de São Paulo de 06 de Abril de 1990. Available at http://www2.prefeitura .sp.gov.br/secretarias/saude/cms/0008. Accessed 22 June 2006.

————. 1998. Lei n. 12.546, de 7 de janeiro de 1998, que dispõe sobre o funcionamento o Conselho Municipal de Saúde de São Paulo. Available at http://www2.prefeitura .sp.gov.br/secretarias/saude/legislacao/0001. Accessed 23 May 2006.

————. 1999. Decreto n.38.576, de 5 de novembro de 1999. Dá nova regulamentação à Lei n° 12.546, de 7 de janeiro de 1998, que dispõe sobre o funcionamento o Conselho Municipal de Saúde de São Paulo.

Sartori, Giovanni. 1973. *Democratic theory*. Reprint ed. Westport, Conn.: Greenwood Press. 479 pp.

————. 1987. *The theory of democracy revisited,* vol. 1. Chatham, N. J.: Chatham House Publishers.

Saule Júnior, Nelson. 1995. *O direito à cidade na constituição de 1988. Legitimidade e eficácia do plano diretor.* Dissertação de Mestrado em Direito PUC-SP, São Paulo.

————, ed. 1999. *Direito à cidade - Trilhas legais para o direito às cidades sustentáveis.* São Paulo: Max Limonad/ Instituto Pólis.

————. 2005. "O Direito à cidade como paradigma da governança urbana democrática." *Instituto Polis.* Available at http://www.polis.org.br/artigo. Accessed 8 May 2006.

Scherer-Warren, Ilse. 2000. *Cidadania e multiculturalismo: A teoria social no Brasil contemporâneo,* vol. 1. Lisboa/Florianópolis: Socius/Edufusc. 2002 pp.

Schmitter, Phillip. 1971. *Interest conflict and political change in Brazil.* Stanford, Calif.: Stanford University Press.

Schumpeter, Joseph. 1942. *Capitalism, socialism and democracy.* New York: Harper.

Selee, Andrew. 2003. *Deliberative municipal governance in Latin America: Causes and consequences.* Academic paper no. 36. Washington, D.C.: Woodrow Wilson International Center for Scholars.

Shils, Edward. 1991. "The virtue of civil society." *Government and Opposition,* vol. 26, no. 1 (January), pp. 3–20.

Silva, Ana Amélia. 1990. "A luta pelos direitos urbanos: Novas representações de cidade e cidadania." *Espaço and Debates,* São Paulo, vol. 10, no. 30, pp. 28–41.

Silva, M. K. 2001. Construção da participação popular. Tese (Doutorado em Sociologia). Universidade Federal do Rio Grande do Sul (UFRG), Rio Grande do Sul.

————. 2002. *Cidadania e exclusão.* Porto Alegre: Editora da Universidade Federal do Rio Grande do Sul.

Silva, Tarcísio. 2003. "Da participação que temos à que queremos: O processo do orçamento participativo na cidade de Recife." In Avritzer, Leonardo, ed. *A inovação democrática no Brasil.* São Paulo: Cortez Editora, pp. 297–334.

Singer, Paul. 1994. *São Paulo's master plan, 1989–92: The politics of urban space.* Washington, D.C.: Woodrow Wilson International Center for Scholars.

————. 1996. *Um governo de esquerda para todos: Luiza Erundina na prefeitura de São Paulo (1989–1992).* São Paulo: Brasiliense.

Singer, Paul, and Brant, Vinícius Caldeira, eds. 1980. *São Paulo: O povo em movimento.* Petrópolis: Vozes/ Cebrap. 231 pp.

Sintomer, Yves, and Gret, Marion. 2002. *Porto Alegre: L'espoir d'une autre démocratie.* Paris: Éditions La Découverte et Syros. 135 pp.

Skidmore, Thomas E. 1999. *Brazil: Five centuries of change.* New York: Oxford University Press.

Snyder, Richard. 2001. "Scaling down: The subnational comparative method." *Studies in Comparative International Development,* vol. 36, no. 1, pp. 93–110.

Sommers, Margaret. 1993. "Citizenship and the place of the public sphere: Law, community and culture in the transition to democracy." *American Sociological Review,* vol. 58, pp. 587–620.

Sposati, Aldaísa, and Lobo, Elza. 1992. "Controle social e políticas de saúde." *Caderno de Saúde Pública,* vol. 8, no. 4 (RJ, out-dez), pp. 366–78.

Stepan, A. 1988. *Rethinking military politics.* Princeton, N.J.: Princeton University Press.

Stepan, Alfred, and Linz, Juan J. 1996. *Problems of democratic transition and consolidation: Southern Europe, South America, and post-Communist Europe.* Baltimore, Md.: The Johns Hopkins University Press.

Stotz, Eduardo Navarro. 2003. "Trabalhadores, direito à saúde e ordem social no Brasil." *São Paulo Perspec.,* vol. 17, no. 1, pp. 25–33.

Suplicy, Marta. 2000. "Um projeto político para a cidade de São Paulo." São Paulo: Instituto Florestan Fernandes.

Tatagiba, Luciana.1999. *Analise da literatura sobre experiências recentes da sociedade civil na formulação de políticas publicas.* Relatório de pesquisa. Unicamp. Campinas.

———. 2002. "Os conselhos gestores e a democratização das políticas públicas no Brasil." In Dagnino, Evelina, ed. *Sociedade civil e espaços públicos no Brasil.* São Paulo: Paz e Terra.

———. 2004. "A institucionalização da participação: Os conselhos municipais de políticas públicas na cidade de São Paulo." In Avritzer, Leonardo, ed. *A participação em São Paulo.* São Paulo: Editora UNESP, pp. 323–70.

Teixeira Ferreira, Luis Paulo. 1988. Entrevista publicada na revista *Movimento Popular.* CPV no. 1. São Paulo: Polis.

Tendler, Judith. 1997. *Good government in the tropics.* Baltimore, Md.: The Johns Hopkins University Press.

Tilly, Charles. 1985. *The contentious French.* Cambridge, Mass.: Harvard University Press.

———. 2006. *Why? What happens when people give reasons . . . and why.* Princeton, N.J.: Princeton University Press.

Tilly, Charles; McAdam, Douglas; and Farrow, Sidney. 2003. *Contention and democracy in Europe, 1650–2000.* Cambridge: Cambridge University Press.

Tocqueville, Alexis de. 1966. *Democracy in America.* New York: Harper and Row.

TRE (Tribunal Regional Eleitoral do Distrito Federal). 1996. *De 1960 até as eleições de 1994.* Available at http://www.tre-df.gov.br/institucional.htm. Accessed 10 May 2003.

Tribunal Justiça. 1995. RGS, 39-1995. Projeto "More Legal." Porto Alegre.

Tourraine, Alain. 1988. *Return of the actor: Social theory in post-industrial society.* Minneapolis: University of Minnesota Press.

———. 1992. *Critique de la modernité.* Paris: Fayard.

UAMPA (União de Associações de Moradores de Porto Alegre). 1986. "A participação popular na administração municipal." Porto Alegre.

UNDP (United Nations Development Programme). 2004. *Human development report 2004: Cultural liberty in today's diverse world.* Available at http://hdr.undp.org/reports/global/2004/. Accessed 2 June 2006.

Van Stralen, C. J. 1996. "The struggle over a national health system: The movimento sanitário and health policy-making in Brazil." Universiteit van Utrecht/ Faculteit Sociale Wetenschappen. Doctoral dissertation.

Verba, Sidney. 1995. *Voice and equality.* Cambridge, Mass.: Harvard University Press.

Vitale, D. 2004. "Democracia semi-direta no Brasil pós-1988: A experiência do orçamento participativo." Faculdade de Direito. Departamento de Filosofia e Teoria Geral do Direito. Universidade de São Paulo (USP). Tese de Doutorado.

Wallerstein, Immanuel. 2002. "Uma política de esquerda para o século XXI? Ou teoria e praxis novamente." In Leite, José Corrêa; Loureiro, Isabel; and Cevasco, Maria Elisa, eds. *O Espírito de Porto Alegre.* São Paulo: Editora Paz e Terra.

Wampler, Brian. 2000. *Private executives, legislative brokers, and participatory publics: Building local democracy in Brazil.* University of Texas, Austin. Doctoral dissertation.

———. 2004. "Instituições, associações e interesses no orçamento participativo de São Paulo." In Avritzer, Leonardo, ed. *A participação em São Paulo.* São Paulo: UNESP, pp. 371–408.

———. 2008. *Participatory budgeting in Brazil: Contestation, cooperation, and accountability.* University Park: Pennsylvania State Press.

Wampler, Brian, and Avritzer, Leonardo. 2004. *Participatory publics: Civil society and new institutions.* New York: Comparative Politics.

———. 2005. "The spread of participatory budgeting in Brazil: From radical democracy to participatory good government." *Journal of Latin American Urban Studies,* vol. 7, pp. 37–52.

Wanderley, L. E. W. 1998. "Estudos da religião no Brasil: Buscando o equilíbrio entre adaptação e criatividade." In Muniz de Souza, B., and Jardilino, E.H., eds. *Sociologia da religião no Brasil.* São Paulo: UMESP/PUC-SP.

Weber, Max. 1968. *Economy and society.* New York: Bedminster Press.

Weber, Max; Gerth, H. H.; and Mills, C. Wright. 1958. *From Max Weber: Essays in sociology.* Oxford: Oxford University Press.

Weffort, F. C. 1980. *O populismo na política brasileira.* Rio de Janeiro: Paz e Terra.

———. 1989. "Why Democracy?" In Stepan, A., ed. *Democratizing Brazil.* New York: Oxford University Press.

Weyland, Kurt. 1996. *Democracy without equity: Failures of reform in Brazil.* Pittsburgh, Pa.: University of Pittsburgh Press. 293 pp.

Whitaker, Francisco. 2003. "Iniciativa popular de lei: Limites e alternativas." In Benevides, Maria Victoria; Vannuchi, Paulo; and Kerche, Fábio, eds. *Reforma política e cidadania.* São Paulo: Perseu Abramo, pp. 182–200.

Whitaker, Francisco et al. 1989. *Cidadão constituinte: A saga das emendas populares.* Rio de Janeiro: Paz e Terra.

Wiarda, Howard. 1974. *Politics and social change in Latin America: The distinct tradition.* Amherst: University of Massachusetts Press.

———. 2001. *The soul of Latin America: The cultural and political tradition.* New Haven, Conn.: Yale University Press.

Zaverucha, Jorge. 1998. "A constituição brasileira de 1988 e seu legado autoritário: Formalizando a democracia mas retirando sua essência." In Zaverucha, Jorge, ed. *Democracia e instituições políticas brasileiras no final do século XX.* Recife: Bagaço, pp.113–48.

Index

Figures, notes, and tables are denoted by f, n, *and* t *following the page number.*